Television and
the Making of
Richard Nixon

Television and the Making of Richard Nixon

WILLIAM T. HORNER

McFarland & Company, Inc., Publishers

Jefferson, North Carolina

Also of Interest
Saturday Night Live *and the 1976 Presidential Election:
A New Voice Enters Campaign Politics,*
William T. Horner and M. Heather Carver (2018)

Unless otherwise noted, all photographs are from the National Archives.

This book has undergone peer review.

LIBRARY OF CONGRESS CATALOGUING-IN-PUBLICATION DATA

Names: Horner, William T., 1968– author.
Title: Television and the making of Richard Nixon / William T. Horner.
Description: Jefferson, North Carolina : McFarland & Company,
Inc., Publishers, 2022 | Includes bibliographical references and index.
Identifiers: LCCN 2022024125 | ISBN 9781476686639 (print) ∞
ISBN 9781476646633 (ebook)
Subjects: LCSH: Nixon, Richard M. (Richard Milhous), 1913-1994—
On television. | Nixon, Richard M. (Richard Milhous), 1913-1994—In mass
media. | Television in politics—United States—History—20th century. |
Communication in politics—United States—History—20th century. | Mass
media and public opinion—United States—History—20th century. | Politicians—
United States—Public opinion—History—20th century. | Presidents—
United States—Public opinion—History—20th century. | United States—
Politics and government—1945-1989. | BISAC: HISTORY / United States /
20th Century | PERFORMING ARTS / Television / History & Criticism
Classification: LCC E856 .H67 2022 | DDC 973.924—dc23/eng/20220527
LC record available at https://lccn.loc.gov/2022024125

BRITISH LIBRARY CATALOGUING DATA ARE AVAILABLE

ISBN (print) 978-1-4766-8663-9
ISBN (ebook) 978-1-4766-4663-3

Front cover: Richard Nixon at a July 1968 campaign rally
in Paoli, Pennsylvania (Ollie Atkins/National Archives)

Printed in the United States of America

*McFarland & Company, Inc., Publishers
Box 611, Jefferson, North Carolina 28640
www.mcfarlandpub.com*

For Heather, Tricia, and Ellie,
the people I aspire to be like.
I love you much more than words can say.

Acknowledgments

Thanks to the University of Missouri and the Truman School
of Government and Public Affairs for more than two decades
of opportunities to do the work I love to do.
Thanks to McFarland for its continued interest in,
and support of, scholarly exploration and inquiry.

Table of Contents

Preface

This book is about the lessons Richard Nixon learned in his political career that led him to craft an approach to dealing with the media that has been modeled by politicians at all levels of American politics. As a presidential scholar, I have read all of Nixon's books that he wrote as a former president, but because of my interest in politics and the media, I have always been particularly fascinated with the book he wrote as a former vice president, *Six Crises*, published in 1962. While I have considered the work his most important, I found that it is not often cited by Nixon scholars. All the crises he discusses are, ultimately, about how the press covered him and lessons he learned in how to deal with the press. They led to a media strategy as a private, but famous, citizen and as a candidate for president in 1968 which endures as the way many candidates conduct themselves today. There are also clear roots for his media strategy as a president to be found in *Six Crises*, though that is not the focus of this book, which is focused on the period from 1952 through 1968.

In this book I draw on Nixon's own writing and appearances in a wide variety of media outlets to see how he developed specific media communication strategies as a candidate to keep himself in the spotlight but to keep the press, who he blamed for his political failures in 1960 and 1962, as distant as possible. The connections inherent in understanding the Nixon style and its origins are important to investigate because they permeate politics today. I have found that while the technologies have changed, the tactics are the same, having adapted to the times. Understanding the intertwining of politics and media is crucial to understanding the political life of the United States. Understanding the media behavior of Richard Nixon is crucial to understanding the politics of the 21st century.

Introduction

I believe that I spent too much time in the last campaign
on substance and too little time on appearance....
—Richard Nixon, 1962[1]

This is not a book about campaign rhetoric or presidential rhetoric. This is not an attempt to argue that any one successful presidential candidate was better than all others as a speechmaker or that any president was a better communicator than the others. This is a book about the media education of Richard Nixon, from the time he was elected to Congress to the point he became president, because the lessons he learned before becoming president had a profound impact not only on his presidency, but on every presidency since then. When he wrote his autobiography in 1962, reflecting on the "crises" which framed his life to that point, he understood a big lesson about how politics had changed during his relatively short career in it. He understood that it was television, and no longer newspapers and other print media, or even radio, where most people got their news and "develop their impressions of the candidates." The way politicians appear on screen matters, perhaps more than anything else in modern American politics. He took that lesson to heart and made controlling his image central to the strategy of the rest of his political life and, in so doing, had a profound impact on all the politicians who followed him. As he wrote, the truth is that "one bad camera angle" can override the words, good or bad, of politicians.[2]

Visual Communicators and American Politics

John F. Kennedy is frequently referred to as America's first television president. In Kennedy, the country had its first president with real screen presence. It was inevitable that someone would come along with this ability and become known as *the* television politician. He bested his opponent,

Richard Nixon, in image-building in at least one of their four televised debates and it forever won him the title of "America's first television president" in the eyes of many scholars and American citizens. But Kennedy was simply a better player of a game Nixon designed, not the designer of the game.

It is likely perverse, in the opinion of many, to make a case that Nixon is in any way a pioneering television politician because Nixon is seen by few as charismatic, engaging, or endearing. But he was, in fact, a pioneer of television in politics in many enduring ways. Journalist Joe McGinniss was embedded with the Nixon campaign in 1968, and though members of the Nixon campaign felt he had betrayed their confidence when his book was published, it is a noteworthy chronicle of the Nixon campaign. In *The Selling of the President 1968*, McGinniss wrote that Nixon was mistrustful of television, even afraid of television.[3] This assessment misses the point. Nixon did not have to *like* TV to know—and he did know—how to *use* TV. Nixon may not have been a natural television performer, but almost none of his career in politics took place without using television. He knew its power and he used it throughout his career.

Other politicians, such as JFK, might have written about the power of television, as he famously did in an essay for *TV Guide*, or looked better on television than Nixon. But Nixon taught others how to *use* television in ways that are still used today. Nixon adapted methods of going over the press which were pioneered by Theodore Roosevelt, who used magazines to go around newspapers, and Franklin Roosevelt, who used radio to go around all print media.[4] That makes Richard Nixon, and not just John Kennedy, a pioneer of the use of television in American politics.

It is not all that important to ask who the best-looking president of the television age was. That was Kennedy or, perhaps, Reagan. What is important is *how* television (and now, newer forms of visual media) is used. We live now in a visual electronic media world and will forevermore. What we should be interested in, if we truly are invested in understanding the ways that politicians communicate with the American electorate, is not how good a performer any candidate is, but how candidates have used the latest technology to forever change the process of campaigning. We rightly credit people such as JFK and Ronald Reagan for being effective on television, but we must also credit Richard Nixon for establishing the way politicians communicate with potential voters in the visual electronic media age. Nixon was a great communicator. This was not because he was great looking on television, or supremely at ease in front of a camera, but because he worked to understand how to make the media work for him and, thereby, left a model for every politician who has come after him to follow.

Electronic communication has been used by presidents since William McKinley. McKinley, who was not known as a great orator or pithy writer, took advantage of a new electronic medium, the telephone, not to build an image, but to protect one. If one looks at the presidential papers of William McKinley, one will find precious little in the way of memos and letters between McKinley and others. Why? Because they realized that they could use the phone to plot and plan without leaving a record that could trail them through history. When McKinley's close adviser Mark Hanna died, his family destroyed all the paper he left behind, at his request. But there was not that much that had to do with McKinley, because they made important decisions on the phone.[5]

FDR revolutionized the use of another electronic medium, radio, to communicate with the American people and, critically, to do so in a way that let him get around the publishers and editors he felt were politically biased against him. Had television been a viable presence in many American living rooms when FDR was president, the discussion could end with him. But it was not. When television came along, the very first politician to use television in the way FDR used radio, to go around the people in the media he saw as his enemies, was Richard Nixon. So, while Kennedy's looks and good humor have earned him the title of a great television president, he was not the only one.

Richard Nixon should properly be seen as the architect of the model for how American politicians communicate with the American public in the age of visual communication. Everyone who followed him was merely tinkering around the edges. This book is an examination of what made Nixon the architect of the strategies modern politicians use in visual electronic communication and how he arrived at those strategies. Much has been written about Nixon as president. Far less has been written of the lessons he learned that specifically prepared him to be the television-focused politician and candidate he was.

Part I: Lessons Learned

ONE

Innovation in Political Communication in the Visual Age

Once television existed, it was inevitable that someone would come along and be a really great performer on camera. That person was John F. Kennedy and, for that reason, he is often dubbed America's first television president. FDR was on television when the technology was too rudimentary and too rarely in living rooms to do him much good. Truman and Eisenhower were both presidents in the television age and they had no talent for broadcasting. But in Kennedy the country had their first president with real screen presence in the television era. Because it was inevitable that someone would come along with this ability and become known as *the* television president, it just happened to be Kennedy, but he was not especially noteworthy as an innovator.

A better question to ask is "Who is the architect of how politicians communicate in the age of visual media?" What is important is not really which of our politicians have looked the best on screens large and small but, rather, *how* television and other communication techniques are used. That is, in some ways, FDR. It is certainly not JFK. When looking for who to credit (or blame) for the current state of presidential communications with the American people, the man who deserves the most notice for the way presidents utilize the tools of presidential communication in the visual media era is Richard M. Nixon.

As political scientist Jeff Tulis demonstrates in *The Rhetorical Presidency*, the rules of the game and the public's expectations of presidents were so different in the 18th and 19th centuries that the office barely resembles the presidency of the 20th and 21st centuries. Presidential behavior changed dramatically, as Tulis demonstrates, with the presidency of Theodore Roosevelt.[1] TR learned how to use the media throughout his early career and really made a study of it when he left his position as assistant

7

secretary of the navy to lead a group of volunteers, the Rough Riders, to fight in Cuba in the Spanish American War. As president, he allowed the press wide access to the White House, on the grounds that he had approval over any direct quotes of him, and, if he did not like what they wrote about him, they were likely to lose that White House privilege. He nurtured relationships with magazine publishers, coining the phrase "muckrakers" to refer to them, and encouraged investigative journalism.

Taft, who considered the role of president to be closely constrained by Article II of the Constitution, did not push the model of presidential communication forward. He believed the president was there to administer the laws passed by Congress and he disagreed strongly with Teddy Roosevelt's stewardship theory of the presidency. Woodrow Wilson, on the other hand, was a radical reformer of both the presidency and presidential communication, bent on making the American system of government much more like the parliamentary democracies so common in other parts of the world. Part of his strategy included a fully developed approach to the news media. Even though he grew frustrated with the press, as he grew frustrated with so many aspects of being president, Wilson became the first president to hold regularly scheduled press conferences.

The trouble arose, as scholar David Michael Ryfe asserts, when reporters did not cooperate with Wilson's agenda. Wilson envisioned the press conference as an opportunity for him to gather information from the journalists, who came from all over the country. The problem was that the reporters expected to get information from him, which he was usually unwilling to give.[2] The problem for Wilson, and even more for the presidents who followed him, was the growing sense of empowerment he gave the press.

As Ryfe observes, "In a process spanning over 15 years, Washington reporters slowly began to see the presidency as a prime source of news." This led the press to see it as their job to represent the citizenry in asking questions of the president and led to their institutionalization, with an accepted physical presence in the White House and the creation of the White House Correspondents Association in 1914.[3] The presidents who followed Wilson—Harding, Coolidge, and Hoover—were much more like Taft than either TR or Wilson when it came to their feelings about making public appeals, although all three did speak to the nation on radio, with Harding being the first president in history to do so.

As historian Craig Allen demonstrates, the title of "first television president" arguably belongs to Dwight Eisenhower. He was not the first president on television, but he was the first president to use it regularly, as something more than a unique new oddity. Allen notes that Eisenhower brought television to the White House in many new ways, including what he called televised "fireside chats," press conferences, cabinet meetings, and hiring the first presidential TV consultant. He notes that the first truly television campaign was Eisenhower's 1956 reelection bid.[4] Allen also argues forcefully that Eisenhower is underappreciated for having a strategy that looks like the way presidents engage with the media today. Certainly, during Eisenhower's time, the nation saw a more sophisticated approach than had previously existed, thanks in large measure to the unpaid efforts of actor Robert Montgomery. For much of Eisenhower's administration, Montgomery was a regular presence, with an office in the Executive Office Building, giving television advice to Eisenhower.

But indeed Eisenhower is not the first television president. The first president to appear on television from the White House was Harry Truman. As historian Franklin Mitchell notes, Truman made a televised speech from the White House to promote food conservation at home to aid Europe.[5] It was not a great performance by either Truman or the production staff, but it was an early foray into a new way to speak to the American people. With time, Truman's presentation skills improved and the technology advanced. Mitchell writes, "None of this technology transformed Truman into a gifted performer, but the improved results pleased viewers and gratified the president."[6]

However, Harry Truman was not accurately the *first* president to appear on television either. That distinction goes to Franklin Roosevelt, who appeared on television when he delivered the speech which opened the 1939 World's Fair in New York City. It was the debut of television to the world at large. FDR did not mention television specifically in his speech, which all but a very few Americans had no way of seeing, but he commented on the growing ease of communication in more general terms, saying, "The magic of modern communications makes possible a continuing participation by word of mouth itself."[7] He was speaking primarily of radio, but television had arrived.

The press took note of the historic occasion if FDR did not. The day before the speech, *New York Times* reporter Orrin Dunlap observed, "With all the exuberance of a boy with a new Kodak, the radio men pick up their electric cameras today and go to the World's Fair to televise the opening spectacle and to telecast President Roosevelt as a 'first' in this new category of broadcasting."[8]

Dunlap was prescient, writing not just about the first president to appear on television, but also about what the future held for television, a medium with an unquenchable thirst for material. He wrote, using radio as a reference, of the "insatiable appetite" of electronic media for material, concluding that for all the weeks of planning which went into preparing to broadcast FDR's speech from the World's Fair, it would be over quickly and there would be an ever-present demand for material if television were to survive.[9] This was no small challenge for the people producing material for television.

Nor was it a small challenge for the people who would appear on television, most especially presidents. Dunlap noted the historic occasion, and the fact that FDR would be remembered as the first president to appear on TV, but he also pointed out exactly what Nixon wrote in 1962 about the impact of one bad camera angle, writing, "On the radio the President may cough and clear his throat before beginning the broadcast, but television is not likely to hide such preliminaries; it will be more natural," and if the president had to blow his nose, or took a sip of water while on camera, it would make it all seem even more natural.[10] And naturalness is often poisonous for politicians.

The day after the speech the *New York Times* reported that FDR's appearance on television was the beginning of a new era and a new industry, "sight-seeing by radio."[11] Still, it was not an event that captivated the globe since almost no one had a television on which to watch the events. As the *Times* reported, there were fewer than 200 televisions tuned in and fewer than 1,000 total viewers.[12]

The event was not only the first presidential appearance on television; it was also the beginning of regularly scheduled television broadcasting in the United States. In the strictest sense, this appearance entitles FDR, who was undeniably *the* radio president, if not the *first* radio president, to the title of "first television president." But he did not make television a regular part of the presidential routine, nor did he develop patterns on television that influenced the behavior of future presidents.

FDR certainly deserves the title of first electronic media president through his pioneering use of radio. He did so for the same reason his cousin Theodore Roosevelt, a pioneer of the print media presidency, curried favor with certain reporters and magazine publishers: to get his message out as unfiltered by what he viewed as hostile news media as possible. FDR's regular presence on radio, with his fireside chats and other appearances, advanced a pattern established by TR. Theodore Roosevelt also chose to speak through outlets that were friendly to the president. TR sought out publishers, especially of magazines, who were friendly to his cause. He also pioneered the way presidents use access to the White House and to themselves to control, or attempt to control, the press. Franklin used radio to avoid the publishers and editors who were hostile to his politics. It was a power FDR recognized early in his political career, during his single term as New York's governor, in a speech he was supposed to deliver to the New York Democratic organization, Tammany Hall.

FDR was supposed to deliver it by phone, broadcast over speakers, from Albany to Manhattan, but when the cutting-edge technology of the day failed, his speech was read by New York Supreme Court Justice William T. Collins. In the speech, FDR noted that the day of the unfiltered political orator, "the golden day of the silver tongue," was killed by the print press, as the people turned to newspapers for news instead of to party orators. But radio, he argued, was turning the tide. He argued that in just five years, the media landscape had changed from one in which 99 percent of people got their ideas from newspapers to one in which at least 50 percent of people listened to politicians from both sides of the aisle articulate their own ideas on the radio, allowing people to make up their own minds.

Radio in politics was a positive development, he argued, because the problem with newspapers was that they were too reliant on data and that people were too dependent on statistics manipulated in print by both parties. FDR concluded, "It is my hope that as the voters listen more and more to the actual spoken word of the orators, they will keep informed more and more on the fundamental reasons which lead them to hold this policy or that policy to be best for our republic."[13] What *Governor* Roosevelt advocated in 1929 was that people find ways to avoid the interpretative tendencies of those journalists who stood in the way of his agenda. As radio became more and more available as the country's first truly mass medium, *President* Roosevelt made the most of radio to help people avoid those interpretive tendencies.

Historian H.W. Brands argues that FDR learned quickly that radio was particularly powerful in the hands of the executive branch and further argues that radio and the power of broadcasting contributed significantly to the expansion of executive power that took place over the course of the 20th century.[14] Brands writes, "Over time Roosevelt's radio audience would come to feel they knew him as they had known no other executive; it was an aspect of his political genius, amplified by radio and sharpened by experience, that he made them think *he* knew *them*."[15]

While Kennedy was not the *first* president to appear on television, he is often thought of as *the* television president because he was the first president to appear comfortable on television. Kennedy's appearance was certainly more natural, relaxed, and confident than Truman's or Eisenhower's. And as FDR understood the power of radio, Kennedy understood, even before he was elected president, that television was revolutionizing politics and the presidency.

Writing in *TV Guide* in 1959, Kennedy observed how much television had changed the nature of every aspect of politics. While some saw it as a negative development, he argued that, on balance, it was a good thing for the country. But the impact of television depended on the people, he concluded, writing, "It is in your power to perceive deception, to shut off gimmickry, to reward honesty, to demand legislation where needed. Without your approval, no TV show is worthwhile, and no politician can exist."[16] To Kennedy, television presented a challenge, both to politicians and to viewers. He was certainly up to the challenge of using the new visual medium to the best possible advantage for himself. It is not as clear that viewers lived up to the challenge he set for them.

Kennedy was a keen observer of the impact the cutting-edge technology of the day would have on the presidency, but it doesn't mean he was himself a revolutionary innovator. Kennedy was also a masterful performer. He had a non-transferable skill as on-camera talent. If it were a transferable skill, then all the presidents who followed him would be equally natural, relaxed, and confident on air. This is certainly not the case. It could not be said of Johnson, Nixon, Gerald Ford, Jimmy Carter, or either Bush that they had the natural skill of JFK. Clinton, and Obama were closer, and Ronald Reagan was at least JFK's equal as a performer. But being a good performer is just part of the picture. More important is understanding how the medium—whatever it is at any given point in history—facilitates the quest for power. And the person who did that in the age of visual media is Richard Nixon.

The political education of Richard Nixon led him to develop his media strategy for a visual media environment. That strategy left an enduring legacy for the office of president of the United States. Like Theodore Roosevelt and FDR, Richard Nixon is a benchmark president who established standards that all other presidents who followed him have maintained. Other presidents certainly made contributions in leading to where presidential media behavior is today.

For example, Woodrow Wilson established the idea that a president's campaigning never really ends, whether it's for office or ideas; Eisenhower, as historian Craig Allen argues, was pioneering in ways to reach the American people with television, but those were largely techniques, not strategies. Kennedy had style and charm that not even FDR had, and he used it on television in ways that most presidents, before or since, could only hope to come close to doing. LBJ used television, knowing it was a way to communicate with the country, but he did so poorly. People did not warm to Johnson, except in those few short months after Kennedy was assassinated. Like Nixon, he held a grudge against the media. He tried to control the media, but it was mostly behind the scenes and primarily a one-man crusade.

But in Richard Nixon we see the creation and institutionalization of a variety of techniques for dealing with and using the media, well before he became president. Most scholars who write about the media behavior of Nixon focus on the boorish, bullying behavior of the presidential years. But, in many ways, Nixon is the media model for the modern politician, who used those tools to become president. He is the politician who established patterns for all who succeed him to follow. The politician who became president with the greatest enduring legacy on how many politicians, including presidents, behave in the ever-changing world of the media is Richard Nixon. Using YouTube, Instagram, Facebook, Twitter, TikTok, and every other Internet-based media platform which is developed is not innovative. It is merely adapting the latest technology to preexisting strategies perfected by Richard Nixon. And this is only part of the legacy of Richard Nixon.

Donald Trump is regularly acknowledged and frequently critiqued for his attacks on the news media and for his threats to create his own media outlets to circumvent the "mainstream media." But in this, Trump is merely following Nixon's gameplan. When Nixon was president, his attack on the media was loud and public, but it began long before he became president. The consequence of his prolonged attack was to begin the erosion of confidence in the news media, to make journalists among the least trusted figures in America. And this is even though it was reporters who told the world of the gross violations of the public trust committed by the Nixon administration. Or, perhaps, it is *because* of this fact. We seem to hate the bearers of bad news more than the news itself. And the resignation of Nixon only threw fuel on the fire of the movement to brand the media as politically biased and untrustworthy. There is an entirely separate book to be written about how Nixon established the model for *presidents* to utilize the media and control the presidential image and message while in office. In fact, Druckman and Jacobs have written such a book in their study of Nixon's attempt to "frame" his image, building on the work of other scholars such as Lang and Lang.[17]

Framing has two meanings in media research, depending on whether one is analyzing framing by the media, or framing by politicians. The way in which the media "frame," or present, an issue may influence how it affects the public. Journalists can frame a story in many ways which generate different reactions in an audience. For example, a story that contrasts the lengthy U.S. military action in Afghanistan with the first Persian Gulf War, judged a success by most, will provoke different audience reactions than a comparison with the much more unpopular Vietnam War.

The way a story is framed in the news media affects the way the audience perceives an event and that can have political consequences. For example, Iyengar and others distinguish between what they call episodic and thematic framing by the media. A story using episodic framing portrays a crime as a single incident; a story using thematic framing reports the crime but explains the incident in a larger context such as long-term trends in crime or the societal causes of crime like a poor economy.[18]

A different type of framing occurs when a politician emphasizes certain aspects of an issue to affect the way people perceive the issue. For example, in discussing programs aimed at the poor, a politician could refer to them as "welfare" or "entitlement" programs, which will make people think in negative terms about them.[19] If a politician refers to these programs as a "helping hand" or an "aid to the needy," people will think more positively about them. When the Republicans in Congress and the Democratic president Bill Clinton spoke of the need for "welfare reform" in the mid–1990s, their plan was well received by many Americans because the word "reform" is generally seen in a positive way by people. But once they saw the details of the reform, some Americans were no longer as supportive.

Another example of framing that involves both politicians and the news media is an issue which was at the center of political controversy for many years: how to define the interrogation tactics used on suspected terrorists. Both the Bush and Obama administrations used the phrase "enhanced interrogation techniques" to describe methods such as waterboarding. It is easy to understand why political leaders who ordered such techniques wanted to distance themselves from the word "torture" and described it in a way that made it seem less negative. To many people, "interrogation" sounds like something which should be done to terrorists and "enhanced" sounds like an improvement. This is framing.

None of this has anything to do with the *substance* of policy making but, rather, only with how people *perceive* an issue. In this media-driven age, politicians of both parties spend a great deal of time trying to figure out how to get the public on their side. Rather than battling to come up with the best ideas, unfortunately, they often battle simply about the best public relations campaign. And, of course, how people *perceive* an issue can have profound effects on policy decisions and elections.

In their book *Who Governs? Presidents, Public Opinion, and Manipulation*, James Druckman and Lawrence Jacobs offer a groundbreaking analysis of presidents' use of media to manipulate public opinion. They are interested in understanding how presidents and other political elites intentionally try to influence public opinion of both policies and of the elites themselves. They identify two primary ways politicians do this: with framing (which they also refer to as priming) and the manipulation of policy to get the best public reaction.[20]

Druckman and Jacobs use the terms priming and framing interchangeably. They define them as the way politicians emphasize certain issues or personality traits. They suggest that elites will emphasize some issues over others, or some aspects of their personalities over others, in an attempt to influence opinion. They write that the main goal of politicians is not to change people's opinions but, rather, the level of importance they assign to the issue. In doing so, politicians play on preexisting beliefs and attitudes.[21] They argue that a politician's personal image affects how the public evaluates them.

Elected officials and candidates for office thus have an incentive to build an image that members of the public will find appealing and/or trustworthy. There are, according to Druckman and Jacobs, four types of personality characteristics that are particularly resonant with the public. These types fall into two basic groups, performance and interpersonal. The performance traits include competency and strength, while the interpersonal characteristics are things such as trust and warmth. People tend to see performance traits as more important, they write, so politicians are motivated to emphasize those characteristics and their ability to handle tough problems.[22] And there are also, of course, strong incentives to counteract negative perceptions.[23] They conclude, "The public's particular perceptions of each politician's personality traits inform their distinctive calculations regarding how to prime image."[24]

There are, Jacobs and Druckman argue, three strategies which elites use to try to prime their image, especially when they are trying to counteract negative public perceptions. First, they write, elites "can directly emphasize the importance of certain images in evaluating candidates." The second strategy is to "employ an indirect priming strategy by invoking visual cues that enhance the salience of images." And third, elites can "emphasize issues that send signals about their image."[25] They point out that the priming of an image is different from the priming of issues. The tools used to draw attention to certain areas are similar, but the purpose of image priming is to highlight aspects of a politician's personality, rather than affecting public opinion about an issue.[26] But, they add, issue priming and image priming are not mutually exclusive, concluding that both are important and depend on the candidate involved and on political conditions.[27]

Druckman's and Jacobs's focus in *Who Governs?* is on the presidencies of Richard Nixon and Ronald Reagan. They write that Nixon was not seen as warm, extroverted, or having much of a sense of humor. In the absence of a warm personality, Nixon and his aides focused on promoting the image of Nixon as competent and performance oriented, and when polls showed his ratings declining in those areas, Nixon became very concerned and urged his staff to find ways to reverse trends.[28]

Druckman and Jacobs argue there are three sets of political conditions which influence how presidents construct their strategies to frame. These are (1) things happening in the real world which influence people's perception of issues and candidates and, thereby, affect the strategies of candidates; (2) current public opinion about specific issues of policy; and, to repeat, (3) the framing or priming of presidential image. They conclude that politicians' decisions about framing their image is informed by the public's perceptions of them and of their personality traits.[29]

Druckman and Jacobs found that as president, Nixon focused his framing on getting credit for his policy positions which were popular, both in domestic policy and foreign policy. Nixon's public opinion data showed that the public did not like him personally and that perceptions of his performance were declining, so he worked to emphasize aspects of his presidency he felt would counteract the slippage. Rather than try to show people he was likable, he focused on building approval for his performance as president.[30] Their analysis was of Nixon as president, and they convincingly demonstrate that Nixon decided as president not to spend energy on trying to make himself more likeable to the American public. However, Nixon tried very hard—*and succeeded*—to make himself seem more likeable throughout his pre-presidential career. Druckman's and Jacobs's assessment of Nixon's media behavior is a valuable contribution to understanding both Nixon and other presidents. But this understanding is broadened by looking at Nixon's earlier life. The roots of everything he did as president can be found in the near quarter of a century of life as a politician he led before finally being elected to the White House.

This book relies on Nixon's own perceptions, as told largely in his own words, to show the lessons that Nixon learned from his life at the highest levels of American politics before he became president. Druckman's and Jacobs's focus on image and issue framing or priming is appropriate. Just as Nixon focused on framing or priming—without using those terms—as president, so too did he focus on them as a politician who aspired to be president. Druckman's and Jacobs's framework for understanding Nixon as president applies well to his pre-presidential days too. To reiterate, they write that image priming focuses on two dimensions: "the performance-based traits of competence and strength and the interpersonal characteristics of warmth and trust." They focus on his presidential years when, ultimately, he was so overcome by the difficulties of being president, as well as scandal, that there was no opportunity for interpersonal characteristics to help. The only hope they saw was to focus on his experience and leadership in a dangerous world. But Nixon understood that interpersonal characteristics matter and, though they were not his main strength, he could use these characteristics to help his standing with the public in his long quest for the White House.

Nixon's importance as a president who used the available media to try to control his image is well-analyzed by Druckman and Jacobs. But it is important to look to Nixon's pre-presidential days to understand how his strategies evolved and even *why* he was compelled to develop them. Nixon's feelings about the media, and his desire to control the media and his media image, did not start with the day he took the oath of office as president on January 20, 1968. Rather, it started far earlier than that, when he was but a relatively unknown member of the House of Representatives.

Many books—hundreds—have been written about Richard Nixon. Many of those books offer psychological analyses of Nixon, and many of them purport to see deeply into the soul of Nixon to comment on what motivated him. But not many analyze Nixon's own words to understand what motivated him and why he behaved the way he did, and why he developed the campaign and media strategies he developed, informing his media strategy in the White House which continues to be the model for presidents and other politicians today. He did more than simply build on a foundation created by presidents such as Theodore Roosevelt and FDR. He redrew the blueprint and passed it along to the generations of politicians who followed him.

To use the terminology of media and politics researchers such as Druckman and Jacobs, Nixon learned about priming and framing early in his political career and engaged in it almost from the beginning. Nixon's autobiography, *Six Crises*, is both an explanation of the lessons he learned in the first two decades of his political career and an attempt to prime the public's perception of him as a brave and decisive leader and, occasionally, a warm, relatable human being. It is also an attempt to frame the news media as both inaccurate in its reporting and hostile toward him personally.

Two

Writing a Book
and the First Lesson

In 1962, Richard Nixon published a book, *Six Crises*. It was not a memoir in the traditional sense but, rather, a book about moments that he viewed as crises in his political life, how he dealt with them, and the lessons he learned from them. The book was written before he ran his campaign for governor of California. The book was written by Nixon, according to his publisher, Doubleday, with the aid of a researcher and an interviewer.[1]

That Doubleday made a point of publicly discussing authorship is directly related to the fact that John F. Kennedy, who was one of the people who urged Nixon to write a book, was plagued by charges that he had not authored his 1955 Pulitzer Prize–winning book *Profiles in Courage*. Accusations that Kennedy was not the author of the book came soon after it was published. One of the most prominent accusers was a journalist who plagued many presidents, including Nixon, Drew Pearson. Pearson, in an appearance on an ABC's *The Mike Wallace Show*, made the assertion that Kennedy was not the author of the book. A lawsuit was threatened and both ABC and Pearson backed away from the charges.[2] But many years later, in his own autobiography, Ted Sorensen suggested that, while Kennedy participated significantly in the production of the book, he did not write it.[3]

Despite Doubleday's efforts at the time of publication, there was also discussion of how much of the writing of *Six Crises* was done by Richard Nixon. One source that, given the day and age in which we live, many people are likely to see as suspect is Wikipedia. In the Wikipedia entry about *Six Crises*, the assertion is made that "like Kennedy, Nixon used a ghostwriter for much of his book. The primary such writer was reportedly Charles Lichenstein." Lichenstein was a Nixon speechwriter and aide. The source for this in the Wikipedia entry is a single *Washington Post* story which states, without any attribution, the following: "Nixon always believed that crisis somehow improves the man, that only through adversity does one learn his own quality, says former ambassador Charles M. Lichenstein, a former Nixon aide and chief ghostwriter for Nixon's first book, 'Six Crises.'"[4]

Biographer Stephen Ambrose provides a fuller account of the writing process for the book and suggests the input of people other than Lichenstein, who he does not mention. He notes that Nixon's syndicated newspaper column was largely written by Stephen Hess and Alvin Moscow, and he wrote that both men also assisted Nixon in the writing of *Six Crises*, along with a third man, Earl Mazo. But, citing Mazo, Ambrose wrote that Nixon did the research for the book, wrote notes and phrases on a yellow pad, dictated that material into a more comprehensible form, and had it typed by his secretary, Rose Mary Woods.[5]

Regardless of the desire some may have to boost or denigrate either Kennedy or Nixon, for the purposes of this analysis, one difference is important to keep in mind about the Kennedy book and the Nixon book. Kennedy was writing a book about senators whose courage made a positive impression on him. Nixon's book was autobiographical. As such, whether he had assistance in writing it or not, the final draft was up to him and it is a valuable resource for understanding who he was in the early 1960s; what he thought about a variety of issues—especially the press and his image; and what motivated his subsequent political moves.

Six Crises came about, in large measure, thanks to the actions of a writer named Adela Rogers St. Johns, and, thanks, Nixon writes, to a suggestion to him from JFK that he write a book. St. Johns was a journalist, novelist, screenwriter and, later in her career, a professor of journalism at UCLA. She was a friend of Nixon and, as Nixon wrote in the introduction to *Six Crises*, she pressed him to write his autobiography. When Nixon failed to act on her advice, she contacted an editor from Doubleday, Ken McCormick, and arranged for him to fly to California to meet with Nixon.[6] As biographer Stephen Ambrose explains, when considering what to write about, he rejected several suggestions, such as Mamie Eisenhower's that he focus on his trips abroad, in favor of focusing on crises. Nixon, Ambrose argued, thrived on crises, and felt he had lived enough of them to fill a book.[7] The title Nixon thought of, Ambrose writes, was inspired by the title of a book written about Eisenhower by one of his staff generals, Walter Bedell Smith. It was called *Eisenhower's Six Great Decisions*.[8] According to Nixon, McCormick told him he would find writing a book to be "easy and enjoyable." However, Nixon found it anything but enjoyable and described writing *Six Crises* as "the seventh major crisis of my life."[9]

Ambrose asserts that the book was complicated, standing as three different things at once: a possible campaign autobiography for the governor's race or the presidency in 1964; a political autobiography; and self-revealing therapy for Nixon.[10] But it was also something else. It was a blueprint for much of the rest of Nixon's career. The lessons he learned from several of these "crises" informed many of his decisions for much of the rest of his very public life. They were lessons about image and how to take charge of it.

In the introduction to the book, Nixon wrote that each of the "crises" were both a personal problem and a problem which had much broader implications and consequences.[11] Nixon admitted the personal nature of his exercise and ends his introduction with a passage noting that there is much to be learned from how someone responds to crisis, "in an age in which individual reaction to crisis may bear on the fate of mankind."[12] In this there seems to be no doubt that Nixon thinks he may be the man to save the world and, at several points in the book, readers definitely get the idea that Nixon feels the voters made a mistake in 1960 in not electing him to the presidency.

The crises which Nixon recounted in the book spanned his political career at the time, from the House of Representatives in the late 1940s, through eight years as vice president. The first crisis is the Alger Hiss case; the second is the slush fund crisis which culminated in the "Checkers" speech; the third is the heart attack which Eisenhower suffered toward the end of his first term as president; the fourth is Nixon's trip to Caracas, Venezuela, where he was subjected to considerable protesting, and which he portrayed as a near-death experience he faced by blocking out fear and reacting not bravely but selflessly[13]; the fifth is his encounter with Khrushchev in Moscow; and the sixth is about his run for President in 1960.

In the last chapter, about the 1960 election, which is almost book-length all by itself, Nixon wrote of the counsel he received from Thomas Dewey, a two-time Republican nominee for president and an elder statesman of the party. Nixon wrote fondly of the objective criticism Dewey regularly offered him and wrote of Dewey's loss of the presidency to Truman in 1948 as a loss to the country. It is impossible to read Nixon's words without seeing that he felt a parallel with the country's failure to elect him. Noting the loss of a man in Dewey who could stand up to Khrushchev and other world leaders, he wrote of the failure to elect Dewey as a loss to America and the free world of his "great talents."[14] The parallel Nixon hoped readers would see with himself was obvious, especially since Khrushchev did not rise to power until 1953.

Despite the criticism he offered of Nixon's writing style and organizational choices, reviewer Denis William Brogan assessed *Six Crises* as an important contribution to the historical record. He wrote that the book gave some useful information about recent events, but its permanent value came from its insights about Nixon's personality.[15] Nixon was an important political figure of the 1940s and 1950s, after all, so there was value in him sharing his view of his role in that time. But there is even more value in the book as a blueprint for the rest of Nixon's political career.

One of the book's great contributions, Brogan pointed out, comes from the insights Nixon gives readers about the importance of image. Brogan wrote that the book made it obvious Nixon was aware of his public image and resented that image. He wrote, "It may be that he has been a victim of 'Friendly's Law,' laid down by Mr. Alfred Friendly of the Washington *Post*, that public characters get like the images Herblock[16] draws of them."[17] If, for example, Brogan wrote, Nixon was negatively affected by his "five o'clock shadow" in the first debate, it was because Herblock and others trained the public to focus on such things.

Nixon was, in other words, negatively affected by what the press said (and drew) about him. Or, at least, that was now Nixon saw it and that is what matters when one thinks about how he behaved during the rest of his career. He was, as Druckman and Jacobs observed more than half a century later, obsessed with image and he worked tirelessly to change Americans' perception of that image.

Brogan continued, noting that the book, itself, was part of an image-rebuilding campaign. Nixon comes across as a victim of negative press coverage and that, Brogan argues, is accurate. He was slandered and maligned to the point that many "otherwise fair-minded people" came to expect nothing but the worst of him. He concluded wondering why Nixon did not do more to deal with the question of why it was so easy to paint him in a negative light.[18] Here, Brogan was mistaken to suggest Nixon did not ask that question. He did ask it and he laid out a plan for countering it. It was the fault of political enemies, and those political enemies included the press.

Columnist Bazy McCormick Tankersley, the daughter of Congresswoman Ruth Hanna McCormick, and the granddaughter of Senator (and William McKinley campaign strategist) Mark Hanna, argued that a very important point was missed in critiques of Nixon's writing style. She wrote that Nixon had given a very real insight into how politics actually work which, she asserts, is rare in books ostensibly about politics.[19] And no matter what one thought of Nixon, Tankersley concluded, in *Six Crises*, he gave readers an intimate look at his political thoughts and his political life.[20] Tankersley and other reviewers felt the book was a must for Nixon to write and it is a must for anyone wishing to understand him. They are correct. The book is a blueprint for the rest of Nixon's career in politics.

The First Lesson: The Alger Hiss Show

Nixon learned very early the power of television. As a Congress-man, first elected in 1946, Nixon became well known as a strong anti-communist. A member of the House Un-American Activities Com-mittee (HUAC), Nixon was at the forefront of the committee's investiga-tion of communists in Hollywood and then, even more significantly, of alleged communist infiltration of the U.S. State Department. The biggest part of the investigation was spurred by a man named Whitaker Chambers, a for-mer communist organizer. At the time of the HUAC hearings, he was a senior edi-tor of *Time*. Chambers tes-tified to HUAC that Alger Hiss, a man who served in several capacities in the State Department before becom-ing the head of the Carnegie Endowment, was a commu-nist and a spy. This led to an investigation of Hiss, much of it directed by Nixon. It also led to a very dramatic hearing—the first Congres-sional hearing ever to be tele-vised—on August 25, 1948, in which Nixon played a very prominent role questioning Hiss.

One should not under-estimate the importance of the fact that the hearing was not only broadcast on televi-sion but was also filmed so it could be shown around the country after the fact. Hun-dreds of people crammed into the hearing room and the halls outside the hear-ing room. They stayed all day,

Alger Hiss booking photograph, 1950.

despite the hot, bright lights brought in for the cameras.[21] But that pales in comparison to the many more people who saw the footage on television and in movie theaters.

In *Six Crises*, Nixon wrote about the fact that television covered the hearings, noting both the power of the medium and, with some regret, that in 1948, most homes still did not have a television. He wrote that it was unfortunate the hearings had not taken place just a little later, noting that millions watched the organized crime hearings Senator Estes Kefauver led in 1951. If more had watched the Hiss hearing in 1948, he asserted, there would have been much less lingering doubt about Hiss's guilt.[22] Unwritten, but implied, is the idea that had more people seen the testimony, rather than read about it as filtered by reporters, the lingering doubts about Nixon would have been disappeared too. That was the power of this new visual medium, as Nixon saw it.

Nixon addressed the importance of these hearings, framing it as an answer to his daughter Tricia's question "What was the Hiss case?" He wrote about the importance of fighting communism, but he also wrote of the academic elites, the "liberalists," and of the news media's responsibility for Hiss not getting the serious scrutiny he deserved. For Nixon, the news media were never far from the root of trouble. Too many people tried to excuse Hiss's behavior when, in fact, he was a communist because he believed in communism. The reason more people did not understand that was the fault of the media and higher education, Nixon wrote, concluding that Hiss was a symbol for "perfectly loyal citizens" worked in the media, higher education, and government bureaucracies.[23]

Nixon had complex feelings about the media's influence on him, personally, in the Hiss case. On one hand, the media enabled his career, which he acknowledged. He wrote that the case brought him fame at a national level and he was given credit for leading the investigation.[24] That fame put him on the path to the U.S. Senate and the vice presidency.

But while Nixon saw the Hiss hearings as his ticket to national prominence, he also saw it as the root cause of what he viewed as the news media's resentment of him. They were angry, he felt, because he took down a liberal, possibly communist, man of prominence. He wrote that what the Hiss case gave, it also took. No political victory was total. The case gave Nixon fame, but left him disliked, not just by communists, but also by intellectuals and journalists even though Hiss's conviction was upheld by the Supreme Court.[25] Nixon saw his crusade against Hiss as the cause of much negativity in his career to that point in 1962. He alleged that, for 12 years, he was the victim of a long-running smear campaign, with people accusing him publicly and through "whispering campaigns" of many terrible things, such as anti–Semitism, alcoholism, and corruption.[26]

Writing in 1962, Nixon saw his action in the Hiss case as a key to his success but also as the beginning of the end his political career. Hiss gave him the vice presidency, but took away the presidency, as Nixon saw it.[27] In the Hiss case, which Nixon called crisis number one, he learned lesson number one: the press was against him. Whether it really was or was not does not matter. What matters is that is how he saw it. And from a Druckman-Jacobs perspective, what he learned was that if he left the framing to the press, it was not an image of competence and strength which won out but, rather, one of meanness, a lack of warmth and trust, and hostility to righteousness and justice.

THREE

The Second and Third Lessons: Checkers and the Crisis Within the Crisis of Eisenhower's Heart Attack

Campaign '52

When Eisenhower made Nixon a candidate for the vice presidency, it propelled him to national prominence even greater than he attained during the Hiss hearings. But securing the nomination did not come easily for Nixon. On the road to being Eisenhower's running mate, Nixon experienced what he called in 1962 "the most scarring personal crisis of my life."

One of America's most famous political scandal stories began innocently enough, as they often do. After appearing on *Meet the Press* on September 14, 1952, Nixon was approached by one of the reporters on the panel, Peter Edson. Edson wrote for a syndication service called the Newspaper Enterprise Association. In *Six Crises*, Nixon wrote that Edson asked him about his "$20,000 supplementary salary," telling him he had not asked Nixon about it on the air because he had not had a chance to do fact checking. Nixon denied having a supplementary salary and told Edson about the fund established on his behalf by supporters in California to pay some of the expenses he incurred as a senator for travel, mailing, and other things. Nixon wrote that he did not give the question any thought right after the show.[1]

But as Nixon embarked on a multi-state train tour of the western United States, Edson published a story about the fund on September 18. It was subsequently picked up by other newspapers and quickly gained momentum. Nixon recalled discussing it with advisers on September 17 and saying, "'Let's wait and see what they do." The wait was short. In *Six Crises*, Nixon characterized the media's coverage of the fund story as an "attack" which began the next morning. In relating the events of the "fund crisis," it is important to do so as it unfolded in the press, because it is the press coverage that created the problem, as Nixon saw it.

Initially, he was not worked up because, as he relates, the most virulent attack came from the *New York Post*, a very Democratic newspaper in his eyes and, therefore, still not a concern. He did not think anything would come of the "smear job" and nothing could be as bad as what he endured in the Hiss case.[2]

On September 19, Nixon issued a statement that described the fund as being set up by supporters to help with expenses that he did not want to charge to the government. He could have, he wrote, used a variety of taxpayer-funded resources, like his Democratic opponent for the vice presidency, Senator John Sparkman of Alabama, but he chose not to do so. He pointed out that he also did not accept fees as a lawyer while serving in Congress. He said, "I prefer to play completely square with the taxpayers."[3]

The *Washington Post*, the newspaper which Nixon would come to hate very much later, took his words and presented them in what seemed to be a positive light on the day that the story was very negatively broken in the *New York Post*. It described the fund in Nixon's terms, as being created to pay for political expenses the government should not be asked to pay, and quoted the administrator of the fund, attorney Dana Smith, a longtime Nixon supporter from California. Smith pointed out that no donor had ever asked Nixon for special favors and no further contributions would be accepted from anyone who did.[4] The article ended with this statement and it seemed designed to put an end to the story.

But it did not put an end to the story. Over the next few days, the momentum grew to take Nixon off the ticket. That momentum was exacerbated by strange signals from the Republican nominee for president, Dwight Eisenhower. On September 20, the *Washington Post*, whose coverage of the story initially seemed to accept Nixon's version of events at face value, published an editorial calling for Nixon to be removed from the ticket. The *Post* had endorsed Eisenhower and now presented this revelation about Nixon as a reason to be concerned that he was not as committed to cleaning up American politics as they thought, concluding, "We still harbor that hope, but it is obvious that his efforts will be gravely handicapped if his running mate exemplifies the unethical conduct that he is denouncing."[5]

Also, on the 20th of September, statements of Dana Smith were published identifying some of the donors to the fund. In an editorial, the *Chicago Daily Tribune*, which leaned Republican on its editorial page, commented on the donors and more generally on the Nixon situation, calling on Nixon to live up to his honorable reputation and be completely transparent about the fund.[6] The *New York Times* scolded Nixon in its own

Eisenhower and Nixon talk in 1952.

editorial, also published on September 20. The editorial did not call for Nixon's removal from the ticket but argued that a vice presidential candidate running a campaign based on decreasing government corruption should hold a higher personal standard.[7]

On September 21, the *Times* published a story summarizing editorial page comments on Nixon from roughly 100 newspapers, most of which, the *Times* asserted, were pro–Eisenhower papers. The story reported that the newspapers disapproved of Nixon's behavior by a 2 to 1 margin and that some were calling for his removal from the ticket.[8] The article contained several quotes from newspapers on both sides of the issue. The *Washington Post* ran a similar story, reporting that some papers were calling for Nixon to leave the ticket while some wanted to "wait and see." It offered summaries of the positions of 20 newspapers from New York and around the country, leading with an argument from the *New York Herald Tribune* that Nixon should offer to resign from the ticket and let Eisenhower decide.[9]

The next day, the *New York Times* published another editorial on Nixon and his fund. The editorial again professed belief that Nixon was not guilty of corruption and that the editors believed the list of donors was complete and that the accounting of how the money was spent was factual and honest. But, at the same time, they questioned Nixon's judgment and suggested reforms to funding Congressional staffing needs should be made.[10] The editorial ended by urging Nixon's continued cooperation with the investigation and with praise for Eisenhower, noting, "He has moved promptly and effectively with both fairness to Senator Nixon and a due sense of responsibility to the public."[11]

Unsurprisingly, the Democrats hoped to make the most of this situation, though there was some hesitance because Stevenson's running mate, Alabama senator John Sparkman, had his wife working on his Senate payroll. Sparkman's defense of his situation was that he hired his wife simply because he could not find good office staff and that he did not spend all his office budget allotment in any case.[12] But on September 21, Sparkman called for a Senate investigation of Nixon's actions, saying that the "Hoey Committee," which was the Senate's permanent investigations committee, should investigate it. Hoey was North Carolina senator Clyde Hoey, chair of the committee. Sparkman wondered aloud what the committee would do to another government employee who did what Nixon had allegedly done and asked what Nixon's response would be to an executive branch employee with a similar fund.[13]

The chairman of the Democratic National Committee, Stephen Mitchell, first issued a statement and then gave a press conference in which he played on a similar theme, asking how concerned Eisenhower could be about corruption in government if this was going on in his own "family." Eisenhower made corruption in the Truman administration a major theme of his 1952 campaign. Mitchell challenged Eisenhower to remove Nixon from the ticket and live up to his own statements about public morals.[14]

The incumbent Democratic president, Harry Truman, was not quiet about Nixon, either. While visiting the Coast Guard Academy in New London, Connecticut, Truman spoke to reporters and drew a parallel between Nixon's fund and what he believed was a similar scandal involving Franklin Pierce's running mate, William R. King, a century earlier in 1852. Truman even suggested a reference, *The Presidency*, by Stefan Lorant, to reporters.[15]

In fact, as reporters discovered after looking at the book and calling Lorant for comment, there was no such scandal involving William R. King. Truman, Lorant speculated, was thinking about a similar scandal involving James Garfield when he was running for president. There was one interesting non sequitur tacked on to the *Washington Post*'s story about Truman's commentary in its final paragraph: "The newspapers read today by Truman on his journey today included *The Washington Post*, supporting Gen. Dwight D. Eisenhower; the Republican candidate, and which suggested Nixon's withdrawal from the ticket."[16] It is presented as news but reads like an editorial suggestion.

A shoe soon dropped for the Democrats. Kent Chandler, a Chicago business executive from the printing company A.B. Dick, issued a demand by telegram, widely distributed to the press, that Adlai Stevenson admit that he created funds like Nixon's for his own political appointees. The *Chicago Daily Tribune* trumpeted this news on September 23, on page one with the banner headline "New Fund Bared; It's Adlai's."[17] Chandler urged Stevenson to make public the names of the donors and suggested that there was nothing wrong with such funds, including Nixon's. Chandler's statement concluded that while Stevenson had his own outside income, "you have found it necessary to provide additional pay in order to induce others not so fortunate to accept responsible state jobs that require honesty, ability, and willingness to serve, when the salary established by the law is insufficient to justify the sacrifice asked of them."[18]

In the face of a growing storm, Nixon issued a new statement and had Dana Smith release the full list of donors to his fund on September 20. His statement asserted that the fund was for political activities; it allowed him to avoid enlarging his Senate staff and charging the cost to taxpayers; it was not for personal enrichment; and the fund was always "a matter of public knowledge."[19] But as the days went by, the speculation continued to ratchet up and the story changed several times: (1) Eisenhower has decided to keep Nixon; (2) Eisenhower will only keep Nixon if he's "clean as a hound's tooth" and he will judge him by a moral standard, not a legal one; (3) Eisenhower is undecided and has refused to speak to Nixon, upsetting the vice presidential nominee.

Nixon referenced Eisenhower's public insistence that Nixon be "as clean as a hound's tooth" with evident annoyance even ten years later in *Six Crises*. He wrote of a meeting with his advisers over the weekend of September 20 and 21, while still waiting to hear directly from Eisenhower. Nixon wrote also of his insistence that he would not speak to Eisenhower's number one man, Sherman Adams, but only to Eisenhower himself. He continued, commenting on Eisenhower's words, writing of how he learned about Eisenhower's "hound's tooth" remark and the implications of that comment, that Nixon would have to prove himself innocent to stay on the ticket. He concluded that he and his advisors were troubled by the way Eisenhower treated them, making them feel like children caught with jam on their faces.[20]

The behavior of Eisenhower and his aides did little to stifle the growing speculation about Nixon's viability as a running mate. It is doubtful Nixon would have agreed with newspapers' approval of Eisenhower's "promptly" acting. Speaking at a rally in Kansas City on September 19,

Dwight Eisenhower made his first public comments on the Nixon situation, reading a prepared statement from Nixon characterizing the fund story as a "smear" and concluding that he believed Nixon, saying that they shared the same standard of public morality.[21] He used this sentence as a launching pad for an attack on political corruption, starting with the history of the Pendergast machine in Kansas City and then tying it to the Truman administration, the Democratic Party and its nominee, Adlai Stevenson.

But while he spoke positively about Nixon at this rally, the press was full of stories about divisions between Eisenhower aides on the Nixon question and indefinite statements from Eisenhower himself. As Nixon noted in Six Crises, he felt much of this confusion was the fault of Eisenhower himself. But he also spread his unhappiness quite easily to the press—through the words of his aides, rather than writing them in his own voice, reporting that his aide Bassett told him 90 percent of the press on the train Eisenhower campaigned from thought Nixon should be removed from the ticket. In the same passage, he also asserted reporters were blaming Eisenhower for not making up his mind "one way or the other," a sentiment with which Nixon undoubtedly agreed. He concluded that although reporters seemed impressed by the favorable reaction Nixon got from crowds when he told his version of the fund story, most media commentators and columnists predicted Eisenhower would remove him from the ticket.[22]

Nixon attributed his strongest condemnations of both Eisenhower's people and the press to statements by Patrick Hillings and Murray Chotiner. Hillings was a member of Congress, having won Nixon's seat when Nixon was elected to the Senate in 1950. Chotiner was a very successful political consultant who worked on most of Nixon's campaigns. Nixon wrote that Hillings told him he owed it to his supporters to stay on the ticket regardless of what Eisenhower wanted and that he should focus on beating the press, not trying to win them over.[23] Nixon's aides were always ready to tell Nixon something he fully believed about himself—that he was very important to the country's well-being and that the press was an enemy to be bested.

He emphasized his feeling of self-importance, writing in Six Crises that he could not submit to a "collective judgment" pushing him off the ticket, because what he decided would affect the Republican Party and the millions of people who supported his nomination. He continued, writing that he felt his decision would affect the future of the United States, as well as the cause of peace and freedom worldwide.[24] He feared that if he left the ticket, Eisenhower would lose, and the far less qualified Adlai Stevenson would become president. Nixon decided he would do everything he could to stay on the ticket, "with honor."[25]

In *Six Crises*, Nixon built up Murray Chotiner as a reliable source and quoted him at length, in condemnation of both the press and Eisenhower's people and, as Hillings did, in praise of Nixon himself. Chotiner, according to Nixon, told him that Eisenhower had no chance to win if Nixon were not on the ticket because Nixon's friends would never forgive Eisenhower and the Democrats would beat Eisenhower to death with the story. He told Nixon that the indecision of the amateurs advising Eisenhower were responsible for the fund story becoming so big.[26]

Chotiner laid out what would be the Nixon blueprint for most of the rest of his political career—with varying levels of success, but with little deviation. Nixon reported that Chotiner told him that he was always able to win audiences over when he spoke to them, so his staff needed to find him the biggest audience they could to allow Nixon to "'talk over the heads of the press to the people.'" Chotiner told Nixon the people supported him, but the press was out to get him.[27] Reality is less important than what Nixon and his devoted aides believed was reality. That Nixon thought the press was against him mattered because it affected how he conducted himself. And it has affected every president since.

The first call between Nixon and Eisenhower did not come until nearly midnight on the night of September 21 and the reporting which followed that call was as speculative as the reporting that came before it. The coverage reported that neither Nixon nor Eisenhower made any comment about what was said between them and continued to speculate about the opinions of Eisenhower's advisers, noting that they were evenly divided between keeping Nixon and dropping him from the ticket.

As the days rolled on, the story picked up momentum, going in many directions, including (1) speculation about how grim things had become inside the Eisenhower campaign; (2) how the GOP would go about replacing Nixon on the ticket; (3) reports of examinations of Nixon's taxes and his allegedly expensive Washington-area home; (4) the fact that Herbert Hoover, Jr., was one of the donors to the fund; (5) Nixon's increasingly strong statements defending the fund as part of his fight against communism and he would not withdraw from the race and (6) what New York governor, and former GOP presidential nominee, Thomas Dewey was telling Eisenhower, frequently described as a political amateur, he should do about Nixon.

Nixon certainly had cause to wonder if Eisenhower was not merely indecisive but actively working to remove him from the ticket. When he learned of an editorial in the staunchly Republican *New York Herald Tribune* which urged him to quit the race, Nixon was very concerned because it seemed to him that it was like an official request from Eisenhower.[28] In *Six Crises*, Nixon vented his frustration at Eisenhower and his team by attributing strong emotions to his advisers, William Rogers (who served Eisenhower as attorney general and Nixon as secretary of state) and Murray Chotiner. The two were angry at the amateurs advising Eisenhower who were unable to identify a purely political attack, Nixon wrote.[29] Nixon added that he felt some of the same emotions but understood it was important not to fly off the handle.[30] It is unnecessary to fly off the handle if you can attribute it to someone else.

Nixon, determined to save his place on the ticket, left his train tour of the west and flew home to Los Angeles. It was announced that he was doing so to prepare an address to be broadcast on NBC television and on the Mutual and Columbia radio networks from 9:30 to 10:00 Eastern time on the evening of September 23, following Chotiner's advice to get before the biggest possible audience. The decision for the final format of the broadcast, as Nixon relates the events, came after two key phone calls. The first was with Thomas Dewey. Nixon wrote that Dewey told him to go on television and have the American people make the decision Eisenhower would not make. Depending on the public's response, Nixon could announce he was staying or leaving and, in either case, no one in the public would blame Eisenhower. Nixon wrote that some of his staff did not like the idea of leaving his fate up to a television audience in case there was an effort to load the deck against him, but his respect for Dewey's judgment won the day.[31] A speech Nixon needed to deliver in Portland, Oregon, interrupted the deliberations about the television appearance.

The second call came from Eisenhower. After the speech Nixon and his staff were again discussing what a television appearance might look like when Eisenhower finally called. Nixon reports the conversation in terms that suggest Eisenhower was unwilling to make the decision about his fate and which also reflected the major points Dewey made to him. Nixon wrote that Eisenhower explained that he felt he would lose either by having his name on a decision to keep Nixon or to drop him. Nixon quoted Eisenhower as telling him to make a nationwide television broadcast and tell all about his life in public service, including any money he ever received. Nixon asked Eisenhower if he would make an announcement after the program as to whether Nixon was still on the ticket and Eisenhower was noncommittal, telling him, "'I am hoping that no announcement would be necessary at all, but maybe after the program we could tell what ought to be done.'"[32]

Nixon pressed Eisenhower for a promise of a statement but Ike remained steadfast, saying they would need three or four days after the broadcast to see what happened and told Nixon to keep his chin up.[33] What is unobserved by Nixon here, but scholars such as Druckman and Jacobs would surely note, is that Eisenhower is essentially telling Nixon they should wait to see what the polls—in the form of telegrammed responses to the speech—told them to do. For Nixon, it was a lesson in manipulating the polls to achieve a desired outcome. Druckman and Jacobs write about him engaging in this behavior as president, but it was a lesson he learned much earlier.

The airtime cost $75,000 and was paid for by the Republican National Committee. Nixon told reporters that he spoke to Eisenhower and got the presidential candidate's approval.[34] His press secretary, James Bassett, spoke about the coming broadcast, calling it an unprecedented financial report by a president. Nixon was going to show the nation he was always law abiding and honest.[35] The staff was fully on board, agreeing this strategy was the best option. As Nixon wrote in *Six Crises*, all his aides agreed that he needed to get his story to the American people and a television broadcast was the only way to effectively do it. The age of campaign trains making whistle stops was coming to an end.[36]

He gave the speech on the evening of September 23, 1952. Nixon's presentation was unremarkable if viewed through the lens of the technological standards of today. With an image of an American flag flapping in the breeze, an announcer reported that the broadcast was sponsored by the Republican National Committee and the Republican House and Senate campaign committees. There was a shot of Richard Nixon's business card and the announcer told the audience they were about to hear a report from Nixon, Republican vice-presidential candidate, who had interrupted his campaign to deliver this important message. The scene shifted to Nixon, sitting at a desk, hands folded and looking uncomfortable, staring into a camera on a set made to look like a home office. Sitting off to the side, occasionally shown on-camera, was Pat Nixon, looking even more uncomfortable than her husband.

But if the setting was awkward and not visually stimulating in a 21st-century context, what Nixon was doing was revolutionary. He set the scene from the beginning, suggesting that he was doing something *normal* politicians do not do. And he made use of a phrase he and many who have followed him politics use frequently: "smear." He told the huge audience that he was there to do something new. Rather than ignore charges against him, or simply deny them, he was going to give his side of the case. The office of vice president was too important, and Americans had a right to know that the charges made against him, of taking $18,000 from supporters in return for favors, was untrue. Implicit in this opening is the notion that there was something new about what he is doing: facing the charges against him to deny them directly to the American people. And he was doing so on a television broadcast controlled completely by him and his team, outside of the influence of the news media that he felt hated him.

Continuing his opening statement, Nixon said flatly that what he did was not legally wrong but posed the question of whether it was morally wrong. He answered the question, saying it would be morally wrong if he used any of the money for personal gain. Did he? To set up his answer to this question, Nixon spent the bulk of the first two-thirds of the broadcast speaking about his family finances, at several points in mind-numbing detail. At times, he spoke in the third person.

In the next section of the speech, Nixon answered the question: none of the money went to his personal use. Rather, he used the money to get his political message to the American public, something he suggested it was his duty to do, to make public all the wrongdoing of the Truman administration. He further argued that by using the fund to pay for publicizing the corruption and communism of the Truman administration he saved the taxpayers of America a lot of money.

Nixon discussed the results of an audit conducted about his use of the fund and gave an extremely detailed explanation of his family finances, starting with his childhood and working up to the present day. See from today's perspective, almost all of it is forgettable: either standard political stump speech material, or mind-numbing details of his personal life most people probably never wanted to know. But in 1952, it was unheard of for a politician to do this on television. And then, about two-thirds of the way through the half-hour presentation, Nixon hit on two effective, memorable, career-saving lines. The first was "Well, that's about it. That's what we have. And that's what we owe. It isn't very much. But Pat and I have the satisfaction that every dime that we've got is honestly ours. I should say this, that Pat doesn't have a mink coat. But she does have a respectable Republican cloth coat, and I always tell her she'd look good in anything." It is delivered awkwardly, and that awkwardness was emphasized as the scene cut to the uncomfortable Pat Nixon. But, uncomfortable or not, it was unlike anything anyone ever heard a politician say simultaneously to so many Americans ever before.

And then Nixon hit the first televised political home run in American political history. He said that the Nixon family did receive a gift from a Texan who heard Pat Nixon on the radio talking about how their daughters wanted a dog. Nixon explained that the man sent them a dog and he said, "It was a little cocker spaniel dog, in a crate that he had sent all the way from Texas, black and white, spotted, and our little girl Tricia, the six year old, named it Checkers. And you know, the kids, like all kids, love the dog, and I just want to say this, right now, that regardless of what they say about it, we're gonna keep it." It was sweet, endearing and very un–Nixon. It instantly became one of the most famous lines in modern American political history and it ensured that Nixon's meteoric rise would continue to the vice presidency.

The remainder of the speech was a campaign stump speech, but one tailored to the situation Nixon found himself in. Many biographies of Nixon point out that he was raised in a family of humble means and that it had a huge impact on him. He may have been resentful of the financial struggles he faced, but he played them up to great advantage in this broadcast. As soon as he was done talking about Checkers, he reminded the audience they were witnessing something remarkable. He said, "It isn't easy to come before a nationwide audience and bare your life, as I've done," and went on to critique the Democrats for opposing a man of humble means. He said, taking a barely disguised shot at the Democratic presidential nominee, that he did not think that inheriting a huge fortune from one's father, as Adlai Stevenson did, should disqualify a man from running for president. However, Nixon added, it was important that people of common means be able to run for president because, as Abraham Lincoln said, "'God must have loved the common people—he made so many of them.'" And, just like that, he put a comparison of himself to Abraham Lincoln in people's minds, directly and unfiltered, via television. Comparing themselves to Abraham Lincoln is something every Republican since Lincoln has tried to do, perhaps none more often than Donald Trump, but Nixon holds the distinction of being the first to do so on television.

Nixon next detailed reports that Adlai Stevenson had his own funds to help him and that his opponent, the Democratic vice-presidential nominee, Alabama senator John Sparkman, put his wife on his Senate payroll, something Nixon made clear earlier in the speech he did not do with Pat Nixon. And then he suggested, on national television, for the first time, that a failure to do what Nixon had just done—explain everything to the people, step by step on television—was tantamount to an admission of guilt that the American people should consider very seriously, because anyone who was going to be president or vice president "must have the full confidence of all the people." The importance of this moment cannot be overestimated. This is the first politician to use national television to do what we see politicians do all the time today: attack charges and allegations head on, with vigor. Nixon's success with this strategy encouraged him to keep doing it and it established a model for generations to follow when accused of anything, whether the charges are true or not. Deny, deny, deny, and shout while you are doing it.

Next, Nixon addressed—and rhetorically attempted to quash—future "smears." He said:

> Now let me say this: I know that this is not the last of the smears. In spite of
> my explanation tonight, other smears will be made. Others have been made
> in the past. And the purpose of smears, I know, is this, to silence me, to make
> me let up. Well, they just do not know who they are dealing with. I am going

to tell you this: I remember in the dark days of the Hiss case some of the same columnists, some of the same radio commentators who are attacking me now and misrepresenting my position, were violently opposing me at the time I was after Alger Hiss. But I continued to fight because I knew I was right, *and I can say to this great television and radio audience* that I have no apologies to the American people for my part in putting Alger Hiss where he is today. And so far as this is concerned, I intend to continue to fight.

And why did he continue the fight? Why did he "bare his soul" to the nation? Why did he decide to stay with the campaign? He answered these questions with patriotism. He did it because he loved America and America was at risk. The only person who could save America was Eisenhower, the man on "my ticket." Nixon was, he argued, part of saving America. It is an even more profound claim than Ronald Reagan's promise to "Keep America Great" or Donald Trump's promise to "Make America Great Again." It is not possible to keep or make America great if it is no longer around.

After discussing the corruption in the Truman administration again and suggesting that Stevenson should not—could not—be president because he was soft on communism, Nixon read a letter from a young supporter, the wife of a soldier, and concluded with a call to action for the viewing audience. Telling them he was not a quitter, and neither was Pat, Nixon told the audience they should reach out to the Republican National Committee to let them know whether Nixon should stay on the ticket or go. And he wanted them to know that no matter what their verdict was, he was going to keep fighting corruption and communism on their behalf. And, of course, they should support Eisenhower no matter what, because he was a great man who was good for America.[37]

The language Nixon used was significant. He did not ask viewers to contact Eisenhower. We know from *Six Crises* that Nixon was frustrated with Eisenhower, feeling he was left waving in the breeze. Nixon asked them to contact the Republican Party and suggested his fate was their decision, not Ike's, to make. And it is true that the party leadership chose Nixon in the first place, in large measure because Eisenhower did not give the question much thought, assuming it was the party's prerogative to make the choice.

Nixon was chosen because of his anti-communist record, to mollify party conservatives who were unsure about Ike. But it is also certainly true that if Eisenhower was fully supportive of keeping Nixon, Nixon's future would not be a question. Nixon knew this, and he found Eisenhower's silence extremely annoying. To force the issue, Nixon did something new and unique in turning to the public to affect public opinion and then using that public opinion to reach a desired outcome. It is exactly what modern media and politics research, such as that of Druckman and Jacobs, suggests politicians of the 21st century try to do all the time—frame a story to their best advantage and prime citizens to prioritize some things over others. Nixon wanted to deemphasize concern about a few thousand dollars in a slush fund and emphasize concern for the very survival of the free world.

It was not a great speech in the tradition of presidential orators like Lincoln, Kennedy, or Reagan. It was nothing we would look at in the 21st century and say, "That's a great television performance." But it does not need to rank as the best, *because it was the first.* Nixon's contribution was not his great charisma or telegenic presence. It was his realization that television would forever change how politicians interacted with the American people. It did and that started with him.

In the aftermath of the televised baring of his financial history and his puppy confessional, Nixon's political fortunes turned around, setting a precedent for every generation of politicians which followed him. Many media outlets reported that the Republican National Headquarters was swamped with telegrams supporting Nixon. The *Wall Street Journal* reported that the response was immediate and that Western Union called it "the biggest flood of telegrams ever sent as a spontaneous result of a television or radio appeal."[38]

One man who commented publicly about Nixon's speech was Lewis L. Carrol, the donor of the cocker spaniel that ensured the speech would forever be known as the "Checkers speech." Carrol said he was "a fighting Texas Republican" and an "Ike-Nixon man" and he had given the dog as a gift to the Nixons "with no strings attached and no price tag" when he read that the Nixons wanted a puppy. As Carrol reported, the dog was "about five months old, pedigreed and registered."[39]

Nixon felt anger for the media who covered him and the slush fund story. The experience helped to build resentments that lasted for decades. One example, cited by Nixon in *Six Crises*, comes from coverage of these events by the *Washington Post*, which was ultimately a key agent in Nixon's downfall two decades later. Nixon's hostility toward the *Washington Post* is evident in memos and other documents, starting from the beginning of his presidential administration, but it began much earlier, in 1952, thanks to the *Post*'s clear assertion, published after the television performance, that Eisenhower should drop Nixon from the ticket.

On September 25, the *Washington Post* published an editorial titled "What Is He Hiding?" It was not technically about Nixon. It was about Adlai Stevenson. In part, it was a stinging condemnation of the Democratic nominee. The editorial suggested that Stevenson's fund for Illinois government employees was every bit as problematic as Nixon's.[40] However, the editorial also included condemnation of Nixon, saying that the level of wrongdoing by Stevenson and Nixon was equivalent.[41] For the *Post*, a revelation about Stevenson did not mean that Nixon was off the hook. While their editorial about Stevenson concluded that Stevenson's reluctance to do anything about "a matter of such importance" disqualified him for the presidency, the paper's editors made it clear they held the same opinion of Nixon.[42]

While the *Post*'s Stevenson editorial was three paragraphs in length, on the same day the paper published an assessment of national press reaction to Nixon's speech, titled "Press reaction split on Nixon," and noting it "ranged ... from 'magnificent' to 'political soap opera.'"[43] To top it off, on the same page on which the Stevenson editorial was printed was a two-column, nine-paragraph editorial reiterating the editorial position that Nixon should be dropped from the Republican ticket. It read, in part, "The central issue, as we view it, remains unanswered by the Senator's talk. It is whether any such private fund can be squared with our American ideals of representative government.... The evil of private funds for public officeholders is that they operate to increase the pressures of private obligation."[44] The editorial reemphasized the fact that corruption in Washington was one of the reasons for endorsing Eisenhower in the first place and that keeping Nixon on the ticket made Eisenhower a hypocrite.[45] The editorial concluded that Nixon was simply a burden to Eisenhower's campaign by refusing to withdraw.[46]

In *Six Crises*, Nixon commented on his reaction to media calls for his resignation from the ticket. He wrote of his initial reaction to being asked by a reporter on September 19 about such editorials. He recollected being asked by a reporter what he thought of editorials in the *Washington Post* and *New York Herald Tribune* calling for him to resign. They were both a surprise to him and he begged off responding.[47] Later, with reflection, he offered an assessment of the editorials. He dismissed the *Post*, saying that the paper had been against him since the Hiss trial. But the *Herald Tribune* editorial was more troubling. It shook his faith that the fund attack was purely partisan and that it would be quickly forgotten. He wrote that while he could shrug off an attack by the *Post*, the *Herald Tribune* "was the most influential Republican newspaper in the East."[48]

The *New York Times*, which would later earn the same ire from Nixon as the *Post*, was more measured than the *Post*—critiquing both Nixon and Stevenson in the wake of the Checkers speech, but not calling for Nixon's resignation from the ticket. The *Times* editorial argued that Nixon was wrong, but that being wrong and acting in poor judgment were not the same as being corrupt. Both Nixon and Stevenson were guilty of serious errors of judgment, as the editors of the *Times* saw it, concluding that the dust-up involving both men was a good thing because it was a lesson to the American people that they needed to clean up public service and public servants.[49] The *Times* also differed from the *Post* in its presentation of comments from newspapers around the country, giving the story this bland and neutral headline: "Excerpts from Editorial Comment on Nixon's Explanation of Fund."[50]

A piece in the *Wall St. Journal*, published on September 25, 1952, was geared toward airing Nixon's grievances—couched as the grievances of his supporters—with both Eisenhower and some unnamed media outlets. The article, ostensibly about a post–Checkers meeting between Nixon and Eisenhower, reported that after the broadcast, Nixon's aides felt he was now much stronger politically and was someone Eisenhower had to treat with respect. The aides also vented about Eisenhower's indecisive treatment of Nixon, saying, "'If Ike can't make up his mind on this, what's he going to do when he's dealing with Stalin?'"[51]

The article continued with a behind-the-scenes look at the Nixon machine, reporting that his aides were angry with the poor advice Ike was receiving from "amateurs," with Eisenhower's handling of the fund crisis, and with the "Eastern newspapers" calling for Nixon to step down.[52] The reporter, William Clark, also noted that Nixon's aides were much more concerned with Nixon's fortunes than they were for Eisenhower campaign.[53] This is fact. The existence of a zealous crew of aides and supporters was both a source of great strength to Nixon throughout his career and, ultimately, a major source of his downfall.

In the aftermath of the Checkers broadcast, the anger Nixon clearly felt toward Eisenhower remained, as evidenced by his telling of the tale in *Six Crises*. But the hostility Nixon and his crew may have felt for Eisenhower was not on public display when the two candidates appeared together at a rally on September 24 in Wheeling, West Virginia. It was a meeting which, according to Nixon, almost did not happen.

But while he put on a good public show, in *Six Crises* Nixon reveals that he had a hard time getting past the personal injury he felt. He wrote that he needed the calm advice of someone from outside his organization because his own team felt the same anger toward Eisenhower he felt. Nixon, who felt too angry to meet with Eisenhower, related that it took a consultation with his friend Bert Andrews, a reporter for the *New York Herald Tribune* who won a Pulitzer Prize for covering the Hiss case, to calm him down. Andrews told Nixon that Eisenhower had no choice but to keep him on the ticket after the Checkers broadcast but that he owed Eisenhower, the war hero general, some deference in making the decision public in his own way. And with that the two men met before the rally in West Virginia.[54]

After a brief meeting on Nixon's plane, in which Eisenhower told Nixon, "You're my boy," the two went to speak to a large crowd. Eisenhower began his remarks to the crowd by apologizing for the late start and blaming the delay on Nixon's late arrival.[55] Eisenhower then proceeded to give a standard stump speech. At the end, he turned to the subject of Nixon and his crisis, saying Nixon was the victim of an unfair and vicious attack. He was, in Eisenhower's estimation, a man of courage and honor.[56] Eisenhower then read a short telegram from Nixon's mother, endorsing her son, and a much longer one from Arthur Summerfield, the chairman of the Republican National Committee, which gave Nixon a full-throated endorsement by the RNC as the vice-presidential nominee. Eisenhower then said, "And now, I give you Dick Nixon."[57]

Using the phrase that annoyed him so much, Nixon told the crowd that the previous night he spoke to the nation to correct people's honest misunderstanding of the situation. He did this, he said, because "as General Eisenhower says, they have got to be as clean as a hound's tooth. They have got to have integrity and honesty, and the people have got to know it."[58] He then described the positive reaction he received for his speech and he praised the American people, saying, "the faith and confidence that I have always had in the fundamental intelligence of the American people was reaffirmed by what I saw today."[59]

Next, Nixon spoke words that he must have choked on while saying them. They were delivered in a way that seemed sincere to the crowd that heard them, but when they are read on the page, it is hard to believe, knowing how angry Nixon was about the whole affair, that they were sincerely felt by him. Nixon told the crowd how proud he was of the way Eisenhower handled the situation. A "lesser man," Nixon asserted, would have simply said he did not believe the charges against Nixon without waiting to hear the evidence. Eisenhower had not done that, Nixon said, because there had been too much ignoring of corruption in the current Truman administration.[60] Nixon could hardly have said otherwise about Eisenhower, but it seems impossible to believe that he wouldn't have preferred for the general to say early in the crisis exactly what Nixon claimed in his speech that he was happy Eisenhower *hadn't* said: that it was a smear against his running mate, Nixon, and that he was going to ignore it.

The *Chicago Daily Tribune* stood out as one of Nixon's friends in the press. Such friends, in Nixon's opinion, were not as plentiful as they should be. While in *Six Crises* Nixon depicts himself as happy with the way Eisenhower ultimately resolved things, the *Tribune* published an editorial on September 25 titled "Nixon Emerges," which took Eisenhower to task for his treatment of Nixon. The editorial opened with praise for Nixon and his Checkers speech. It credited him with gathering the largest audience for any candidate in the campaign and asserted his was the most effective speech given by any Republican in the race, concluding, "and it is not likely to be surpassed in impact as the campaign goes on."[61]

The editorial continued, attacking the way Eisenhower handled the situation, suggesting it led to doubt about his ability to judge others and creating the impression he doubted Nixon's integrity.[62] The conclusion the *Tribune's* editors arrived at is rather overwhelming in its dramatic assertion: "It would hardly be an exaggeration to say that in the public mind, the Republican ticket is now Nixon and Eisenhower rather than Eisenhower and Nixon."[63] It is unlikely many Republicans would have agreed with such an assessment, but such a sentiment no doubt raised Nixon's spirits.

In *Six Crises*, Nixon noted the lingering effects of the "fund" crisis, thanks in no small measure to the press. He wrote of the aftermath of the speeches he and Eisenhower gave in Wheeling noting, once again, a lesson learned about the importance of visuals in modern American politics. His aide Bill Knowland came over to congratulate Nixon for the speech. Nixon, at his emotional limit, began crying and buried his face in Knowland's shoulder. This exchange was captured by a press photographer and the resulting picture, Nixon wrote, "was forever to characterize the fund speech and my reaction to it."[64]

Nixon wrote that while the fund crisis was over after a week, he and his wife would have to live with the consequences of it for the rest of their lives. These words were written in 1962 and are like the words he used at the end of his chapter about the Alger Hiss case, and they bring readers back, full circle, to the beginning of the chapter on "The Fund," in which he characterized the crisis as "the most scarring" of his life. He certainly would not agree with that statement following his resignation from the presidency in 1974, but the fact that he characterized this crisis in such profound terms in 1962 speaks volumes about how troubled he was by these events and how much he felt they were going to dog him going forward.

In the final pages of his chronicle of "the fund" crisis, Nixon wrote of the positives of the crisis: It brought his team together and it saved his political career. But Nixon spent many more words writing about the negatives and airing grievances against the news media. He noted that there was plenty of criticism of his broadcast in the press. There was nothing in politics, Nixon wrote, which was "akin to 'total victory.' The speech itself was smeared and labeled 'a carefully rehearsed soap opera.'"[65]

Nixon doesn't name the source of this description, but lines similar to it appeared in editorials in newspapers such as the *New York Post*, which began the hubbub over "the fund," and commented derisively, "Sen. Nixon staged his private soap opera before a nation-wide television audience last night," adding, "Undoubtedly there were some, including Gen. Eisenhower, who regarded the performance as a thrilling evening in the theater; others may have felt, as we did, that the corn overshadowed the drama."[66] The *St. Louis Post-Dispatch* wrote that Nixon's program "had many of the elements of a carefully contrived soap opera."[67]

In *Six Crises*, Nixon framed the news media as an entity hostile to him and to his presence in positions of power in American politics. Repeatedly, Nixon referred to negative reporting about him as smears and made efforts to show that the press was inaccurate and, he implied, deliberately so. Even when news media outlets acknowledged their errors, they did so only after it was too late for the corrections to do Nixon any good.

In making his nationally televised address which saved his place on the Eisenhower ticket in 1952, Nixon undoubtedly learned valuable lessons about the power of television in American politics and he worked to re-frame his image and prime Americans to see him in a different light. Historian Kevin Mattson observes that Nixon managed to change his image to that of a family man at a time such an image change was critical for his future. But Mattson also notes the bigger impact of what Nixon did, calling him "a man out to save his career on television screens across America.... And a man who projected a political style that remains with us to this day."[68] It is essential to understand that Nixon learned a critically important lesson from this experience: Television gave politicians the ability to change their political fortunes. It was both a lesson of opportunity and a cautionary tale for Nixon.

But the most important lesson Nixon learned about television in 1952 was that it worked to his advantage because he took complete control of it, rather than letting reporters filter things for (and against) him. Following this experience, Nixon continued to harbor resentment and distrust for the media. By the end of the fund crisis, Nixon's resentment for the coverage he received in the media was set in concrete. The impact of the "smear" endured. He wrote that his honesty and integrity was challenged throughout his years as vice president and into private life when he and Pat bought a house in Beverly Hills. He wrote that people had the impression that he spent his time as vice president hiding money away, allowing him to buy the house when, in fact, he worked 80 hours a week.[69]

Nixon concluded his chapter on the fund crisis in a tone that is ironic in hindsight, given how the rest of his career went. In martyr mode, Nixon wrote of how friends asked him how he was able to endure being attacked so frequently over his career.[70] He wrote that he told those friends that people go into the political arena voluntarily and while undeserved attacks were hurtful, honest people should still take a chance and enter public service because, "if men with good and honest reputations do not take such risks, they leave the field of public service to the second-raters and chiselers who have no reputations to worry about."[71] And Richard Nixon, he wanted readers to know, was neither a chiseler, nor a second-rater. He was building the image of an upstanding, honest man. And a fighter.

Nixon went on at some length about reputations. He wrote that for those men with good and honest reputations, their reputations are their most important asset, and those reputations were, Nixon asserted, always at risk from "smear artists" and "rumor-mongers." It was impossible to keep up with "a concerted smear campaign." He then gave advice that he did not follow himself in the fund crisis or anytime in his career. He wrote that it is usually a mistake to publicly deny rumors, or to try to sue for slander and libel because it only helped to "spread the smear." The smears get the front page, he asserted, while defenses against them were relegated to "the deodorant ads." He concluded that a person in public life had to expect to be smeared and know that in most cases the best thing to do was to ignore the smears and hope they went away.[72] But in reality, Nixon never ignored rumors and charges, just hoping they would go away. He fought them fiercely and, as his career evolved, he developed sophisticated strategies and a team of advisers to help him fight the "smears" of the media.

Nixon wrote in *Six Crises* that the fund crisis was an exception to his general rule that politicians should just walk away from smears because it was an "exceptional situation."[73] But if that statement is to be taken at face value, it means that Nixon and his support staff viewed nearly every situation as exceptional, because Nixon always fought like a tiger, no matter whether the charges were true, false, trumped up, or devastatingly accurate. And it is a lesson that many politicians who have followed Nixon have continued to implement: deny, deny, deny, and smear the press for smearing you.

The major lesson from crisis number two was the same as from crisis number one: the press was out to get Richard Nixon and the only way to combat that was to go on the offensive. And he developed many ways to go on the offensive that have been emulated by his successors, at all levels of politics, in the video age. In the fund crisis chapter of *Six Crises*, Nixon worked to frame the press as biased and inaccurate and to prime people to see him as honest, forthright, proactive, determined, and courageous.

Lessons of the Heart (The Third Crisis: Eisenhower's Heart and "Monday Moods")

Richard Nixon began the third chapter of his book *Six Crises* with a quote and a paraphrase of Charles Dawes, the vice president under Calvin

Coolidge, one of the architects of William McKinley's successful campaigns for president and a winner of the Nobel Peace Prize. The vice presidency, Dawes said, was the easiest job in the world and its responsibilities were limited to presiding over the Senate and checking up regularly on the president's health. Nixon was never content as vice president to limit his duties to those two functions. He established an office in the Executive Office Building, next door to the White House, which no previous vice president had done, and he played political and diplomatic roles for the administration. Nixon was an ambitious entrepreneur who always had his eyes on the prize of the top job. But he knew he had to be careful about letting that ambition show too much.

On September 24, 1955, Richard Nixon was informed that Eisenhower suffered a heart attack while on vacation in Denver. Eisenhower remained in Denver, at Fitzsimmons Army Hospital until November 11, and the job of being vice president became more complicated. The chapter is not really about Eisenhower. It is written by Nixon *about* how Nixon was affected by, and responded to, Eisenhower's heart attack. In large measure, it is about his resentment of the way he was treated in service to Eisenhower.

The heart attack pre-dated the adoption of the 25th Amendment to the Constitution, which both makes the line of succession clear in case of a vacancy in the presidency or the vice presidency and lays out the conditions under which a still-living president may either voluntarily transfer the powers of the office to the vice president or involuntarily have those powers taken away.

Nixon's early instinct, if the ordering of his chapter is a reliable clue, was to worry about his own reputation. He begins writing that he knew vice presidents could not look like they were trying to grab power when the president was ill. That statement is fine. But the next sentence suggests that Nixon's main lesson learned was that he needed to step carefully because everyone was out to get him. He wrote that he was in a more difficult position than previous vice presidents in similar situations with a seriously ill president. He wrote that many considered him too young for the responsibilities of the job. He also felt that he was a longtime "whipping boy" for people wanting to indirectly attack the popular Eisenhower.[74]

The resentment was clear. That Nixon saw himself as a replacement target for the benevolent figure of Eisenhower clearly bothered him. The "crisis" in this chapter of Nixon's book, and of his life, was not the possibility that he could have to take over the reins of power but, rather, how he felt he was perceived by the American public. The heart attack chapter was, once again, an effort to frame a different image.

Nixon wrote that in the first days of Ike's heart crisis, as the country wondered about the president's health, he was facing his own crisis.

Eisenhower recuperates at Fitzsimmons Army Hospital in Denver in 1955.

It was unlike any Nixon faced before and being unsure of what to do was very stressful.[75] The problem, as Nixon saw it, was that in situations such as the Hiss case or the fund crisis, the course of action was obvious. But Ike's heart attack was a different kind of crisis for Nixon. One of the most telling parts of the passage where he analyzed this crisis was his discussion of public opinion polls. He wrote that he always adhered to a political philosophy of not following public opinion or being politically expedient. Rather, he wrote, he always did what his instinct told him was the right thing to do. The usefulness of public opinion polls, Nixon argued, was to help politicians speak to the people more intelligently, but they should not be a guide for politicians' behavior. This is a sentiment with which Druckman and Jacobs, and other scholars who have examined Nixon's obsession with polls, would clearly take exception. The politician must lead, not follow, Nixon argued, except in this case, Nixon wrote that in the heart attack crisis he knew he could not lead too much, lest people resent his behavior as a power grab.[76] As he writes in *Six Crises*, Nixon was primarily concerned with how he would be perceived. If some saw him as indecisive, he wanted them to know it was by design and he was in fact very decisive.

Nixon wrote, "The crisis was how to walk on eggs and not break them.

My problem, what I had to do, was to provide leadership without appearing to lead."[77] Nixon professed repeatedly in this chapter that he didn't want to do anything that would *seem* as if he was trying to grab power. However, that does not mean he had no interest in power. For instance, as it became clear Eisenhower would survive, the question shifted to whether he would run for reelection in 1956 and that raised all kinds of political issues for the vice president. Nixon wanted to be there to take over the mantle if that opportunity arose and, he wrote, "my problem remained how to exert leadership without seeming to do so."[78] He argued that one of the biggest problems he faced was avoiding making comments to the press. He tried to do so, Nixon wrote, but they were impossible to avoid in his trips between the White House and the Executive Office Building.[79]

When Eisenhower returned to Washington on Veteran's Day, November 11, 1955, after two months of recuperation in Denver, it was a nationally televised event. He went to his farm at Gettysburg to continue his recuperation, and on November 21 and 22, members of the administration met with him at Camp David. Nixon was there and, once again, resentment for the way Eisenhower treated him is apparent in *Six Crises*. Nixon notes that Eisenhower offered no thanks to anyone at the meeting, especially to him. He wrote that not offering personal appreciation was typical for Eisenhower. Only if someone did something extraordinary did Ike express appreciation. Nixon wrote that Eisenhower evidently did not consider the vice president's very hard job of walking "a tightrope" as Ike recovered worthy of personal words of thanks.[80] Nixon adds that no thank you was required, as he was only doing his duty as vice president, but this is hard to believe. If no thanks were expected, there was no need to mention it in his book.

Nixon continued to air grievances with Eisenhower in this chapter, much as he did in the chapter on the fund crisis. According to Nixon, Eisenhower's real crisis was not his heart attack but his inability to decide whether he was going to run for a second term. In explaining this personal crisis of Eisenhower's, Nixon took the opportunity to engage in some critiquing of the boss, describing him as a tantrum-prone bully behind closed doors. It was not unlike things aides and confidants would say about Nixon himself but, of course, this was in a book published two years after leaving the administration. Nixon wrote that Eisenhower was volatile, moody, given to "tailspin[s] of emotion" and that aides decided whether to speak with him based on what mood-predicting color of suit he was wearing, noting there was "one particular sports jacket he would wear when in a 'Monday mood.'"[81] It is, in the language of 21st-century media and politics research, an effort to frame a new image of Eisenhower from benevolent grandfather to petulant grump and to make Nixon look like a rudder necessary to keeping the administration balanced.

In describing Eisenhower's "should I run or not" interlude, Nixon writes that the press predicted Eisenhower would not run and added, rather self-servingly, that they were saying Nixon was now the heir apparent for the presidency. He described a president who spent several months worried, depressed, or both. On December 26, Nixon had a meeting with Eisenhower in which the president expressed the opinion that (a) Nixon was not popular enough to run for president in 1956 if Ike did not run and (b) that Nixon should consider serving in some capacity other than vice president in a new administration. Nixon's career would be better served, Eisenhower told him, if he served as attorney general or in some other Cabinet-level position.

Eisenhower was also not impressed with Nixon's poll numbers. Nixon wrote that Eisenhower told the vice president he was disappointed Nixon's popularity wasn't higher.[82] Ike further told Nixon that he wanted to meet with him periodically to talk about his popularity, saying, "'We might have to initiate a crash program for building you up.'"[83] Nixon took this to mean that Eisenhower thought he would be a drag on the ticket as Eisenhower's running mate if Ike chose to run again in 1956, but Eisenhower told him this wasn't the case.

But that was privately. When Eisenhower made his announcement on February 29 that he was going to seek a second term, he demurred on questions about whether Nixon would be his running mate. Eisenhower said that it would be up to the Republican National Convention to pick a presidential candidate first. Nixon complained in *Six Crises* that these comments caused speculation to run rampant and gave Nixon the impression Eisenhower wanted him off the ticket. In response, Nixon told various people that he was prepared to announce he would not be running with Eisenhower in 1956. Other people heard of this, he wrote, and insisted that he do no such thing, so he held his tongue.[84]

And then Nixon got the sign he was evidently waiting for—he received more than 20,000 write-in votes in the New Hampshire primary for vice president. But Eisenhower still refused to say he wanted Nixon as his vice president. Nixon wrote with frustration that Eisenhower told him the choice was up to the party, not the president.[85] Eisenhower also continued to tell the press that he was waiting for Nixon to indicate whether he wanted to stay on the ticket, "to chart his own course."

So, Nixon wrote, he did some "intense soul-searching" and called Eisenhower to tell him that he was honored to remain as vice president and had only remained silent because he didn't want to force himself on Eisenhower against his wishes.[86] What Nixon really wanted, it seems, was for Ike to ask him to please be on the ticket, but with that request not forthcoming, he told Eisenhower he wanted to stay on the team. Eisenhower told him he was delighted to hear the news and they made an announcement the same day from the White House. Nixon then suffered a minor effort, led by Minnesota governor Harold Stassen, to "dump Nixon" from the ticket. It was never a serious threat, but it was never forgotten by Nixon.

In general, the very idea that it was possible, however briefly, that Nixon would not be asked to join the ticket in 1956 was a very serious crisis to him. He called the uncertainty about his place on the ticket for 1956 a "personal crisis." He also wrote that it was minor in comparison to Eisenhower's heart attack, "for the outcome was never really in doubt," but it is not at all clear that it was never in doubt. After the fact, Nixon was trying to dismiss something he, in fact, took very seriously. He wrote at length that the problem arose because he allowed himself to relax too much in the aftermath of the heart attack crisis and that left him vulnerable to a different kind of attack on his ability to survive politically.

In an advice-giving mood, Nixon wrote that it was important to take time to relax and reenergize. If people did not do that, their tempers would be short and their judgment flawed. If that sentiment was accurate, then Nixon was quite regularly short on rest and relaxation. It is difficult to imagine a scenario in which he would take Eisenhower's lack of enthusiasm more calmly. The lesson from this crisis was, once again, that if Nixon did not look out for Nixon, no one else would.

The rest of the chapter on the heart attack is an exposition on the need for a constitutional amendment to account for presidential disability. However, concerns about presidential succession are not the main takeaway from this chapter of *Six Crises*. The main takeaways are the lessons Nixon learned about communication and protecting his own flank because he felt no one else was going to protect it. He was troubled by Eisenhower's ambivalence about him, and he was troubled that despite his best efforts, there were still people within his own party who did not like him. It was an important lesson in keeping as much control of the message as he could. He needed to make sure that the public saw him in the frame of decisive and capable leader, and he needed to prime them in the importance of that criterion when they considered him as a potential president.

FOUR

Nixon's South American Adventure

In the spring of 1958, Nixon was asked to make a trip to Argentina by an assistant secretary of state, Roy Rubottom. In chapter four of *Six Crises*, Nixon explained that his inclination was to say no to this request because he thought he had better, more important things to do at home. Namely, he expected to play a key role in the coming 1958 midterm congressional elections, and he did not want to waste any time with a trip out of the country. The reason for the trip, as the State Department saw it, was for the United States to properly recognize the democratic election of a new leader of Argentina, Arturo Frondizi, who was replacing the political faction led by Juan Peron. There was, as Nixon wrote, a perceived need to demonstrate that the United States was not sympathetic to Peron.

Rubottom, as Nixon described, organized a pressure campaign which included players such as Under Secretary of State Christian Herter, Secretary of State John Foster Dulles, and Eisenhower himself to convince Nixon to go. Nixon felt he had no choice but to say yes and, when he did, the agenda was expanded to include stops in several South American countries: Uruguay, Peru, Paraguay, Bolivia, Colombia, and Venezuela. This chapter of *Six Crises* is ostensibly about the trip, but it serves two strategic purposes: (1) to, once again, show the press to be reporting stories that are different from reality as Nixon saw it and (2) to bolster a frame of Nixon as a brave leader, uncowed in the face of violent protesters.

In his preparation for the trip, Allen Dulles, the brother of Eisenhower's secretary of state, John Foster Dulles and the first civilian to head the CIA, told Nixon that there were some concerns about the possibility of protests in some of the countries he was going to visit. But since these did not include predictions of violence, Nixon told the reporters who inquired about the trip that it was not worth coming with him. The consequence of this, Nixon added, was to make the press angry with him. He wrote,

"They probably will never stop needling me for that prediction. The trip produced one of the top news stories of the year."[1]

Nixon's first stop on the trip was Uruguay. From his perspective, the arrival in Montevideo went very well. But the next day, he was surprised to see that the press coverage featured pictures of protestors, some holding signs saying things such as "Fuera Nixon," which roughly translates to "Nixon Go Home." In *Six Crises*, Nixon described the journey from the airport to his hotel as uneventful, noting that he didn't know until reaching the hotel that any people, students at the University of the Republic, had been holding protest signs, and he certainly didn't consider it significant.[2] But, Nixon added, when he awoke the next morning, one of his aides, Bob Key, told him that the press was focusing on the protesters, not what Nixon saw as the warmth of his reception. He wrote, with evident annoyance in *Six Crises*, that all the headlines were about the negative signs and pickets.[3]

And, indeed, there was attention paid to the protestors. One curious difference in Nixon's story about the drive versus the press reports about it is that while Nixon seems to not even have seen protestors, the press coverage suggests it would have been impossible not to see them. In the *Washington Post,* Stanford Bradshaw reported that Nixon was greeted with jeers telling him to go home and accusations of the United States oppressing Latin American countries.[4]

The headline in the *New York Times'* story about the arrival was "Uruguayans Jeer and Cheer Nixons." The first paragraphs of the story were positive, belying Nixon's impression that there was nothing positive in the coverage, but the kind of coverage that drew Nixon's ire *did* come in the fourth paragraph, with a description of students yelling, "Get out, Nixon," and throwing leaflets about North American imperialism at him. From here, the story varied notably from Nixon's recollection in his book.

Nixon wrote that he did not notice the protestors at all, but the press account suggests a different scenario—that he saw them and ignored them. The story reported that Nixon smiled and waved at students who were yelling at him about negative American influence on the Uruguayan economy. It is possible that Nixon really didn't know what he was seeing on the parade route, but then, at the luncheon following his arrival, several invited guests also unambiguously spoke up with concerns about U.S. policy and the rapidly worsening Uruguayan economy, something which Nixon didn't mention at all in his book.[5] While Nixon wrote nothing about Uruguayans protesting, he did complain about the reporting, noting that he had learned early on that "the unusual or the controversial event always makes 'news' over the expected or routine occurrences, even though the latter may be a more accurate picture of the true situation."[6]

Nixon's response to hearing about the protests was to stop his motorcade on the way to the airport the next morning at the University of the Republic, walk into its law school, take over a classroom, and start a dialogue with students. In Nixon's version of this event, it was a triumph of diplomacy. He wrote that he was swarmed with well-wishing students wanting to shake his hand and get his autograph and he engaged in a question-and-answer session. He wrote that he spoke with them for nearly an hour about a variety of complaints against the United States, saying that he was able to address each concern honestly and directly.[7] Although he was unhappy with the press coverage overall, the coverage of this event, at least in the *Washington Post*, concurred with Nixon's assessment.[8]

Writing strangely in the third person, as he sometimes also spoke, Nixon wrote, "The real enemy for Nixon was always Communists," and he made it clear that it was communists who were the troublemakers in Uruguay. He wrote that while the communists were not able to pack the room where he was speaking, they packed the route back to his motorcade, shouting and protesting. But, Nixon writes, they were successfully opposed by other students.[9]

Nixon reported in *Six Crises* that his advisers were very happy with how he handled things at the university, and they were off to their second country of the tour, Argentina, where he was to show American support for the new president, Arturo Frondizi, as he was inaugurated. In the book, Nixon's discussion of the ceremony was covered in one sentence, noting that his schedule in Argentina allowed him to attend the inauguration and do other things.[10] But what he did not mention was that he missed the swearing in.

As was reported by the reporters traveling with Nixon, he arrived at the ceremony after Frondizi took the oath. For example, the *Chicago Daily Tribune* reported that the vice president and his motorcade did not allow enough time for the 40-block drive from the U.S. Embassy. He was hooted at by the crowd outside as he ran in late. He went in and was taken around to a side entrance, where he slipped in and sat between the representatives from Bolivia and the Vatican.[11] Considering that the ostensible reason for the entire trip was to demonstrate American support for Frondizi, it was an embarrassing diplomatic gaffe. Nixon also neglected, in his one-sentence explanation of events at the inauguration, to mention that Frondizi took the opportunity in his speech to criticize U.S. trade policy.

Nixon's take on his time in Argentina was that it was mostly spent giving speeches which addressed the concerns of labor unions and the need for them to resist communist infiltration. Just as he visited a university in Uruguay, he also made a stop at Buenos Aires University. Here, again, he was faced with some opposition. He took pains to describe the difference between American university students and *some* Latin American university students. He wrote dismissively that in Latin America there were many professional students who were likely communists working to indoctrinate younger students.[12]

Once again, if there was any difference of opinion in the rooms where he spoke, as Nixon saw it, it had to have been inspired by communists. Nixon described one of his interactions with a student whose credentials he doubted. He wrote that he was not trying to convert communists but rather to keep others from being persuaded by anti–U.S. propaganda.[13] There is, of course, no way to measure if he was at all successful, but it reads well in his book.

From Argentina, Nixon traveled to Paraguay. He was there for just a day largely because, he wrote, there were diplomatic concerns it would seem like the United States supported the dictator who ruled the country, Alfredo Stroessner. After a day in Paraguay, he went to Bolivia. The reception in Bolivia, Nixon reported, was pleasant, save for "a few Communist hecklers carrying anti–American signs."[14] The main message of Nixon's time in Bolivia was to promise U.S. economic aid for the poverty-stricken nation.

So dire was the state of the nation's economy, Nixon reported, that the president of Bolivia, Hernán Siles, pointed at the pictures of his two predecessors on the walls of his office and explained to Nixon that one committed suicide and the other was hung from a lamppost by an angry mob: "'I often wonder what my fate will be,' he said with a wry smile."[15] The story is a little odd, because neither of Siles's predecessors met the end described in the story. Nixon either did not know that or, unlike his drive to correct errors in the news media, felt no such need to correct the president of Bolivia.

While he was in Bolivia, Nixon took time to suggest that, once again, the proper message was not being heard by the proper people. Meeting with reporters traveling with him, Nixon discussed what he saw as "a woeful lack of understanding" of America's economic policy among opinion leaders in the countries he visited. A reporter noted that Nixon complained about feedback he was getting that the United States did not do enough to help Latin American, saying that the United States needed to increase exchange programs and bring more opinion leaders to the United States so incorrect impressions of the United States could be fixed.[16]

So far in Nixon's trip, after stops in four of the eight countries he was to visit, there had not been much of a crisis, though missing the ceremony which motivated the entire journey certainly was embarrassing (and, unsurprisingly, not discussed in his book). The next nation on Nixon's itinerary was Peru. There were several possible problems facing Nixon as he landed in Lima despite a long history of positive relations with

Peru. But Nixon was assured by Roy Rubottom, his State Department handler, that there was nowhere in the hemisphere he would get a warmer welcome.[17]

This did not prove to be true. After what Nixon described as a "gracious" reception at the airport, the motorcade headed into the city. Sensing "an air of suspense and uneasiness," Nixon was nevertheless able to make it to his hotel without complication. After a day of official engagements, Nixon was supposed to go to speak at San Marcos University. However, both Peruvian and American officials tried to get him to skip the engagement because there were rumors that protests would take place, and he was urged to go instead to Catholic University, where the student population was less likely to take on the characteristics of a mob.

Nixon wrote of his reluctance to leave the impression that he was intimidated by communist bullies, but he also did not want to overrule those advising him who knew more about the situation.[18] Peruvian officials did not want him to go and that night, before he went to bed, he polled the aides travelling with him, along with the U.S. ambassador to Peru. His personal staff advised him not to go. The ambassador told him that from a personal safety standpoint, he should not go, but from a U.S. standpoint, he should go, because it could have negative public relations effects if he did not.[19]

Nixon described a sleepless night of indecision. In the same passage, he displayed knowledge of another lesson learned from this crisis: the value of self-aggrandizement. Nixon explained that as he tossed and turned throughout the night (something which evidently plagued Nixon frequently, if his reports in *Six Crises* are a representative sample), he thought about Eisenhower. He wrote that he knew the indecision he was feeling was far more exhausting than "tomorrow's action would be" and described at length a conversation he had with Eisenhower about "the decision-making process."

Nixon related a story Eisenhower told him about the inner turmoil Ike endured in deciding to go forward with the Normandy invasion and the subsequent calm he felt once the decision was made and was thus in good shape for the many subsequent decisions which had to be made. Nixon wrote of his own decision in similar terms, reporting that he assessed all the factors in the context of what he hoped to achieve. He made it clear that he was not concerned for his personal safety or about the concerns of Peruvian leaders advising him not to go. There were more important things at stake, as a leader of a world power, including not appearing to be bullied by communists. Leaders needed to make their own decisions, he wrote, relying on their own intuition and "considerable experience" and "not count noses" of advisers.[20] And, just like that, Nixon made

Eisenhower's decision to initiate the key military action in World War II equivalent to his own decision to visit a college campus in Lima. Nixon framed his choice as being made selflessly in the interest of the United States and in the image of the very popular Dwight Eisenhower.

After laying a wreath at the tomb of a Peruvian hero, Jose de San Martin, Nixon gave the order to go to San Marcos University. As the motorcade made its way to the university, the students mobilized and, according to Nixon, as they got closer to the school, the chants changed from "Fuera Nixon" to "Muera Nixon," from "Nixon Go" to "Death to Nixon." Because the approach to the school was blocked, Nixon ordered the motorcade to stop about 50 yards from the gate and Nixon and two aides got out of the car, in the middle of the crowd, to walk. Nixon wrote that he tried to speak with them and walked "directly into the mob." Once again, Nixon saw the older students as the problem, stirring up the younger students from the rear as they saw Nixon calming things down.[21]

The danger of the situation quickly escalated. Nixon was informed that the crowd began throwing stones and they made their way back to the car. Nixon wrote that before getting in the car, he stood up in the convertible as it started to move, braced by a member of his Secret Service detail, Jack Sherwood. As his words were translated into Spanish by his interpreter, Colonel Vernon Walters, he wrote that he shouted at the protesters, telling them they were the worst kind of cowards who were afraid of the truth. He described feeling the "excitement of battle" in control of his temper as he "lashed out at the mob." Nixon explained that those close enough to hear became quiet and listened to him, but rocks were still being thrown from the back of the crowd.[22] It was, as Nixon described, a moment of extreme bravery in the face of a mob, although there was an important difference between one aspect of Nixon's description of events and some of the press reporting. In his book, Nixon wrote that as they left San Marcos, "the rocks were flying around us." But in the press, it was reported that "a dozen or so rocks came flying from the back of the crowd."[23] It is not pleasant to have even one rock thrown at you, but there is quite a difference between a dozen or so rocks, as described by the news media reports, and the showering of rocks that Nixon described in his book.

The delegation then went to Catholic University where, as predicted, the reception for Nixon was much calmer. But later, when Nixon returned to his hotel, which was near the tomb of General San Martin, another mob was waiting. They had torn up the wreath Nixon laid and blocked access to the hotel. Nixon, his Secret Service detail, and aides got out of the car and made their way, on foot, through the crowd to the hotel, but not before a man, identified by Nixon as "one of the most notorious Communist agitators in Lima," spat in his face.

Nixon closed his description of his visit to Peru with a final bit of self-aggrandizement, as he explained that he had 12 hours left to go in the country. He wrote, "I knew that if what had happened this morning were to have any meaning, it would depend on what I did and said during the balance of the day." His military aide entered the room and, according to Nixon, said, "Sir, I have never been so proud to be an American as I was today. I am honored to be serving under you."[24]

Nixon wrote that for the rest of the day, he received a hero's welcome everywhere he went. At the press conference he gave that day, he told the audience that he did not blame Peru or most of the students at San Marcos University but, rather, just "200 trained agitators" for the violence. It is a line worth noting, because it is one that Richard Nixon would use later in his career, as a candidate and as a president facing protestors of his own. Thanks at least in part to Nixon, blaming trained (and paid) agitators has become a commonplace accusation in 21st-century politics.

For once, the press coverage of the day in Peru was universally laudatory as Nixon saw it. Nixon was widely hailed for his bravery in the face of frightening adversity. What happened in Peru after he left, as Nixon described it, was the near elimination of the communist insurgency because the government finally cracked down on them. He reported hearing from Leonard Bernstein, in Lima with the New York Philharmonic, that the audience stood and applauded the playing of the "Star Spangled Banner" for "several minutes." And, Nixon reported, the Peru incident played well for him personally. Referring to it as gratifying, he wrote of the congratulatory notes and phone calls he received, including one from Eisenhower, who praised his calm, courageous behavior and told Nixon it greatly improved his reputation at home.[25]

Nixon was not wrong—the press was laudatory. One newspaper which he would come to see as a nemesis, the *New York Times*, published an editorial which agreed with his notion that communists were behind the aggression against him and gave a heroic interpretation of his performance, arguing that communists wanted to damage the United States and its allies and Nixon was more than just courageous. He was, the editorial argued, "patient and thoughtful," setting an example for all to follow.[26] That is a review any politician would relish seeing in print, and Nixon certainly did.

After calm visits to Ecuador and Colombia where, Nixon asserted, the communists had been knocked off their game by the events in Peru, the next stop was Venezuela and here, Nixon was told, there was the possibility of violence, perhaps even an assassination attempt. Nixon was determined to go to Venezuela anyway, he wrote, not because he was brave but because of the sensitive political situation in Venezuela. The recently deposed dictator of Venezuela, Perez Jimenez, and the chief of his secret police, Pedro Estrada, had been granted exile in the United States. That fact, Nixon wrote, was great propaganda for communists and put the United States in a sensitive spot diplomatically. He wrote that the State Department felt Nixon had to visit and show support for the new government.[27] Nixon expected Venezuela to be difficult, but he did not think anything that happened could be worse than what he experienced in Peru.

He mused in *Six Crises* about mobs and how to deal with them. It is another lesson learned by Nixon which he applied later in this trip and later in his career. Nixon's experience in Lima, he thought, was a graduate course in handling mobs. His master's thesis, he wrote, would have made the following conclusions: (1) mobs do not behave intelligently; (2) mobs are made up of cowards and one cannot show fear to cowards; (3) since mobs are stupid it is important to surprise them and do something unexpected; and (4) such unexpected behavior will throw mobs off enough for the person being protested to escape safely.[28]

The trouble in Venezuela started as soon as Nixon and his entourage, including his wife Pat, got off the plane at the airport in Caracas. They were shouted down and spat upon as they made their way to the motorcade. The head of his Secret Service detail directed Nixon toward an enclosed car rather than the convertible which waited for him. Nixon observed that if they opted for the open car, they could have been killed. The drive from the airport to the city was blocked several times by protestors. Nixon, who was riding with the Venezuelan foreign minister, lectured about the danger of communists when the foreign minister said the new government did not want to do anything that could be seen as suppressing free speech. Nixon wrote, "I could see that he believed what he was saying and I dropped the diplomatic double-talk and let him have it with both barrels." While the car was blocked and beset with spit and rocks, his wife, Pat, and the wife of the foreign minister were trapped in a car behind them. Pat, Nixon wrote, was as calm as if she were stuck in traffic on the Hollywood Freeway. Nixon then explained that he displayed the same level of calm, contrary to the panicky Venezuelan foreign minister, demonstrating how he put his lessons learned about mobs in Peru into action in Venezuela.[29]

Nixon asked in *Six Crises*, "What does a man think of at a time like this?" Nixon says he thought of how to get out of danger and of the importance of controlling his fear and staying calm. He wrote that while the foreign minister was "near hysterics," Nixon knew "I must be as cold as the mob was hot. The test of leadership is whether one has the ability, as Kipling once said, to keep his head while others are losing theirs."[30] And in *Six Crises*, Nixon was determined to show that *he* met Kipling's standard, but only as Nixon interpreted Kipling. The full poem, "If—," with the part Nixon paraphrased, is actually suggestive of a standard Nixon bridled against, in the sense that he rarely seemed to actually "make allowance for" the doubts of others. The line in Kipling's poem reads, "If you can keep your head when all about you are losing theirs and blaming it on you, If you can trust yourself when all men doubt you, But make allowance for their doubting too."[31]

Nixon ordered his driver to leave the motorcade, since it was not providing much security anyway, and head to the American embassy instead of their scheduled destination. He described meeting with Venezuelan president Jimenez and the ruling junta and greeting them with "courtesy but with deliberate coolness." His assessment of the situation was that the new government had not put enough emphasis on developing an adequate police force. It is another lesson—or pre-existing belief—that Nixon would implement later in his career. He wrote that freedom and order must be balanced. Both suffer if one is neglected in support of the other.[32] For Nixon as a candidate and as a president, the emphasis was on showing the American public how he would impose order. His critics would say he was doing so in response to what Nixon saw as a little too much freedom.

At a press conference, Nixon told the assembled crowd of journalists that what happened to his motorcade was not an expression of political freedom but, rather, of communist-inspired violence. He said that those who rioted were not loyal Venezuelans but, rather, loyal to an international communist conspiracy. Similarly, Nixon might argue, those who later protested in America did not represent the "silent majority" and the loyalty of the protesters was certainly in question. And this kind of law-and-order argument has survived the test of time, being used by Donald Trump in both 2016 and 2020. Those who agree with the leader are right and should be allowed to exercise their free speech; those who do not agree are a lawless mob.

The Nixons left Venezuela and stopped for a night in Puerto Rico before returning to Washington. This extra stop was added, Nixon wrote, so a proper welcoming ceremony could be prepared, something he clearly felt was in order: a hero's welcome. He wrote that 15,000 people, including Eisenhower, his Cabinet, and congressional leaders from both parties greeted them at the airport. It was, Nixon wrote, the end of an ordeal, a trip he did not want to take because he thought it would be boring.[33] It was, indeed, a hero's welcome, with Ike breaking protocol to be there. The day before Nixon returned, Eisenhower said of his plan to go to the airport to greet Nixon, "While it would be creating a precedent, because of my admiration for his calmness and fortitude and his courage in very trying circumstance, I would like to make some special gesture."[34]

But the chapter on this crisis was not complete. For Nixon, all the lessons he learned about mobs and dealing with pressure situations were overridden by his enemies: other politicians and the press. The final five pages of the chapter are devoted to how he felt he was blamed for poor Republican performance in the midterm elections. The tone he struck in describing the election is one of victimhood and of bad things happening to him personally.

Once again, for Nixon, it was all about Nixon and he found a way to find crisis in triumph. He wrote that the chapter was really a story of how a crisis affected an individual, not government policy. He cautioned that public officials should never believe in undying or enduring support. A crisis may generate support for a leader, but when the crisis cools, so does the support. There was, he wrote, no better example of this phenomenon than what happened to *him* after he got back from South America.[35]

Nixon wrote of his self-sacrifice, noting that he realized there was no one else to campaign nationally for the party. But if he did this, he said, he knew he would be endangering all the good will and popularity his South American adventure garnered him. He wrote that after weighing the plusses and minuses, he had no choice but to hit the campaign trail. His responsibility was to the party—not the country—and he wrote, "I had to risk my political prestige to avoid a disaster, if possible, knowing full well, as in 1954, we would probably lose, and I would be the big-name target for the defeat." And it was a bad defeat. The party lost 48 seats in the House of Representatives and 12 seats in the Senate.

One of the few highlights for Republicans, Nixon noted, was the big victory by Nelson Rockefeller in the gubernatorial race in New York. Nixon wrote with resentment about a commentator on television who called Rockefeller the big winner and Nixon the big loser. And Nixon, who would harbor negative feelings about Rockefeller throughout his career, learned his final important lesson of Venezuela—that he had no friends, he was surrounded only by enemies, especially in the worlds of politics and the news media.

Nixon took space in *Six Crises* to call out Rockefeller, saying that what Rockefeller said about Nixon changed to benefit Rockefeller.[36] For Nixon, there were no friends, no allies; there were only fickle people taking advantage of him when they could and distancing themselves when they thought it would help them. Nixon's lesson learned, once again, was that only Nixon cared about his own image. And strategically, that translated into Nixon working to frame the right image. Nixon learned that no one other than Nixon was going to look out for Nixon. He was going to have to be the steward of his own image and reputation. Writing *Six Crises* was part of that image-defining mission, and he carried it on for the rest of his life.

FIVE

Nixon Makes a Crisis Out of His Visit to the Soviet Union in 1959

In 1959, Nixon was sent by the Eisenhower administration to visit the U.S. Trade and Cultural Fair in Moscow. This was the first such exhibition by the United States in the Soviet Union and was, as Nixon described in chapter five of *Six Crises*, an outgrowth of a 1955 summit in Geneva, Switzerland, between Eisenhower, English prime minister Anthony Eden, French prime minister Edgar Faure, and two Soviets: Communist Party general secretary Nikita Khrushchev and the Soviet premier, Nikolai Bulganin. Khrushchev assumed the role of premier, while remaining general secretary, in 1958. The Geneva summit was considered a first step in trying to ease post–World War II East-West tensions, although the Cold War would become much more intense over the next few years.

As the United States' official representative heading to Moscow, Nixon wrote in *Six Crises* that he did all he could to prepare for meeting with Khrushchev, who had a reputation as an extremely difficult man to interact with. Using a baseball analogy, he described Khrushchev as a pitcher who "throws a bewildering assortment of stuff ... all delivered with a deceptive change of pace."[1]

Meeting Khrushchev was eye-opening for Nixon. The Russian was, he wrote, the first head of government to meet him with a "tirade of four-letter words" that were embarrassing for the interpreter to translate.[2] Given the language Nixon was heard using on the White House tapes, this must have been quite a string of words. On the morning of his first full day in Moscow, Nixon went to the Kremlin for what he thought was supposed to be a brief courtesy meeting with Khrushchev, with more substantive meetings scheduled for later. However, it turned into a much longer meeting in which Khrushchev went on the offensive and became quite animated.

After the meeting in the Kremlin, Nixon was supposed to tour the American trade and cultural exhibition. Khrushchev accompanied him and they toured the grounds with Khrushchev sparring with Nixon as they were followed by a large group of the press.[3] They walked into a building that housed a model of an American television studio and, according to Nixon's account, they found themselves accidentally on a stage in front of television cameras. There, an executive from Ampex asked them each to say something on camera which could be used as a greeting to fair visitors. To a casual observer, it may have seemed quite casual and unplanned.

But the visit to the television studio was not entirely happenstance. Herb Klein, who later became the first-ever White House communications director (another important and enduring innovation of Nixon, the precedent-setting electronic media president), oversaw the American media which accompanied Nixon to Moscow. Klein explained the TV studio encounter came about because executives from NBC and Ampex asked him to get the leaders to come in so they could show them the invention: videotape. Klein agreed and herded the pack, including Nixon and Khrushchev, through the exhibition. When they got to the television studio, they entered. As Klein recollected, "What the Ampex people had said to me was that they thought they could come in, and they could talk about the trip and ask about their families and just have polite conversation so that they could see how Ampex worked."[4] What happened, however, was that Khrushchev looked around, saw an opportunity, and launched a verbal attack on Nixon.

As Nixon saw it, Khrushchev was reluctant to speak on camera at first because he worried about being tricked, but when he saw a group of Soviet workers and the large group of press following them, temptation got the better of him. Nixon wrote that Khrushchev took the chance at free TV as quickly as an American politician, and instead of using it to greet visitors to the exhibition, the Soviet leader attacked Nixon. Nixon was not troubled by the fact that Khrushchev went on the attack, which, he wrote, was nothing, but that he did so on television.[5]

Klein's perspective of this exchange agreed with Nixon's perspective: the exchange did not go well for the vice president, and it was all captured on videotape, in living, breathing color. Klein explained, "So when we left there, I felt ... that it was great to have him on film with Khrushchev, but on the other hand I thought that he had been weak in his debate with him. So, I said to him, as we were walking along, 'If you're going to get into any more debates, you'd better get tougher because he pushed you around.'" Nixon responded with a simple "Okay."[6]

Nixon was frustrated, feeling constrained by the requirements of diplomacy from responding to Khrushchev in the same tone the premier was using with him. Nixon's frustration increased when he watched the videotape. Khrushchev was rude and aggressive, while Nixon felt like he was fighting with a hand tied behind his back.[7]

Another account of the incident comes from William Safire. Safire would later be a speechwriter for Nixon, but at this time he was a press agent, and his client was the company All-State Properties, Inc., which built the model American home for the exhibition. He worked for Nixon in both the 1960 and 1968 campaigns and then joined the Nixon administration as a speechwriter. In his autobiography of his years working with Nixon, Safire wrote that the problem was that people expected Nixon to be a fighter, but he was, in fact, behaving as his normal diplomatic self in the TV studio and being deferential to Khrushchev. The consequence, Nixon worried, was that his tough guy reputation as someone who could stand up to the Soviets would be forever damaged by 20 minutes of videotape. Safire wrote, "Nixon came out of the TV studio sweating profusely, knowing he had 'lost,' and anxious to find a way to make a comeback."[8]

The tour of the exhibition grounds continued and, according to Nixon, Khrushchev continued to press throughout the tour, ending at the All-State Properties' model of a modern American home, filled with all the newest appliances and technology.[9] The leaders and their gaggle of press ended up in the kitchen. There, as Herb Klein explained, Nixon pointed out the refrigerator and Khrushchev dismissed it, claiming that the Soviets invented refrigeration. This began a back-and-forth argument between the two men. Klein, who left the house looking to see where to take the tour next, realized what was happening and tried, fruitlessly, to squeeze back into the kitchen. What happened in the kitchen was covered by the press as well. At the window, he saw William Safire passing press cameras in and out of the window. This second confrontation, according to Klein, went much better for Nixon. Noting that the reporters praised Nixon, Klein said people who read about the kitchen debate the next day saw that "Nixon had really stood up well and dominated it and had shown Khrushchev how to debate. The whole thing was pro–Nixon."[10]

For his part, Nixon, still unhappy about the TV studio debate, was unsure how the kitchen debate had gone. However, he was reassured by what he described to "widely differing sources," who both told him he did well. One was reporter Ernie Barcella from United Press International, and the other was the Soviet official Anastas Mikoyan, who Nixon met in Washington before traveling to Moscow. According to Nixon, Mikoyan pulled him aside and said, "'I reported to Mr. Khrushchev when I came back from Washington that you were very skillful in debate and you proved it again today.'"[11]

Thanks to that kind of positive feedback, in terms of thinking about the kitchen debate as a *debate*, a contest which could be scored and a winner determined, Nixon saw himself as having bested Khrushchev. But the fact that round one, which Nixon lost, took place in front of television cameras, while the second debate, which Nixon won, was captured only by reporters taking notes and still cameras, left a lasting impression on Nixon, who understood that the moving image was quickly becoming the most powerful element in American politics.

Nixon's own recollection of the encounter in his 1978 autobiography *RN* also characterizes the kitchen debate as a win. In his autobiography, Nixon wrote, "Unlike our encounter in the model television studio, our 'kitchen debate' was not televised, but it was widely reported—with a dramatic photograph showing me prodding my finger in Khrushchev's chest for emphasis."[12] It is not a surprise that Nixon wanted to emphasize the storyline of winning his conflict with Khrushchev for posterity, but it belies a clear interest in the importance and power of the moving visual image. And it is clear from this passage of his autobiography that what Nixon cared most about was the visual, moving or not.

Attempts by Nixon's people to suppress the video from the first debate failed. The news of the kitchen debate was widely circulated in the United States by the time CBS broadcast the footage of the TV studio debate two days later, but the problem, according to Herb Klein, was that when Americans saw it, and saw Nixon being dominated by Khrushchev, they thought it was the kitchen debate.[13] And this was certainly how it was reported. In its news coverage of the TV broadcast, the *New York Times* acted as if it was all one debate, rather than a play in two acts, noting only that the "unusual exchange" between the two leaders was broadcast on network television, without pointing out that there were two different unusual exchanges.[14]

Similarly, television critic Jack Gould, evaluating the TV history that was made, referred to "the taped telecast of the debate between" Nixon and Khrushchev and called it "an item of unusual viewing. Its first-hand glimpse of the two men engaged in their now celebrated tilt was a vivid supplement to the earlier newspaper accounts."[15] Gould, like other journalists, presented it as one big event and not two separate events, much to the frustration of people such as Klein and Nixon.

However, while Gould blended two encounters into one, he still saw an overall victory for Nixon. He wrote both of Nixon's weak performance and his comeback, without having seen the comeback. It is an interesting blend of what Gould saw and what he read becoming one in his mind. Gould wrote, "The Vice President at the outset seemed very unsteady in the extremely difficult situation but later regained his aplomb. Once again television showed how it could personalize a historic moment."[16]

William Safire saw the way Gould and many Americans synthesized the two separate encounters and took it as a lesson in public opinion formation. Because the story about the second encounter in the kitchen was reported first, along with a photo that became famous of Nixon thrusting a finger at Khrushchev's chest, it created an impression that Nixon bested Khrushchev. When the video was broadcast a couple of days later, people's impressions were already set and did not change because they viewed the video footage with the mental frame that Nixon stood up to the Soviets. That he appeared to be deferring to or, as Safire wrote, "kowtowing" to Khrushchev had no impact.

To Safire, this was an important lesson. He wrote, "That meant that the writing press would remain important in the coming Age of Television, influencing viewers' opinions of what they say. Something to remember."[17] Safire's analysis of the events may be the correct analysis, since print journalists like Gould covered the broadcast of the footage as confirmation of Nixon's triumph over Khrushchev, but one thing is clear: Nixon didn't see it that way. The experience taught Nixon another lesson he would never forget: the moving image matters more.

In concluding his discussion of the kitchen debate, Safire made it clear that Nixon saw things very differently. Safire wrote that Nixon would never agree with an analysis that emphasized substance over image. He quoted Nixon saying, "'What's on the tube is what counts.... I've never been able to get anybody in my press operation who understood the power of television.'"[18] Television was proving itself to be a source of great influence on people and Nixon knew it, which made him obsess about a bad TV moment like the first debate with Khrushchev.

The problem, as Herb Klein tried to articulate, came from the possibility that what people saw with their eyes on the television screen was not exactly what happened or, at least, was not everything that happened. The kitchen debate took place nearly a decade after the Checkers speech. Unlike the fund crisis speech, which Nixon controlled entirely and used to his great advantage, he saw this video with Khrushchev as far more powerful than newspaper stories in building people's impressions of him. And, as Klein related, its dissemination was entirely out of Nixon's hands. The vice president feared that it showed him being bested in a moment of direct confrontation with America's greatest enemy. Nixon was saved, as Safire saw it, by the fact that another confrontation happened very soon after and he was covered in that conflict as having bested Khrushchev. But even if Safire is correct, it is important to remember that what everyone seems to agree upon—Nixon, Safire, and Klein—is that it was another kind of visual image, the photos of Nixon poking at Khrushchev, and not the words that were written, which made the difference. It was another lesson in the power of visual images, the power of television and controlling one's own image on television.

The rest of the chapter of Nixon's Khrushchev crisis is about the dangers of communism and fighting communism was certainly an important theme of Nixon's entire career. But the lesson he learned was another one in the importance of media. Even if the perception of many people was that Nixon was tough, thanks to the image of Nixon pointing his finger at Khrushchev, he worried tremendously about losing control of the moving image that showed otherwise.

Six

Campaign '60
as a "Crisis," Part One

Television played an outsized role in the 1960 presidential election. Each election cycle brings new opportunities to engage with new technology. In 1960, TV was still new enough to politics to bring surprises. Nineteen sixty also brought two young men as presidential candidates who were familiar with television and the changes it had made, was making, and would make in American politics.

The election of 1960 is often treated by both scholars and the public at large as an election whose outcome was determined by television. Specifically, the outcome is seen as being decided by the first-ever televised presidential debates. It is not wrong to consider the debates an important factor in the election. It is certainly true that they affected the outcome of the election. More important are the lessons they taught Richard Nixon.

But the debates were not the only source of lessons for Nixon from the 1960 campaign. Nixon also learned the value of entertainment television during the 1960 campaign, and this had a more profound impact on both the career of Richard Nixon and the future of presidential candidates' elections than the debates. Nixon never engaged in another debate, but he used entertainment television throughout the 1960s, establishing a model for generations of politicians which followed.

Nixon and Kennedy were not even close to the first politicians campaigning for office, even for the presidency, to appear on television shows. The two-time Democratic presidential nominee Adlai Stevenson, for example, appeared on two different Edward R. Murrow documentary-style news programs during the 1950s: *See It Now* and *Person to Person*. But appearing on entertainment-oriented shows was new and different. For Nixon it would turn out to be a critical part of his winning political style in 1968.

Late Night Comes to Presidential Campaigns— Nixon Does It Before the "TV President"

Nixon and Susskind, Round One

On the evening of May 15, Richard Nixon made an appearance on the late-night talk show hosted by David Susskind, *Open End*. The show was called *Open End* because when it premiered, each episode ran until the host and his guest ran out of things to talk about. Susskind's interview show was rebranded *The David Susskind Show* in 1967, but he remained continuously on the air from his first show, in October of 1958, until his death in 1986, interviewing more than 7,000 people.[1] Probably his most famous, or infamous, interview was with Nikita Khrushchev in October of 1960. Landing one of the world's most powerful leaders was, according to Susskind, "a shot in the dark, just a written request and he said yes."[2]

But before he interviewed Khrushchev, Susskind interviewed the man who famously "debated" Khrushchev in Moscow, Richard Nixon. Nixon's episode began at 10 p.m., Eastern, on May 15 and ended at 1:45 a.m. on May 16, 1960. As Susskind biographer Stephen Battaglio put it, the in-depth nature of Susskind's questions and Nixon's lengthy answers made it close to four hours long and, possibly, "the longest television interview ever recorded."[3] Before the marathon interview took place, Susskind said he deeply researched the career of Nixon, reading several books about him. He said he saw the opportunity to interview Nixon, which took several months of requests to get Nixon to agree to, as a "tremendous responsibility" and "a chance really to dig, to ask the things that are in people's minds about Mr. Nixon—to challenge him on those issues where, to date, confusion and obfuscation appear." His plan was to ask Nixon about a wide range of things, including his views on domestic and foreign politics, as well as "his ideas on how he is regarded by the public."[4] He certainly did that.

As Susskind biographer Stephen Battaglio notes, the open-ended format of *Open End* appealed to politicians who liked to talk without being constrained, as was the case on shows such as *Meet the Press*.[5] Nixon appeared with Susskind after Adlai Stevenson appeared on the show. Stevenson, the presidential nominee of the Democratic Party in 1952 and 1956, did not declare his candidacy in 1960, but said that if he were "drafted" by the party, he would accept the nomination. This did not happen, but Stevenson was actively involved in trying to get himself drafted at the convention. Of his interview with Stevenson, Susskind said, "he had been my political hero, and then, after the interview, well..." he was not.[6] During the build-up to the 1960 campaign, Susskind also interviewed Nelson Rockefeller and Hubert Humphrey.

While he might have felt that Stevenson was once his hero, Susskind never felt strongly about Nixon, but he was complimentary in comments before the interview, calling him "astute, courageous and an unusually effective politician of good manners and good taste."[7] Susskind predicted that after the show Democrats would be angry that Nixon did not embarrass himself and Republicans would be mad that he made Nixon occasionally uncomfortable.[8]

During the interview, Susskind asked Nixon a wide variety of questions about diplomacy, foreign policy, relations with the Soviet Union and nuclear weapons. He also asked several very pointed political questions which pressed Nixon to address the unstated question of whether he was a viable presidential candidate. For example, Susskind said to Nixon that he was very partisan and frequently very extreme. Susskind told Nixon that he heard a lot of talk about him being the "New Nixon" and asked Nixon if he regretted any of his previous "extreme partisanship and extreme vitriol." As he would do two years later in *Six Crises,* Nixon took the opportunity to complain about the way the news media covered him, noting that he had been exposed to significantly more scrutiny than most. In a nod to appearing open to criticism, however, he did add that he was sure he had made mistakes in the past and that it was fair to examine all the past behavior of a candidate such as himself in detail and "discuss it vigorously and in a way that will bring it home to the people."[9]

Susskind also asked him a couple of questions about the party's liberal champion, New York's governor, Nelson Rockefeller. He asked Nixon if he could envision being a running mate with Rockefeller. Nixon responded by saying, first, that any differences which existed between he and Rockefeller were smaller than people thought and that he and Rockefeller got along well, especially on foreign policy. Second, he pointed out that Susskind's question was purely hypothetical since Rockefeller made it clear he had no intention to accept a vice presidential nomination and that he did not plan to attend the Republican Convention. Nixon continued at some length, saying how much he admired Rockefeller's decision and urged Susskind—and others—to respect Rockefeller's decision.[10] It was a deftly handled opportunity by Nixon to defuse a potential rival, but Susskind was not finished. He followed up with another question about Rockefeller, asking Nixon if he was upset that Rockefeller had not yet endorsed Nixon. Nixon said no, praised his leadership of New York, and said that he was sure Rockefeller would work hard to help the Republican ticket succeed in New York.[11]

Susskind also asked Nixon about religion, wondering what the Republican Party would do if Kennedy ended up with the Democratic nomination. Would the Republicans, Susskind wondered, need to nominate a

Catholic for vice president in response? It was an early chance for Nixon to deal with the religion issue which would loom large during the campaign, especially for Kennedy (and it also foreshadowed an exchange between Nixon and Susskind eight years later when both appeared as guests on Merv Griffin's show). Nixon told Susskind that trying to balance the ticket in that way would be obviously cynical and would be rejected by many people in the country. While there were many Catholics fully qualified for high office, Nixon said, they should be judged on their merits and not chosen merely as an effort to balance a political ticket.[12]

Another question asked by Susskind was particularly relevant because he asked the same question again eight years later when both he and Nixon were guests on *The Merv Griffin Show*. In 1960, Susskind told Nixon that his previous two victories were "coincident" with the victories of the very popular President Eisenhower, a national hero. The implication was that Nixon was not popular or a national hero. Susskind continued, asking Nixon how he would attract disaffected Democrats and independent voters and "disabuse" such voters of their "traditional view of you as someone who deeply distrusts him, questions his patriotism, his judgement and everything else."[13] In other words, he was telling Nixon such voters did not like him and he appeared not to like them, so why would they vote for him?

It was a question Nixon would be asked many times by many people before finally winning the presidency. Showing poise, Nixon responded by saying that all he could do was share his positions on the issues with voters, along with "the splendid progress this Administration has made," and that some people would like what he had to say, and some would not. He concluded, "I will present this as honestly and as effectively as I can, and it may be that it will win; it may be that it won't. That's the only way I know how to do it."[14] It was, perhaps to Nixon critics, a surprisingly forthright answer.

Critic Jack Gould's review of the show focused on three primary points: its length, its historic nature, and Nixon's performance. Despite his concern about the show being too long for most people, Gould was full of praise for the historic nature of the exercise, "taking politics out of the realm of press-agent oratory." And, Gould noted, it was during this performance that Nixon voiced his willingness to debate whomever his Democratic opponent might be, should he become the Republican nominee. If the legal obstacles of the equal time rule could be overcome, debates would "benefit the viewer and in all probability reduce the heavy cost of campaigning."[15] As Susskind biographer Stephen Battaglio observed, the offer by Nixon was historic, setting "television history in motion."[16]

Finally, Gould lauded Nixon for his abilities on television, which would never be a compliment handed out liberally to Nixon. He wrote that Nixon was able to deftly respond to many questions about complicated issues, managing to appear both independent of and loyal to Eisenhower. Nixon also, Gould noted, had an instinct for television that led him to the conclusion that things were going on too long. He wrote that when Nixon wondered aloud whether a large portion of the audience had gone to bed, "his was the television veteran's seventh sense: in the stillness of the studio there is no sound louder than distant sets being turned off."[17]

Most important, Gould paid Nixon something of what Gould perhaps thought was a backhanded compliment, but it is a crucial observation in making the case that Nixon is the politician who did more than any other to make the visual electronic image an integral part of American politics. Gould wrote that around one in the morning, Nixon was finished making his positions on several issues known and turned to talking politics. It was something he did, Gould observed, with "zest and relish." Gould wrote, "The evening's lecturer had become a personality, with the camera accenting in a fascinating way the quality of intuitive ability rather than of innate warmth."[18] And that, of course, was the entire point about Richard Nixon. He did not exude warmth, ever. But he did know how to make the most of that deficit through an effective use of television. Nixon understood inherently that what television gave him was an opportunity to frame an image of himself.

Next, Nixon Makes Paar

Today it is a given that presidential candidates will make the rounds of television talk shows, daytime and late night alike, to promote their candidacies. Not many serious candidates skip them. When Mitt Romney refused to do talk shows in 2012, it generated an enormous amount of press coverage. This is a sea change from the middle 20th century, when one might have considered a candidate who did talk shows to be anything *but* a serious candidate. Before 1960, talk show appearances simply were not a part of campaigning for president. But in 1960, both Kennedy and Nixon appeared on *The Tonight Show* with Jack Paar. Kennedy appeared first, on June 16, 1960, as he politicked for the Democratic nomination. Nixon appeared in August, after he had the Republican nomination locked up.

Kennedy's appearance came on the same day he attended the 1960 Harvard University commencement ceremony and his 20th undergraduate reunion. At this point, he was also in the process of wrapping up the presidential nomination. By mid–June, getting the Democratic nomination was something that veteran political observer James "Scotty" Reston of the *New York Times* predicted was all but a certainty. While the "old pros" of the party could have still taken the nomination away from him, it was highly unlikely since the "old pros" did not agree with each other on an alternative to Kennedy. Reston saw Kennedy's appearance with Paar as part of a carefully designed plan of action to grab the Democratic presidential nomination while other candidates spun their wheels. He wrote that the appearance was part of Kennedy's effort to raise his profile and "try out his ammunition" on Nixon.[19]

Early in the interview, Paar joked about whether it was okay if he called Kennedy "John," because his daughter would be impressed. The answer was "yes." He asked Kennedy a question that is a good one to ask of every presidential candidate—the "why" question (which would famously derail the campaign of his brother Ted in 1980). It should be an easy question, not one which derails an ambitious politician, and JFK handled it well. Paar asked him why someone who had it all and who could do anything he wanted went into politics.

Kennedy responded seriously and at length. He spoke of his early career as a journalist, covering a United Nations conference in 1945. He realized there that "all of the great decisions" which would affect the fate of Americans and of its allies would be made by the U.S. government. The United States, he told Paar, was the only "guardian at the gate" against the spread of communism. As an interested citizen, he wanted to be part of the process. He did that by serving in the House and the Senate but, he believed, "the presidency is the key office." The president, and not the Congress, would determine whether people lived in peace and what U.S. relations with the rest of the world would be like. He was running for the presidency, he said, "for the same reason I ran for the House: because this is the place where action is going to take place affecting the lives of our people and every people for the next four and eight years."[20]

This was an important media appearance for Kennedy, exposing him to an audience that may not have been so attentive to politics. At the time he made it, there were reasons many Americans may have doubted Kennedy, despite his frontrunner status. Chief among these were his youth and his Catholic religion. Paar, apparently supportive of Kennedy's candidacy on air, threw him an easy-to-hit pitch when he asked the "why" question and Kennedy had a ready answer for it, which was remarkable in its unabashed enthusiasm for wanting the presidency because of the power that comes with the job.

Kennedy's appearance on *The Tonight Show* engendered an incident of what we would today call "trolling." Had it happened in the 21st century it would have been in the form of social media posts. Happening as it did in 1960, it came in the form of an open letter, written by Pennsylvania Republican senator Hugh Scott to Kennedy. It was released en masse to the press, sort like a tweet. In it, Scott sarcastically updated Kennedy on the hard work of the Senate while he was out of town attending Harvard's commencement and appearing on *The Tonight Show.*

Before he left on his trip, Kennedy used a floor speech in the Senate to lay out his ideas about foreign policy and to criticize Eisenhower's foreign policy. It was a campaign speech and Senator Scott noted it sarcastically. There was a feeling, backed by statistics to a degree, that Kennedy was absent from the Senate a great deal of the time as he campaigned for the presidency. In 1959, his attendance was fourth lowest in the Senate and that number decreased further in 1960. He also had the lowest attendance of any Senator in 1955, due to health problems.[21]

Scott wrote, "I am sure you will appreciate this note because it indicates that we in the Senate took very seriously the lecture you had delivered to us only two days before on the importance of leadership and the need to do something about the missile programs and about modernizing the armed forces."[22] Senator Scott wrote he was prompted to write the letter "after 14 weary hours on the Senate Floor," when he "came home after midnight and flicked on his TV set. On the screen appeared the face of Sen. John F. Kennedy.... Looking happy, rested and relaxed, Kennedy was exchanging witticisms with entertainers on the Jack Paar show in New York City."[23]

Scott went on at some length, describing the Senate's "real busy day," which included the passage of a defense appropriations bill, approval of what would become the 23rd Amendment giving electoral votes to Washington, D.C., a foreign aid bill, and a housing bill.[24] He invited Kennedy to stop in the Senate if he had time or, if not, to just send another Kennedy in his place.[25] The obvious sarcasm is entertaining, but it also speaks to the unique nature of Kennedy's appearance on the Paar show.

To Scott, a senator engaged in the serious business of the Senate and a liberal Republican who was supportive of a great deal of civil rights legislation, seeing one of his colleagues on late-night television, having missed a momentous day in the Senate, was clearly galling. He also made it clear that he did not feel particularly positive about presidential campaigning taking place in a forum such as *The Tonight Show.* Notably, John Kennedy did not appear on *The Tonight Show* again after his nomination, though he was invited by Paar and indicated he would make a second appearance.[26] Perhaps Senator Scott's sarcastic rebuke was still ringing in his ears.

Scott's treatment of Kennedy had no impact on Nixon, who accepted the opportunity to appear on the entertainment show after laying claim to the nomination of his party for president. In fact, Nixon requested the appearance. NBC and Paar were happy to oblige, but not before Congress took up the issue of the equal time rule. Nixon's appearance on *The Tonight*

Show did not happen until August 25, the day that President Eisenhower signed legislation suspending Section 315 of the Communications Act of 1934, which required all candidates for an office to receive equal television time and comparable advertising rates, in its entirety for the 1960 campaign.

At the time, network executives hoped, maybe assumed, that the suspension of the equal time rule would become permanent. It did not, but the temporary suspension had a profound impact on the 1960 election, clearing the way for those first-ever televised presidential debates between only the Democratic and Republican nominees. When Congress approved the suspension on August 22, 1960, it was over the objections of organizations such as smaller political parties and the ACLU, which feared that suspension of the rule would lead to a monopoly of access to the airwaves for the major parties at the expense of minor parties. The networks, however, carried the day, characterizing the ACLU's concerns as "insuperable."[27]

Almost immediately after the press conference, NBC announced that Nixon would be on *The Tonight Show*.[28] Paar went to Washington to tape the segment with Nixon in front of a live studio audience at NBC's Washington studio on the evening of August 25. *New York Times* reporter James Loftus wrote that Nixon came on stage smiling and wearing "the usual studio make-up."[29] This reference to "the usual studio make-up" may seem surprising given the fact that one of the major flaws of his performance in the first debate with Kennedy in 1960 was that he refused to wear studio make-up.

One reporter, Willard Edwards, wrote glowingly of Nixon's performance. Edwards's description of Paar is also important for, once again, it draws attention to the historic nature of this kind of campaigning. His description of Nixon was much more positive than his words about Paar. Edwards wrote, "The people who sit up late saw a television show Thursday midnight which featured Vice President Nixon, Republican candidate for President, and Jack Paar, a temperamental entertainer regarded by many listeners as a comedian." Edwards noted that there were serious questions about Eisenhower, the future of the United States in a "troubled world," and the differences between Nixon and Kennedy. Edwards added, "He also responded to such questions as whether he liked Mexican food, how he handled his laundry on long campaign trips, the reaction of his children to political attacks upon him, and whether he and Kennedy were personal friends."[30] While clearly feeling Nixon did well on the show, Edwards also commented negatively on the entertainment and comedy aspects of the appearance, noting that "Paar indulged in a number of wisecracks, some of dubious quality."[31]

Paar did, indeed, crack a lot of jokes, but he started Nixon off with a very serious topic which was material for a famous Kennedy television ad. At a press conference where he discussed signing the bill suspending the equal time rule, President Eisenhower was asked by reporter Sarah McClendon to list important decisions Nixon had contributed to during his administration. Much to Nixon's embarrassment, Ike insisted that in eight years as vice president, Richard Nixon made no important contributions to decisions, since making decisions was Eisenhower's power alone.[32] When reporter Charles Mohr followed up, Eisenhower stuck to his answer. When Mohr then asked for an example of any Nixon ideas which Eisenhower had used in deciding, Eisenhower's response, which became fodder for an effective Kennedy campaign commercial attacking Nixon's supposed experience advantage over Kennedy, was "If you give me a week, I might think of one. I don't remember."[33]

It was with this statement by Eisenhower that Paar began the interview. He said he was going to ask a tough question and mentioned Eisenhower's words at the press conference. Paar suggested that perhaps Ike's answer meant that Nixon did not really have such an experience advantage over Kennedy as he claimed. Paar continued, saying, "Forgive me for asking that, but they want to make me really powerful, and I don't want to be really." There is no mention of who "they" were, but it was a very different opening from the one Kennedy got from Paar. When Kennedy appeared with Paar, he was asked questions about policy, but it certainly did not begin with a question that got to the very core of Kennedy's qualifications for office. With Nixon, Paar's approach was to start with a very "tough question," and it certainly was tough.

However, Nixon was clearly ready for the question, and he answered it with confidence. One cannot help but wonder if Paar really helped Nixon, whether he intended to or not. Nixon was poised and certainly seemed very at ease sharing the stage with Paar. Nixon responded as if Ike's answer was perfectly natural. Yes, the president consults with advisors, including the vice president, but when a decision must be made, the president makes it alone. He added that his experience as vice president included participating at the highest levels of the administration, including the Cabinet and the National Security Council, "being asked my opinion on matters where I have experience and then participating in the discussions which lead to a decision by the President."[34]

If Paar preferred Kennedy, he certainly gave Nixon a chance to make the point that he was more qualified for the presidency than Kennedy. After complimenting Nixon for being unwilling to let religion be an issue in the campaign, he asked about Kennedy's age. Nixon pointed out that they were only four years different in age and said that it was not age that was important but the difference in their attitudes about the issues and their experience.

After telling Nixon that a lot of people he knew told him that they did not think there was much difference between him and Nixon, Paar asked Nixon how he felt he was different. Nixon answered that the differences would become clear through the course of the campaign but suggested there were important clues in the two convention acceptance speeches. The differences included experience and issue positions. Nixon predicted that many Democrats would vote Republican in 1960 because they did not agree with the Democratic platform.[35] Nixon then offered a critique of the Democratic platform.

At the end of the interview Paar gave Nixon room to circle back to the first question of the interview, allowing him to address the experience question once again. Paar suggested to Nixon he was the most active vice president in U.S. history and asked him, given his experience as vice president, if he thought that the vice president should be increased. Nixon responded that he thought one of Eisenhower's major contributions as president was increasing the responsibility of the vice presidency, "so that instead of being a gavel-pounder over the Senate, he actually is used in foreign policy, in domestic policy, and in a lot of other important matters."[36] It was an opportunity for Nixon, in a polite way and in third person, to refute the idea, born from Eisenhower's dismissive comments, that he didn't contribute much to the Eisenhower administration.

Nixon was clearly happy with the way his appearance went because he wrote a letter, publicly released, to Paar, thanking him for the experience and noting how many people on the campaign trail told Nixon and his wife that they saw the show and how much they liked it. It was no wonder, Nixon noted, that Paar's ratings were so high.[37] One thing was different about Nixon's appearance with Paar from Kennedy's: it did not cause a sarcastic attack from anyone in the opposing party accusing him of not doing his job. The appearance was, for Nixon, a lesson in the value of using a medium mainly considered to be for entertainment in the serious business of campaigning.

On November 1, Nixon's running mate, vice presidential nominee Henry Cabot Lodge, was a guest on *The Tonight Show*, making Lyndon Johnson the only one of the four candidates not to make an appearance. Lodge was the Eisenhower administration's ambassador to the United Nations, after serving in both the House and Senate representing Massachusetts. Nixon chose him as his running mate with the clear hope that he would counterbalance Kennedy's support in New England. While on with Paar, during the "serious" part of the interview, Lodge maintained the theme he presented throughout the campaign, that Nixon had "the maturity and understanding to keep the United States out of war and moving toward a 'new plateau' of achievement."[38] Throughout his day in New York and with Paar, Lodge spoke about Nixon as someone who knew how to stand up to communist leaders and made a connection to the Truman administration, blaming Truman for the then-growing crisis in Berlin, and arguing that if Truman had been stronger in backing the Soviets down when he was president, the nation would be much better off.[39] Lodge also joked with Paar about his enjoyment of jazz. He saw this as an advantage in the election, telling Paar, "The jazz vote's a big vote."[40]

The 1960 campaign made appearing on entertainment television a standard for campaigning in America. Not everyone thought that was a positive development. Television critic Jack Gould offered some pointed criticism of the state of entertainment and politics in 1961. Gould wrote bitingly of both Kennedy and Nixon appearing on Paar's show to explain why they should be president to "vaudeville's statesman." Gould concluded, "The thirst for appeasing TV to obtain publicity is a symptom of an era and a social environment that has touched the mighty and the small alike."[41]

A prominent observer of American politics wrote about this new phenomenon—candidates campaigning on late night television—in prescient ways that have much to say about the state of campaigns in the United States in the 21st century. The observer was the veteran political reporter for the *New York Times*, James "Scotty" Reston. Writing after Nixon's appearance with Paar, Reston noted the historic nature of the show, observing that all presidential elections create new precedents. In 1960, he wrote, the precedent was candidates running for office on a late-night talk show. Reston asked, "What other generation of Americans has ever had the opportunity of hearing the Vice President of the United States discuss the survival of the Republic with a night-shift comic?"[42]

Obviously not seeing this as a positive development, Reston wrote that the entry of late-night television into the campaign process *changed* the process in negative ways. He wrote that prior to the appearance of *The Tonight Show* in the campaign, there was one important question to ask about Nixon and Kennedy: who was better suited to deal with Khrushchev? The new question was who was a better guest with Jack Paar? Continuing in a sarcastic and disapproving tone, he suggested, "From now on, it will be important to analyze not only who has the best speech writers but who has the best gag-writers," and went on to suggest several amusing exchanges that could have taken place between Paar and Nixon or between Paar and Kennedy.[43]

Reston wrote with continued derision but also pointed out an issue which politicians like Donald Trump now tweet about daily—balance in the jokes comedians tell about them. Reston wrote that comedians leaning toward the Democrats would be hard on Republican candidates and vice versa, in a kind of entertainment equal time competition.[44]

Reston foresaw what has become reality—politicians avoiding serious journalistic interrogation for lighter, entertaining fare that makes them look good. Ending in a tone that was both scolding and prescient, Reston wrote of what he called "the rigged political show." He was not using the term as some politicians use the word "rigged" to suggest that the deck is stacked against them but rather that a politician like Nixon would use an appearance on an entertainment show to improve his standing with audiences which was, of course, exactly what Nixon was trying to do.

Reston criticized Nixon for not being able to find the time for more than three hours of debates with Kennedy as he found time for talk shows.[45] Reston wrote that serious people, such as historians and philosophers, wanted to ask the candidates serious questions but the candidates gave priority to comedians. He concluded, "Just who gains from all this and why these two deadly serious and intense young men want to prove that they are funny and relaxed is not quite clear. It is a precedent, all right, and anybody who wonders why is obviously a stuffed shirt."[46]

Reston's tone was frequently sarcastic and derogatory, but he was right—campaigns in America would never be the same after 1960. In many ways, Reston was proven correct repeatedly. Politicians regularly appear on entertainment shows with comedians. They also seem to be genuinely more concerned, or just as concerned, with being seen as funny and relatable as they are with being seen as serious people with leadership potential. Being funny has become a criterion for leadership potential. And in many ways, that started with JFK and Nixon. But it was far more important for Nixon. Kennedy was seen by many as a natural wit. Nixon was never accused of being a natural wit, so it was a perception shifter for people who saw him showing a sense of humor on television and perception shifts have an enduring impact on people. Nixon learned the lesson that at least *appearing* engaging was important, and he did so repeatedly throughout the 1960s.

What is clear in the thoughts of both Reston and Gould is that while the marriage of entertainment and politics was a reality after the 1960 election, there was good reason to question the wisdom of that marriage. It is hard to imagine what they would say about the state of things today.

SEVEN

Campaign '60 as
a "Crisis," Part Two

Televised Debates

The televised debates between Kennedy and Nixon in 1960 were the first televised debates between the major party nominees for president in history. There was a televised primary debate between Kennedy and Hubert Humphrey in West Virginia during the 1960 Democratic primary campaign, but it paled in comparison to the spotlight on the Kennedy-Nixon debates which, with the hindsight of history, many observers of American politics argue determined the outcome of the election.

Critics argue that Nixon looked like a man from an older generation in his televised debates with John Kennedy in 1960. Nixon was just four years older, but to many observers, Kennedy looked like he understood the visual medium, while Nixon looked like someone who had no understanding of the power of television. The first of the four debates drew the largest audience in 1960 and continues to receive the most attention today. It is always clips from the first debate that are shown to demonstrate what a disaster the debates were for Nixon's campaign. Nixon's performance was much better in the subsequent three debates, but the first debate created an enduring image of Nixon as sweaty and uncertain, and that image dogged him throughout the rest of the debates and the campaign.

Given his experience in 1952 and during the Eisenhower administration, Nixon's evident mishandling of the debates, especially the first, is surprising. Whatever happened during that first debate in 1960—including illness, a distracting knee injury, and an unfortunate refusal to use more than a minimal amount of television make-up—Nixon certainly did understand the power of television *that he could control.* As Ambrose observed, "Television had been a central concern for Nixon ever since his 1952 Checkers speech, and he had learned long ago that the appearance

77

he made on the screen was as important as the policy or argument he presented."[1]

In *Six Crises*, Nixon wrote extensively of the 1960 campaign, beginning with what he saw as a maxim of politics: a candidate must give credit to advisors for successes and take personal responsibility for failures.[2] It is not clear he thought that trade-off was fair, but clearly, the decisions Nixon made regarding the first-ever televised presidential debate played a role in what was an extraordinarily close campaign. Kennedy won the popular vote by just over 100,000 votes, although his margin of victory in the Electoral College was 303 to 219.

Nixon's tone in his discussion of the debates and the campaign is quite bitter in *Six Crises*. In his chapter on 1960, he makes what can be interpreted as several negative comments about his opponent without mentioning his name. For example, he wrote that the most important thing for a candidate to do in a campaign is to be himself and not try to pretend to be someone else. He wrote, "Whenever he does, he gets out of character and loses the quality that is essential for political success—sincerity and credibility."[3] Implicit in this and in comments explicitly mentioning Kennedy was a dismissiveness of Kennedy as disingenuous but not of his teleogenetic nature.

In Nixon's assessment of Kennedy's strengths as a presidential candidate in January of 1960, he included his intelligence, energy, and "particularly effective television personality." Here we see, once again, Nixon's understanding of the new age in which he lived. The other items in Nixon's list of Kennedy's assets were his "unlimited money," which allowed him to hire a talented campaign team and, most important, "the weakness of his opponents … you can't beat somebody with nobody."[4] In other words, Kennedy beat losers to capture the Democratic nomination. Of course, he also beat Nixon to capture the presidency.

Kennedy's other "advantage," as Nixon saw it, was also framed in such a way that it was really a criticism of Kennedy and an excuse for himself. He wrote that Kennedy had the *advantage* of inexperience, meaning that the fact that he had done so little left very little to criticize. Nixon wrote, "All that voters could judge him on was what he said, rather than what he had done, and voters quickly forget what a man says. They remember much longer what he has done."[5] Nixon no doubt felt that he was being held to an unfairly different standard, thanks to his eight years as vice president. To summarize, then, Nixon's opinion of Kennedy, at the time of his writing *Six Crises* in 1962, was that Kennedy was a flashy, inexperienced, spoiled rich kid who lucked his way into the presidency. Kennedy was an image; Nixon was substance. Nixon found competing with an image frustrating, but it reinforced a lesson for him—image matters a great deal.

Given the fact that television saved Nixon's place on the Republican ticket in 1952, and that he clearly understood the importance of using television, appearing well on television, and projecting the right image, it is no small irony that he lost in 1960 to a candidate who used television even more effectively. In Kennedy's 1958 essay for *TV Guide*, "A Force That Has Changed the Political Scene," he not only predicted how important television would become in politics, but he wrote of the importance image had assumed in politics. And there was nothing wrong with that, as far as Kennedy was concerned.[6] Kennedy wrote that qualities such as honesty and intelligence were important parts of a candidate's image, no matter what scornful intellectuals and politicians thought. Kennedy believed that the images and impressions viewers developed watching candidates on television were "uncannily correct." He wrote, "I think, no matter what their defenders or detractors may say, that the television public has a fairly good idea of what Dwight D. Eisenhower is really like—or Jimmy Hoffa—or John McClellan—or Vice President Nixon—or countless others."[7] It is hard to know Kennedy's true intent in including Nixon's name with both an honorable figure such as Eisenhower, who had a highly respected image in 1958, and with more dubious persons like Arkansas senator John McClellan and Jimmy Hoffa. McClellan headed the Senate's investigation into organized crime, including the infamous Teamster boss Hoffa, but he was also a very vocal opponent of all attempts to desegregate the South, including Little Rock's Central High School.

In the summer of 1960, when Congress passed its legislation allowing the television networks to temporarily waive Section 315 of the Federal Communications Act of 1934, known as the equal time rule, it was specifically to allow for debates between the Democratic and Republican nominees for president. The rule reads, in part, "If any license shall permit any person who is a legally qualified candidate for public office to use a broadcasting station, he shall afford equal opportunity to all other such candidates for that office in the use of such broadcasting station."[8]

Under ordinary circumstances, the rule required that all candidates for federal offices be provided with the same access to television and radio airtime. In 1960, there were presidential candidates from third parties on ballots across the country. These parties included the Socialist Labor Party, the Socialist Workers Party, the Prohibition Party, the Constitution Party, the Conservative Party, the Afro-American Unity Party, the American Vegetarian Party, the American Beat Consensus, the Tax Cut Party, and the States' Rights Party, whose nominee was Orval Faubus, then the Democratic governor of Arkansas. In theory, networks hosting a debate would have been obliged to allow all these candidates to participate. However, with this legislation, Congress allowed the networks to broadcast debates between the two major party nominees without having to include any third-party candidates. For the first time in history, the temporary recission of Section 315 cleared the way for televised debates between Republican and Democratic nominees in the United States.

As the campaign began in 1960, the upside for participating in debates was clearly higher for Kennedy. As scholars Lang and Lang note, Kennedy not only had to bring his own party back together after a fight for the nomination with Hubert Humphrey and supporters of Adlai Stevenson, but he also had to overcome several Nixon advantages: experience, name recognition, prestige and, though he was only four years older than Kennedy, maturity.[9]

Kennedy's desire to debate Nixon was strategic, of course. During the Democratic primaries, he refused to debate Hubert Humphrey before the Democratic primary in Wisconsin in April because he had a notable advantage over Humphrey in the form of strong Catholic support and could only suffer from a debate. But in the West Virginia primary, held in May, the race was much closer, and Kennedy's Catholicism was seen as a possible disadvantage, so he agreed to a televised debate against Humphrey, which gave him valuable experience Nixon did not have. When it came to the general election Kennedy had every reason to put himself side by side on television with Nixon.

With the benefit of hindsight in 1962, Nixon wrote that the pressure to participate in debates—which he never referred to as "debates" but, rather, as "joint appearances"—quickly became something that could not be ignored. If he declined to participate, he felt, he would have been accused of being afraid to defend the Eisenhower administration's record as well as his own.[10] Of the "joint appearances" themselves, he wrote that Kennedy had both more to gain from the debates and an advantage in the debates. Kennedy was less well known than Nixon and stood to gain more from the audience attention. Kennedy was advantaged, as Nixon saw it, in that he was in position to attack Nixon's record while Nixon would have to be on defense. Nixon wrote that he happy to defend the Eisenhower administratio but added, "I knew from long experience that in debate, the man who can attack has a built-in advantage that is very hard to overcome. Almost automatically, he has the initiative and is the aggressor."[11]

At the first debate, Nixon arrived in rough shape. Journalism scholars Seltz and Yoakam noted that Nixon was sick and running a temperature. He was exhausted by the campaign and by a busy day prior to the debate. He was very skinny, having lost a great deal of weight following knee surgery, and he simply did not look good. Seltz and Yoakam noted that even if Nixon had used make-up, it would not have covered Nixon's obvious exhaustion. This image sank in with those watching the debate on television before Nixon even spoke a word. Seltz and Yoakam noted that since Nixon did not give the visual picture which viewers expected as the "fighting commando of the Republican cause," it made them focus on the visual picture he did present and wonder what was wrong. This meant, they wrote, that, "for the first time, they were more conscious of his appearance than of what he was saying."[12]

Seltz and Yoakam observed that television make-up would have helped, but they also noted that Nixon appeared unsure of himself: his eyes darted around uncertainly, and he was sweaty. He also was not helped by the way the debate was shot on camera. They wrote, "with the tight shots used by Hewitt these things were more obvious."[13] Hewitt was Don Hewitt, who directed the coverage of the debate and later created *60 Minutes* for CBS.

In Chicago, both candidates eschewed the help of a professional make-up artist, CBS's Frances Arvold.[14] However, Kennedy was very tan from campaigning in California, and the lack of make-up was not a problem for him, while both Arvold and the senior lighting director for CBS, Robert Barry, counseled the Nixon team that Nixon really should use some make-up. One of his advisers, Everett Hart, put a pancake make-up called "Max Factor's Lazy Shave" on Nixon's face to try and cover his heavy beard, but nothing else was done. According to Stelz and Yoakam, Nixon and his advisors were "satisfied with his looks."[15] It would be wrong, many might argue, to say a presidential election was lost for lack of professionally applied make-up, but one cannot lose sight of the unprecedented nature of the largest role TV had ever played in an election.

Regardless of make-up, the post-debate feeling shared by Nixon and his aides was that the event did not go Nixon's way. As Nixon wrote, in trying to analyze the debate objectively, "I felt that Kennedy had done extremely well.... But also, from a great deal of experience with television, I knew that appearance may at times count more than substance," so he asked each of his aides what he felt was the key question, which was how each appeared on television.[16] It is clear that Nixon's real feeling about Kennedy was not that he performed well on the issues, but that he had done well on image. And Nixon, an early learner of lessons about the power of television, knew the importance of image in the television age.

The reviews of Nixon in the first debate were not positive, even from those closest to him. One of the first people he spoke to was his longtime secretary, Rose Mary Woods, who told him that her parents had called and asked if Nixon was sick. Later, Nixon reported that his mother, Hannah, called and, like Woods's parents, asked if he was feeling okay. Woods told him she agreed with their assessment of his appearance, though "she thought I had had the better of the argument on substance."[17]

Nixon spoke with a doctor friend, Malcolm Todd, who told him he looked weak, pale, and tired on television during the debate because he was, in fact, all those things. He told Nixon that he had to focus on getting well by reducing his schedule and eating more before the next debate. "We have to lighten up the schedule, get more food into you, and get you up to par before the next debate." He prescribed a daily milkshake for Nixon to help replace some of the weight he lost during the campaign.

Nixon found unanimity among the members of his campaign staff that he did not look well onscreen in the debate. Nixon concluded that he made a basic mistake, writing, "I had concentrated too much on substance and not enough on appearance," forgetting the maxim that a picture is worth a thousand words. He concluded that the lesson for the remaining debates was clear: his image had to be better. It was not acceptable, he wrote, to blame that on technical problems. If the technical people were not doing a good job, it was the campaign's responsibility to find better technical people.[18] Once again, the overarching takeaway lesson for Nixon was that the visuals were decisive, not the words.

Nixon wrote in *Six Crises* that he could blame his "poor physical appearance" on television on the fact that he was sick but argued that he felt just fine when the debate began. He was mentally alert and even his injured knee was not bothering him. So, he asked, what was the problem? He admitted that while some of the problems were of a technical nature, with hindsight, he saw that many of the issues were avoidable. He concluded, "The TV camera is like a microscope: it shows not how one feels but what his physical condition actually is."[19] The camera saw everything and what it saw, Nixon realized, did not look good.

After the disaster of the first debate, the question was what could be done in the remaining debates. Nixon wrote that he disagreed with his media advisers who told him that audiences would build throughout the series of debates and that he could recover from a poor first debate performance. But Nixon claimed he felt the first debate would have the largest audience and each debate would have a smaller audience as the novelty wore off and he lamented that he gave his best debate performance, which covered foreign policy, in the last debate, which had the smallest audience.[20]

Nixon felt that the first debate had an enormous impact on the subsequent debates and, most likely, on the outcome of the election. He was far from alone in that assessment. A study by Lang and Lang found that 89 percent of the people they surveyed felt Kennedy had either won or tied Nixon. They also reported that the Gallup poll conducted after the debate found that of people who watched the debate, twice as many thought Kennedy won as thought Nixon did. Their conclusion based on this data was devastating.

Lang and Lang wrote, "The single most important result of the debate lay in its destruction of the image, so widely held, of Richard Nixon as champion debater and television politician par excellence," and the impact of this, Lang and Lang found, was to help undecided voters make up their mind and to affect the attitudes of committed partisan voters about the fitness of each man for the presidency.[21] While they did not conclude that many votes of strong partisans were changed by the debates, they hypothesized that what changed—and could well have had a decisive impact in such a close election—was the impact on undecided voters and on the enthusiasm of campaign workers for the two candidates.

Nixon was fixated on the numbers. Although he felt confident that he bested Kennedy in the three final debates, he was deeply troubled by the idea that fewer people were paying attention. Nixon wrote that the audience for the first debate was approximately 80 million people, but that the audience for the remaining three debates was around 60 million each time. As Nixon saw it, that meant there were 20 million voters who could, possibly, have made their voting decision based on the first debate and, in an election decided by a margin of just over 100,000 votes, 20 million was a very meaningful number of voters. It is not clear that Nixon's audience numbers are accurate, but what is clear is that he *believed* the numbers were accurate and he took away yet another reason to believe in the power of television and image.[22] He believed the first debate cost him the election and, in an election so close, he could well be right. It was something he would work to never let happen again, in a variety of ways related to controlling his image. Chief among those ways was to not participate in debates in 1968 or 1972.

Nixon continued to lose undecided voters to Kennedy after each of the three final debates. In a study conducted before and after the second, third, and fourth debates, Ben-Zeev and White found that Kennedy gained support steadily after each debate while Nixon lost support and did not recover it. They found that Kennedy picked up support during the debates while Nixon simply held his own. They also found that the percentages of debate viewers hewed closely to vote outcomes. For instance, in Chicago, the margin of people who thought Kennedy won the fourth debate was 64 percent to 36 percent, and the vote in Chicago was 66 percent for Kennedy and 34 percent for Nixon. They concluded, "When viewers of each debate are compared with non-viewers, it becomes apparent that most of the 'within debate' changes in favor of Kennedy are due to the viewers."[23] In general they found that for those who watched the debates on television, the debates "tended to shift opinion in favor of Kennedy." Further, they found that increases for Kennedy came from undecided voters and not from the ranks of those who supported Nixon prior to the debates. Kennedy gained, they found, about 4 percentage points per debate.[24]

In *Six Crises*, Nixon came to a similar conclusion. He cited the objectivity of the assessment of two journalists, Charles Lucey and Jack Steele of Scripps-Howard, who wrote that Nixon started slow and finished fast in the series of debates, but that the deficit from the first debate was too much to overcome. They wrote that while Nixon was able to greatly reduce Kennedy's advantage from the first debate, "on balance, the four debates also left Mr. Kennedy with a big political plus. He slugged it out on fairly even terms and gained exposure before vast audiences."[25] Nixon was the incumbent vice president and the voice of the outgoing administration in this campaign, while Kennedy was a young senator. For Kennedy, the debate was mostly upside. For Nixon, it was mostly downside. This was a lesson Nixon learned and remembered.

What Lacey and Steele wrote, and what Nixon clearly believed, is that Kennedy, the challenger, was at an advantage in this kind of contest because the expectations of him were lower. Merely performing competently was seen as a success for a lesser-known candidate or for a candidate who faced concerns about his youth and inexperience, as did Kennedy. The challenger, Nixon asserted, would be free to attack. The incumbent, or the representative of the incumbent party, would be forced to defend, putting the challenger at a distinct advantage.[26] Nixon predicted that John Kennedy would learn that unpleasant lesson in 1964 "when the shoe would be on the other foot."

With an annoyed tone, Nixon noted that Robert Kennedy said his brother would never give equal exposure to an opponent as Nixon had done and would not be participating in debates in 1964. Though he would refuse to participate in debates in 1968 and 1972, Nixon was clearly thinking about running in 1964 when he wrote *Six Crises* and argued "my view is that debates between the major party candidates will be a feature of all future presidential campaigns, regardless of the candidates' own desires."[27] No doubt, he assumed that if he debated Kennedy in 1964, he would have the advantage of being the challenger which Kennedy benefited from in 1960.

Nixon assumed when writing *Six Crises* that debates were there to stay, but he also suggested a prescription for better debates. He called for debates without moderators and with a longer period of two hours. It would, he argued, allow for more in-depth discussion. These would be like the Lincoln-Douglas debates of the Senate race in Illinois in 1858.[28]

What this meant was that for Nixon, the chief way of improving debates in the future, which he assumed voters would insist on seeing, was to remove journalists. This was a major part of Nixon's political formulation going forward. Removing journalists from the debates was something he strove to do for the rest of his political career. Nixon learned three major lessons from his 1960 campaign "crisis." The first was to eliminate journalists whenever possible. The second came from the debates and from Jack Paar: both the debates and the late-night appearances taught Nixon that it was crucially important not to sacrifice image for substance.

It became clear later that Nixon also learned a third lesson: control of his own visual image could be even stronger if he could eliminate not only the media but also his opponent. While Nixon wrote of the inevitability of televised debates in every future presidential race, both he and LBJ were able to effectively use the equal time rule to avoid them in 1964, 1968, and 1972. Nixon relied heavily on television, but it was television he controlled as much as possible from there on. There were no debates or "joint appearances" with his opponent in 1968 or 1972. Nixon instead engaged in town hall forums in which he controlled the agenda and, most important, his image.

EIGHT

A Seventh "Crisis" and More Lessons about the News Media: Running for Governor in California in 1962 and the Debut of Nixon's Manifesto

Following the presidential election, Nixon moved his family to California where he joined the law firm of Adams, Duque & Hazeltine. The job was taken with the idea that Nixon would continue to be active in Republican politics, both in California and at the national level, though at the time he took the job, in March 1961, he avowed that he was "not a candidate for governor" of California.[1] And, truth be told, Nixon did not really *want* to run for governor of his home state.

Nixon's decision to run for governor was a tortured one. According to Nixon in his autobiography, *RN: The Memoirs of Richard Nixon*, he never really wanted to do it. When he decided to run, he asked for Eisenhower's endorsement and, as Eisenhower did so many times, he held back, telling Nixon he could not have it until after the Republican primary was over. It seems mean-spirited because, at least according to Nixon, he was only running for governor on Ike's advice.

Nixon wrote that Eisenhower counseled him to run for governor, win, and then run for president again in 1964, two years into his term as governor. Nixon asserts that he would not have done that; that had he won, he would have felt duty-bound to serve out his term as governor. But he also asserts that his heart really was not in running for governor, even though he really did not think he would lose to the incumbent Democrat, Pat Brown. He was confident of winning, despite what he felt would be "the all-out opposition of the Kennedy administration" who "would do everything they could to stop me from getting a new political lease on life by winning the governorship."[2] It often seems that, to Nixon, everything was a conspiracy against him, as opposed to simple partisan politics. But what is important about that is how his frequent use of terms such as "conspiracy" and "smear" have become regular parts of the lexicon used by modern politicians to delegitimize critics, either of the other political party or in the media. In his assessment of the 1962 campaign, the conspirators were both the press and the Kennedys.

In *RN*, Nixon described his campaign announcement press conference as two announcements: that he was not running for president in 1964 and that he was running for governor in 1962. But, according to Nixon, the reporters didn't believe him and accused him of being disingenuous about 1964.[3] He may have been sincere about not planning to run for the presidency in 1964, but he was still disingenuous, for he wrote in *RN* that the real problem was that he didn't want to be governor.[4] If true, it is just as well, because he lost the race to the incumbent governor, Democrat Pat Brown.

After the loss, Nixon gave an angry press conference in which he blamed the press for favoring Pat Brown and for misreporting (or deliberately not reporting) things about the candidates and the campaign in ways

Nixon, wife Pat and daughters Tricia (beside Pat) and Julie with Checkers at home in California in 1962.

which favored Brown. As he did in his assessment of the 1960 debates in *Six Crises*, Nixon also placed a great deal of blame for his loss in 1962 at the feet of his campaign staffers. As reporter James Reston wrote, "Even in his farewell address, he insisted on taking responsibility for 'any mistakes' in the campaign, and then blamed his 'magnificent' staff for blowing the election. Similarly, he said he 'respected' the reporters while accusing them of betraying their responsibility."[5] Nixon's conclusion, once again, was that he could not trust anyone but himself.

None of Nixon's biographers (and not even Nixon himself) devote many pages to his gubernatorial run. But for Nixon, the campaign was, ultimately, more conclusive proof that the denizens of the press were out to get him. Among many complaints Nixon had about media coverage of the campaign was the fact that one of his longstanding antagonists, columnist Drew Pearson, became the center of a major firestorm during the gubernatorial campaign. The story involved Nixon's brother and an alleged loan he received from Howard Hughes when Nixon was vice president. The implication was that Hughes made the loan to gain favor with the Eisenhower-Nixon administration. The loan was made in 1956 and Pearson first broke the story late in the 1960 presidential campaign, in a column published on October 26.

The issue of the loan to Don Nixon, which was for $205,000, returned dramatically during the 1962 gubernatorial campaign when Nixon made a joint press conference appearance with Pat Brown at a national conference of United Press International editors and publishers in San Francisco on October 1. This was not a debate in any shape or form, but it was the closest the two candidates got to having one. It was truly what Nixon liked to call a "joint appearance."

The main ground rule of the press conference was that the questions could only be about policy, but that was violated when Nixon was asked by Tom Braden, the publisher of the Oceanside, California, *Blade-Tribune* "whether he thought it was proper to permit a member of his family to receive a 'secret loan' from a major defense contractor, the Hughes Tool Company."[6] Nixon was given the opportunity to skip the question, but he insisted on addressing it, accusing Pat Brown of spreading the story and challenging him to produce evidence of wrongdoing if he had it. Brown declined to take the bait.

Drew Pearson, however, continued to fan the flames when he followed up on the skirmish with a column on October 8, writing that Don Nixon had received a loan "the average citizen could not get."[7] Pearson returned to the loan story the very next day, with his October 9 column titled "Some New Facts on Don Nixon Loan." In the column, Pearson addressed—and dissected—claims made by Nixon regarding the loan during his press conference with Pat Brown, arguing that the Nixon was lying. He argued Nixon traded his influence as vice president to help his brother and, if he did, Nixon was not fit to be Governor of California.[8]

On November 2, just four days before Election Day, Pearson wrote a column which called several aspects of the Nixon campaign into question, including, once again, the loan from Howard Hughes to Don Nixon. Pearson also wrote of a doctored photo made to make Pat Brown look bad. He alleged that Nixon supporters had been distributing a picture of Brown "bowing apologetically before Premier Khrushchev." Pearson argued that the photo had been banned from publication by California courts and was, in fact, an altered photo of Brown bowing to a Laotian girl making a presentation.[9] Pearson suggested "a lot of Californians" were asking questions about Nixon. It was not a helpful column so close to Election Day. However, as irritating as Nixon clearly found Pearson, he was but one example of what Nixon viewed as a concerted effort of the press to oppose him. He made this abundantly clear in his post–Election Day press conference.

The press conference was perhaps sincerely meant to be a political farewell in the heat of the moment after losing the election. But looking back, with the knowledge of all that would happen later, the transcript of the press conference reads not as a farewell but as a manifesto, one which became a blueprint for generations of American politicians, Donald Trump being just one of the most recent examples. Watching the press conference, one sees Nixon seething from the moment he comes to the podium. Nixon's press secretary, Herbert Klein, spoke first, announcing that Nixon was conceding the race to Pat Brown.

Nixon took the stage and began a lengthy attack on the press. He said, "Good morning, gentlemen. Now that Mr. Klein has made his statement, and now that all the members of the press are so delighted that I have lost, I'd like to make a statement of my own. I appreciate the press coverage in this campaign. I think each of you covered it the way you saw it. You had to write it in the way according to your belief on how it would go. I don't believe publishers should tell reporters to write one way or another. I want them all to be free. I don't believe the F.C.C. or anybody else should silence [word lost in transmission]. I have no complaints about the press coverage. I think each of you was writing it as you believed it."[10] His words about government regulation of the press, even though he denied having such desires, undoubtedly caught the ears of wary reporters and became prescient seven years later when Nixon took office and used the apparatus of the federal government, including Herb Klein, his White House communications director, to pressure the news media through investigation and threatened regulation.

Nixon's phrasing was important. Nixon was sure to point out the role played, as he saw it, by reporters' beliefs. It was obviously not true that Nixon had "no complaints about the press coverage." Nixon had many complaints, the most significant of which was that the press cost him a victory. While Nixon said he had "no complaints" about the media coverage of the 1962 campaign, he in fact had a laundry list of complaints. After his opening remarks, Nixon began with comments about Brown, saying several nice things about the governor while pointing out that Brown did not reciprocate in saying nice things about him. He defended Brown's patriotism while the press questioned his. Nixon defended Brown's motives even though he disagreed with them and did not get the same courtesy in return. He wanted the record set straight and for reporters to report it.[11] Nixon felt he never, or almost never, got a fair shake from his opponent or the press covering the campaign. In fact, it appears that Nixon saw his opponent and the press as one and the same.

To drive the point home, he put a spotlight on the *one* reporter he thought covered him fairly. Nixon said, "One reporter, Carl Greenberg[12]— he's the only reporter on *The [Los Angeles] Times* that fits this thing, who wrote every word that I said. He wrote it fairly. He wrote it objectively. I don't mean that others didn't have a right to do it differently. But Carl, despite whatever feelings he had, felt that he had an obligation to report the facts as he saw them. I am saying these things about the press because I understood that that was one of the things you were particularly interested in. There'll be no questions at this point on that score. I'll be glad to answer other questions."[13] The phrasing Nixon used is important. Reporters had the right to do what they wanted to do, and they did so. Only one chose objectivity as his standard, as Nixon saw it, and even that reporter, Nixon seemed to assume, did not really like him.

Nixon next praised his campaign volunteers, spoke about the domestic political situation, commended other Republicans who won elections the night before, and said he had no regrets about running and losing. He said he had no hard feelings for Pat Brown or the people of California. And then Nixon returned to his thoughts about the news media. He said that he did not begrudge reporters their personal views, but he clearly did. In his words, it is possible to see a blueprint for the kind of control over the message Nixon and his team would impose in the campaign of 1968 and later in the White House.

Suggesting an end to his remarks that was far from coming, Nixon said that he noticed when he began speaking some reporters seemed annoyed with what he was saying about them. But he did not care because he felt his "philosophy" of the press never got its due, "and I want to get it through." He then said that he thought he was unique among politicians in *not* complaining about the press in the entire 16 years of his career.

Never did he complain to a publisher or editor about someone's reporting, Nixon said. He continued, "I believe a reporter has got a right to write it as he feels it. I believe if a reporter believes that one man ought to win rather than the other, whether it's on television or radio or the like, he ought to say so. I will say to the reporter sometimes that I think well, look, I wish you'd give my opponent the same going over that you give me."[14] And it was clear Nixon felt his opponents never got the "same going over."

Nixon continued, with an angry smile on his face, "And as I leave the press, all I can say is this: For 16 years, ever since the Hiss case, you've had a lot of—a lot of fun—that you've had an opportunity to attack me and I think I've given as good as I've taken. It was carried right up to the last day."[15] As is clear from tapes and the memos of Nixon's years in the White House, one thing which drove him and his aides up a wall was what they felt was unequal treatment of Nixon in comparison to his political opponents.

Nixon made this point very clear in these 1962 comments. As an example, he told a story of accidentally saying that he was running for governor of the United States, which the *Los Angeles Times* reported. But it had not reported a similar slip of the tongue by Brown, misstating the name of a member of the Democratic ticket in California. Nixon also noted, not insignificantly for this analysis, that his "flub" was one of the very few he made, "not because I'm so good on television but because I've done it a long time."[16] Although Nixon claimed he was not bitter about this unreported flub by Brown, he clearly *was* angered by it. Nixon's lesson learned, again and again, was that the press was biased against him. All he could do on that day in 1962 was complain about the bias. In 1968, he did all he could to eliminate it or, at least, to make it irrelevant by closing out the press as much as he possibly could.

Nixon then laid out a philosophy about what he saw as a crucial difference between print and broadcast news media. He said, "I think that it's time that our great newspapers have at least the same objectivity, the same fullness of coverage that television has. And I can only say thank God for television and radio for keeping the newspapers a little more honest."[17] His feeling about the fairness of broadcast media being higher than that of print did not last, but it does reflect the importance he assigned to broadcast news media in modern American politics, largely because he saw broadcast media as a way for the public to at least hear and see him speak.

After praising the broadcast media, he called for newspapers to do a better job keeping opinion in the editorial section and out of the news section. He said that newspapers, especially the big city newspapers, "have a right to take every position they want on the editorial page, but on the news page they also have a right to have reporters cover men who have strong

feelings whether they're for or against a candidate. But the responsibility also is to put … a fellow on, who at least will report what the man says.
That's all anybody can ask."[18] In these comments, he specifically referred to
Carl Greenberg again as an example of a fair reporter. Newspaper editors
could have opinions about candidates, but they had to report on every candidate fairly, Nixon repeated, noting specific newspapers, such as *The New
York Post* and the *Louisville Courier Journal,* which, Nixon said, "people"
told him he should be concerned about. But no, Nixon insisted, he was not
worried about those papers. Their editors had the right to think what they
wanted, if their reporting of each candidate was fair.[19] One can only imagine what the editors of the newspapers Nixon listed thought about being
singled out in this. He would do the same after becoming president. But
then, he was president, with all the power that office brings.

With that, Nixon wrapped up with his famous words, saying he was
exiting the political stage, never to return. He concluded: "The last play.
I leave you gentlemen now and you now write it. You will interpret it.
That's your right. But as I leave you, I want you to know just think how
much you're going to be missing. You won't have Nixon to kick around
anymore, because, gentlemen, this is my last press conference, and it will
be one in which I have welcomed the opportunity to test wits with you.
I have always respected you. I have sometimes disagreed with you. But,
unlike some people, I've never canceled a subscription to a paper and also
I never will."

In his next sentence, Nixon made clear how he felt about the press, if
he had not already. He said, "I believe in reading what my *opponents* say
and I hope that what I have said today will at least make television, radio,
the press, first recognize the great responsibility they have to report all
the news and, second, recognize that they have a right and a responsibility, if they're against a candidate, give him the shaft, but also recognize if
they give him the shaft, put one lonely reporter on the campaign who will
report what the candidate says now and then. Thank you, gentlemen, and
good day."[20] And with that, Nixon left the political stage. But only briefly.

Nixon was obsessed with football, so "last play" could have been
a sports metaphor. Or, since he spoke of the press writing it, maybe he
meant it as a theatrical metaphor. Really, it does not matter which metaphor was in Nixon's head as he spoke. Either metaphor suggests a script of
one sort or another, and if one carries Nixon's metaphor of a stage play or
a game plan forward, what he was really doing was writing the script for
how he would deal with the news media in the future.

A few days after the election, on Sunday, November 11, Howard K.
Smith hosted a program on ABC titled *The Political Obituary of Richard
Nixon.* One of the guests on the program was Alger Hiss, which Nixon

found quite irritating. In his autobiography, he claims that more than 80,000 people contacted ABC to complain about Hiss's inclusion in the program. But ABC was not alone in kicking dirt on Nixon's political grave or offering harsh criticism for his dramatic exit stage right with the press conference. The *Washington Post* covered his press conference with the headline "California Loser Angry at Press" and noted that an "embittered Nixon" said goodbye to public life.[21] The *New York Times* reported that Nixon conceded defeat, made "bitter denunciation of the press," and "also made some acid remarks about his victorious gubernatorial opponent." In the story's third paragraph, it was asserted, "A failure to win his native state had been widely assessed before the election as impairing, probably irreparably, the 49-year-old Republican's viability in national politics."[22]

In his memoir *RN*, Nixon wrote of his "last" press conference after he resigned from the presidency, with the hindsight of knowing that it was neither his last press conference nor the end of his political career. What he wrote succinctly sums up the lesson he learned from the gubernatorial campaign and how it informed the rest of his political career regarding the press. He wrote: "I have never regretted what I said at the 'last press conference.' I believe that it gave the media a warning that I would not sit back and take whatever biased coverage was dished out to me. In that respect, I think that the episode was partially responsible for the much fairer treatment I received from the press during the next few years. From that point of view alone, it was worth it."[23] The lesson learned from this crisis was, again, to not let the press write his story. Nixon ended this campaign knowing that if he were going to try politics again, he would be the author of his own story. And, until the scandal around Watergate got out of control, that is exactly what he did.

Nixon is a difficult, maybe impossible, puzzle box to open. There have been hundreds of books written about him. They have been written by people who purport to have known him and by historians, journalists, and political scientists. There are psychological analyses that diagnose Nixon with a variety of mental illnesses or conditions, but none were written by anyone who conducted therapy sessions with Nixon, making their conclusions purely speculative.[24] What can be said about this press conference and why he gave it? It is tempting to say it was delivered as part of a grand plan, a blueprint that led the way to the presidency in 1968. Such an assertion may be foolish. But that does not mean that what Nixon said should be taken lightly, for even if it was not delivered with the intent of being a manifesto, that is what it became for Nixon.

It is said that Nixon's speech at his "last" press conference was made in anger, that it was impromptu, that it was off the cuff. It is certainly true that he did not have prepared remarks in front of him on the podium. But it is also true that in his remarks, he established a blueprint for his eventual election to the presidency.

What is clear is that, even in defeat, Nixon had no intention of forgetting about politics. At the start of the press conference, he made it clear that he was still a leader of the Republican Party. Despite the list of personal grievances he revealed to the press gathered before him, he paused to demonstrate that a topic foremost on his mind was how well the Republican Party did on Election Day 1962, not just in California, but across the country. He spoke about Republican losses in the Senate, gains in the House of Representatives, and several Republican gubernatorial victories.

Nixon also spoke about the state he just lost, California, saying it would be revitalized under new leadership. Not his leadership, but someone else's, he said, asserting it was without any bitterness. This could be read as retirement from politics, or it could be read as Nixon telling the state of California what it could do with its governorship, because Richard Nixon was on to bigger and better things.

He then spent a while talking about the 1964 presidential election, calling it a horse race in several states. Hanging in the air was an unanswered question: Would he be one of the horses? And finally, before returning to the subject that filled most of his press conference—critiquing the press—he introduced a campaign issue for 1964 and beyond: Kennedy's poor handling of "the Cuban situation" and several other issues. In his next few sentences, Nixon raised doubts about how Kennedy would handle Cuba, Khrushchev, NATO and the Warsaw Pact, atomic testing, and China going forward. He ended this laundry list saying he thought that if Kennedy could handle "all of the woolly heads around him—if he can just keep them away from him and stand strong and firm with the good Irish fight of his, America will be in good shape in foreign policy." Nixon's tone clearly suggested he doubted Kennedy would stand strong and firm.

Nixon turned to domestic policy, telling the press that he was answering "questions" which hadn't actually been asked because "I know that some of you will ask them." Nixon stated that the economy was not going well and that classic Republican prescriptions, such as tax reform and "relying on individual enterprise and individual opportunity," were the way to improve it. With these comments on both foreign and domestic policy, Nixon offered a road map for the next campaign. Republicans made gains in the midterm election and Nixon told them how to build on them.

Nixon also addressed his own alleged political future, or lack thereof. He introduced that topic with a deceptive "one last thing," since he was only halfway through his long monologue. Nixon said: "What are my plans? Well, my plans are to go home. I'm going to get acquainted with my family again. And my plans, incidentally, are from a political standpoint, of course, to take a holiday." Nixon's real plan was, indeed, a holiday from politics, not retirement. And it turned out to be a short holiday.

Nixon's words "You won't have Nixon to kick around anymore, because gentlemen, this is my last press conference" did not prove to be true. It certainly was not the end of his political career. It also was not his "last" press conference, although he gave precious few of them for the rest of his political career. Why? Because much of the rest of his career was fashioned around the idea of controlling the press and not letting it control him. The denizens of the press would not have him to kick around any longer because he was not going to give them the opportunity to do the kicking. Nixon would be the master of his own image as the 1960s moved on. And that plan worked quite well for him until it did not. But the plan did not fail because the plan was flawed. We have seen the plan enacted quite well by many politicians since Nixon. The plan failed because the man enacting the plan was flawed.

NINE

Lessons Nixon Learned from LBJ

Nixon learned many lessons throughout his political career. He learned from his mistakes and his successes. He also learned from the mistakes of the man who filled the office he would soon fill, Lyndon Johnson. And he had ample reason to pay attention to LBJ, because Nixon was often publicly targeted by Johnson during the 1960s as a "chronic campaigner."

LBJ and Richard Nixon are often compared as being of similar personality. It is certainly true that they were both often negative and chafed mightily under criticism, especially from the press. But they reacted to it quite differently. The ways Nixon developed for responding to negative press endure to this day, influencing generations of politicians. Johnson's approach was more personal and less successful than Nixon's and, as a result, was less enduring. In addition to all the lessons Nixon learned from his own life which informed his behavior, he also had the opportunity to observe, for five years, the behavior of LBJ as president and to develop very different strategies.

Lyndon Johnson took every negative portrayal, every bit of bad news, as a personal slight. Johnson battled with the press throughout his presidency. So did Richard Nixon. But Nixon also knew better than Johnson how to get his points out through the media, despite the media. In part he learned from life experience, but he also learned from the model of LBJ himself.

As president, Richard Nixon would often have Vice President Spiro Agnew or other administration officials fight the media on his behalf, and in very public ways, making speeches and giving interviews. The Nixon administration also developed a variety of systematic ways of dealing with the press. It is only with the hindsight the Nixon tapes provide that one understands how much Nixon loathed the press personally. Johnson, on the other hand, preferred to take on the media in personal contests with reporters and worked behind the scenes, playing political power games and antagonizing individual reporters. Reporter Helen Thomas described Johnson's treatment of reporters in an oral history project about the Johnson administration. Thomas explained that she thought Johnson behaved in ways that were "deliberately sadistic" and designed to show the press who was boss. It lost him friends and was, she said, "a lousy way to do the nation's business."[1]

It is no secret that Johnson paid a great deal of attention to any slight he perceived in media coverage of him. Biographer Robert Dallek wrote that Johnson worked hard personally to make sure the only news out of the White House was what he wanted it to be. Johnson tried to direct coverage by raising national security, pressuring publishers to print pro-administration stories, planting questions at press conferences, and harassing reporters he did not like. He also intimidated his aides by recording all their phone calls from the White House switchboard to make sure they were not speaking to reporters.[2]

Helen Thomas told a story about an issue unimportant to the country or to world affairs but which nevertheless put her fully in Johnson's doghouse. Thomas broke the news that Johnson's daughter Luci was engaged to be married, causing the entire family to refuse to speak to her for weeks. And there were, she said, many other times when she knew he was angry with something she had written. Johnson was always paying attention to what reporters reported, and when he was unhappy, "you always got the message."[3] Johnson was not capable of tuning the press out. Instead, he was obsessed with it and even the mildest of stories got his attention. Historian Randall Woods notes that *New York Times* reporter James "Scotty" Reston "perhaps best summed up LBJ's impossible relationship with the Fourth Estate. 'If you don't tell the precise truth about him, which is almost inevitable, he thinks you are dishonest, and if you do, he feels you are disloyal.'"[4]

After LBJ left the White House, when Spiro Agnew delivered his first speech critiquing the media, Lyndon Johnson's fourth, and final, presidential press secretary, George Christian, addressed Johnson's feelings about the press, saying that Johnson was often angered by the coverage he received, but he asserted that Johnson never went to the extent Agnew did to issue such an aggressive, threatening, public challenge to the press. Christian referred to a speech Johnson delivered to a meeting of the National Association of Broadcasters the day after he announced he was not running for reelection in 1968 as evidence of a supposedly more restrained approach.[5] In the speech, Johnson told the press they had a sacred trust to tell the truth and not what was popular. In the long speech, the only applause he received was when he promised that if he were in power, the government would never try to restrain the press through legal means,[6] but this said nothing of his many personal efforts to intimidate, block, and manipulate the press.

Of the speech, Christian said, "It's in the nature of the way he did business. On occasion, his feelings of anger were every bit as strong as those of the present Administration. After all, we did get some punishing treatment. But he chose to make his feelings known to reporters and networks personally, on a sort of man-to-man approach. He never considered making a broad, frontal attack. It never got to the nationwide TV speech level."[7] Christian saw the NAB speech as very different from Agnew's approach, pointing out that Johnson didn't make his speech until after he announced he was not running for reelection and that he spoke with more moderation, not taking the same sharp tone as Agnew always did.[8] Perhaps Johnson didn't take the same sharp *public* tone as Agnew in his speech to the NAB, but as reporter Robert McFadden noted in his interview of Christian, "Mr. Johnson did react" to every slight he perceived in press coverage.[9] Did he ever.

One insightful impression of Johnson comes from journalist John Chancellor, who knew Johnson both as a subject (Chancellor covered Johnson as a reporter, including a short time as the NBC White House correspondent) and as a boss (he served in the Johnson administration as the director of the Voice of America from 1965 to 1967). As a reporter covering the White House, he remembered that Johnson "was obsessed with press relations" and recalled many instances of Johnson getting personally involved in reporting about his administration.

One such story involved a report on NBC about Maxwell Taylor, who at the time was serving as the U.S. ambassador to South Vietnam. Chancellor was asked by NBC News to confirm the story, so he reached out to a Johnson aide, Jack Valenti, and asked about Taylor. Valenti gave answers that seemed to confirm the story, so Chancellor went on the air and said that although the White House did not confirm or deny the rumor, it seemed likely Taylor was leaving Vietnam but hat it would not mean any change in U.S. policy. Chancellor said, "Then I went back to my little cubicle there in the press room and the phone rang, and it was the President. I tell this because it illustrates how he worked. He was furious! He said, 'That's not true. Why didn't you ask me? I'm a hundred yards away from you right now. Why didn't you just come in and ask me?'"[10]

Taylor did not leave Vietnam for several months after this. Chancellor offers no speculation on this, but given the many known occasions when Johnson changed his mind to ensure that reporters were wrong, one cannot help but wonder if Taylor stayed on longer in Vietnam because Johnson was angry that the story broke ahead of time. It would be natural to react to such an assertion with skepticism, except for the fact that there are many clear cases of Johnson unambiguously changing policy because he did not like the reporting.

One remarkably revealing glimpse into Johnson's views of the press that covered him comes from a long interview with historian William Leuchtenberg, conducted in 1965 but not published until 1990. In speaking with Leuchtenberg, Johnson claimed that he paid no attention to news columnists, but then proceeded to show that to be a lie worthy of Pinocchio.[11] He was completely obsessed with the media, as several points of Leuchtenberg's description of his interview with Johnson demonstrate. Leuchtenberg observed, for instance, that Johnson had a special television console with three screens which allowed him to watch all three evening news broadcasts at once, switching the sound on and off between them with a remote. Throughout much of his interview, Leuchtenberg reported that the president frequently stopped to listen to certain stories. Johnson lashed out frequently at the press, pointing out specific journalists, such as Rowland Evans and Drew Pearson, who had especially offended him. Johnson called on an aide to give Leuchtenberg a copy of a memo detailing the inaccuracies of certain journalists and told Leuchtenberg, "If the livelihood of *The New York Times* depended on its accuracy, they would be shot at sunrise." Johnson was so distracted by his anger about the news media, according to Leuchtenberg, that he was almost incapable of concentrating on the legislation which was supposed to be the subject of the interview.

Leuchtenberg observed that once Johnson started his commentary on the press, he was loath to let it go. Johnson complained about columnists but dismissed them as having little influence. He told Leuchtenberg that he kept records of "lies" in the press. In the past week alone, Johnson said, the *Washington Post* published 11 lies. He complained about "well-informed sources" being quoted in the paper and said, "'That just means what they want to say. Someday we'll have to pass a law *stopping* them from using 'well informed,'" and added, "'They don't have the horsepower to really defeat me, or they would.'"

In summarizing his hour-and-a-half interview with Johnson, Leuchtenberg concludes with words that could well be used to describe President Trump, simply by replacing the examples Leuchtenberg cites. He wrote that Johnson was consumed by news coverage and waging war against it. Johnson was also determined to show the world he was much better than predecessors such as JFK and FDR. Leuchtenberg described it as "a conviction of his own centrality in the universe bordering on egomania."[12]

Assessments of Johnson's approach to the press vary depending on who is making the assessment. It is perhaps not surprising that George Christian, as a former aide to Johnson, saw Johnson's behavior in benign terms. Christian's views were summarized by the *New York Times'* Robert McFadden who, quoting Christian, wrote, "'There were many newsmen who he talked to when he thought they had done something to injure him.' In addition, he added, Mr. Johnson was 'not loath to talk to the networks' about his misgivings, and occasionally made 'one-liner' public criticisms at his news conferences. However, he declined to 'make a concerted issue out of it,' Mr. Christian said. 'He felt he could achieve fairness in other ways.'"[13] However, more objective observers note that Johnson was obsessed with the press and did make a "concerted issue out of it." He simply chose to do so behind the scenes most of the time and largely aimed his aggressive action against individual reporters who offended him.

While Johnson did not make a continuing *public* attack on the media in the way the Nixon administration did, Christian's defense of Johnson characterizes the boss's behavior as more benign than it really was, given what is known about his behavior in response to what he saw as sins of the press, behind the scenes or not. Johnson was obsessed with media coverage personally, to the extent that he could not have a continuous conversation with Leuchtenberg without pausing several times and getting angry at the national news broadcasts.

Reporter Helen Thomas made this observation about Johnson: "He so hoarded information; he didn't like anyone to know, even those who would be in his camp."[14] John Chancellor would have concurred with that assessment. He remembered preparing a story and recording a bit of material standing in front of the White House on a Sunday. Johnson spied him from a window and had a guard bring Chancellor to the phone so he could ask him what he was doing a story about. Chancellor told him and LBJ gave him a briefing on the issue. Chancellor noted that reporters would be thrilled with such an inside source, but as Johnson spoke, the words did not ring true to Chancellor. Nevertheless, since it was Johnson speaking, Chancellor reported what he said, only to find out after the story aired that Johnson had lied to him. Chancellor remembered, "I've rarely been as angry. I really was just furious!"[15] The most revealing part of this anecdote isn't that Johnson lied to a reporter. It is that it did not matter what the subject was. Johnson happened to look out a window at the White House, saw Chancellor, and involved himself in the reporter's business and did so mendaciously, just because he could.

The hoarding of information extended to his staff. Johnson frequently got very angry at reporters who reported things he did not like or did not want made public. That anger was even more frequently directed at the people who worked for him as potential sources of information for reporters. Asked if she thought Johnson's staffers were hard to get information from, Helen Thomas said they were too scared to say much to reporters. Johnson frequently told his staffers that they were not brought into his administration to get their names in the papers. Thomas spoke words that have been more recently said about Donald Trump. She said that Johnson's aides did not want to risk his wrath. They knew he hated for them to be quoted, so they were extremely reluctant to speak to the press. Thomas said of LBJ, "He wanted to know everything that was going on. He ran the White House. And he ran everyone with it. He had a total knowledge—or thought he had total knowledge—of what was going on."[16]

Chancellor saw Johnson's attempts to control the media as an inescapable consequence of his personality. Chancellor said, "Kennedy understood media much better than Johnson did.... I know he knew that he had failings in this, that he wasn't very good at it, and he was constantly trying to overcome it. Various presidential press conference techniques were used, an endless array. They were forever tinkering with the television equipment in the East Wing of the White House, various kinds of glasses were used, barbers were used. All of this is perfectly legitimate. As a matter of fact, it's necessary for a president to try to present himself as well as he could. But Johnson, I think, never got the secret. He never could overcome it."[17] Chancellor felt there was a very good reason that Johnson couldn't overcome it—it was his "basic personality."[18]

Chancellor explained, "Lyndon Johnson's troubles with the media and troubles with the press were directly related to the fact that he was not so much a politician as a legislator, as a parliamentarian ... every action he took in his public life was designed to produce legislation." This led, Chancellor thought, to a "conspiratorial nature." He explained, "And Lyndon Johnson was, and I say this with admiration, the sneakiest of them all. He was just marvelous at accomplishing good things in devious ways."[19] But what worked so effectively in Congress didn't translate well to the very different and much more public stage of the White House. Chancellor said, "you put him in the public spotlight of the presidency where the public's business pretty much has to be conducted in public. I found that Lyndon Johnson was totally unfit—his life had not prepared him to operate in the presidential spotlight where things have to be done in a quite different way. Lyndon Johnson ran the White House and the country the way he had trained himself to run the Senate. Only the country and the White House aren't the Senate."[20]

While it worked for LBJ to buttonhole reporters he could take by the hand in the halls of the Senate, it did not work so well at the White House. But he continued to try the personal approach that worked so well for him as a legislator, and he became ever more frustrated when it did not work the way he wanted it to work. The consequences, as Chancellor saw them, were disastrous. He said, "It's perfectly all right to have sort of a grudging admiration, along with mistrust, for a parliamentary leader who has got to do a lot of finagling and string pulling in order to get things done. But that measure of that sense of uneasiness and mistrust can kill a president, and it did Lyndon Johnson."[21] Chancellor's theory makes a great deal of sense and is certainly at least partly correct. And it explains that while the stories of Nixon and LBJ ended the same way, they got to their similar endings in very different ways. Nixon was a legislator early in his career, but never in the way LBJ was a legislator.

For Johnson, controlling the press was about making the world see him as its center, at least in part because as the Senate majority leader, he was the center of that world. And LBJ tried to do it one reporter at a time. In response to the question "Did you get the feeling that Johnson tried to capture certain newsmen?" reporter Helen Thomas put it this way: "I felt that he always wanted to be understood and wanted to be loved. I know that's a cliché answer, but I think he really did, and he wanted to be personified, and he wanted to be in the newspapers in the right light, according to his view. So, I think that the press was a transmission belt for him and a nemesis."[22] Johnson wanted to be loved, hated it when he was not loved, and blamed the press for it.

The way Nixon handled press relations, especially as a candidate and in his first term in office, was different from Johnson. LBJ tried to force people to love him. He was outraged and mystified when they did not. Nixon instinctively understood that it was not likely he would ever be loved. This is a core part of his personality Druckman and Jacobs zeroed in on in their research.

What was needed, as Nixon understood it, was a *system*, not a personal lobbying effort because he understood the limits of his personality. This is not to say he did not get personal sometimes. There were, to be sure, journalists on the "enemies" list. But, in general, Nixon was much more systematic in dealing with the press than LBJ. The *how* of how Nixon handled the press is important not just for understanding Nixon individually but also for understanding his long-term impact on the relations between politicians and the press and how politicians interact with the news media. Nixon did, at times, take a personal approach. But far more important, he took an *institutional* approach and, in so doing, established a model that every president who succeeded him has followed, along with countless politicians at other levels of government. There was much to be learned from the Sisyphean efforts of LBJ, pushing rocks up the hill against every individual journalist or media outlet he felt had wronged him, only to have them—as he saw it—roll right back down over him.

LBJ's behavior toward the press was controlling and almost entirely on a micro level, face to face either with offending reporters or with other reporters in the expectation it would get back to the reporter with whom he was angry. There was some of this same behavior by Nixon, especially as

Watergate caused things to unravel, but early on what Nixon learned from Johnson was the need for a structure, a systematic way of dealing with the press. Micromanaging the press consumes all one's time. Nixon eventually fell into that trap too, as his system was unable to stop the press discoveries inspired by Watergate, but he learned enough from Johnson to try and avoid it. And in so doing, established a model for those who followed.

Part II: The Lessons Applied

TEN

The "Wilderness" Years Were
Not the "Non-Media" Years

From November 7, 1962, until he took the oath of office and became the 37th President of the United States on January 20, 1969, Nixon was a "private citizen," though he was never truly out of the public spotlight. Many historians have referred to these years as the "wilderness" years. But for Nixon, the middle years of the 1960s were a period of image rebuilding. This was a process which began for Nixon just a few months after the so-called "last press conference."

After Nixon left the stage in California, not to be kicked around anymore, he did a curious thing: he made an appearance on the *Jack Paar Program*, a primetime show on Friday nights. It was Paar's new show after he decided to leave *The Tonight Show* at the end of March of 1962. Paar's new show was like what he did with *The Tonight Show*, and he was never shy about putting politics center stage.

For Nixon, it was a first step in a six-year campaign to repair his image. It is something that today experts would call a "textbook move" for a politician with image problems. But at the time Nixon did it, he was writing the textbook. He went on an entertainment-oriented talk and variety show. Much of the appearance was quite serious in tone, and he made clear then and there that he had no intention of staying on the sidelines. He told Paar that while he was relocating to New York to practice law, he planned to "reserve as much time as possible for the purpose of discussing public affairs."[1] It was, he said, the beginning of his effort "to call the shots as I see them."[2] That meant, primarily, critiquing the Kennedy administration and, following JFK's assassination, the Johnson administration. He did this in speeches, interviews, and other appearances by the dozens throughout the 1960s, creating a role for himself as what today's world of cable news networks might call a "wonk." Or, alternately, as a statesman without a portfolio. It is a model created by Nixon for the world of television which many politicians who are in between jobs frequently follow.

105

Nixon continued his Paar appearance with material from the middle of his "last" press conference—attacking Kennedy on the question of Cuba. He said Kennedy failed to take decisive steps to "eliminate the Communist cancer from Cuba,"[3] and he said that if Kennedy did decide to take strong action, he would have the bipartisan support of Republicans. Nixon, purportedly a non-politician, laid out a detailed plan for sanctions he thought should be carried out: a blockade of oil deliveries to Cuba, foreign aid sanctions against countries which engaged in trade with Cuba, removal of Soviet troops from the island and inspection of missile installations on the island. He dismissively called the Kennedy administration a public relations success and said it was "brilliant from the point of salesmanship," but "the product doesn't live up to the words."[4]

Nixon continued in this vein at some length, saying Kennedy failed by not providing air support to the Cuban rebels during the Bay of Pigs invasion and noted that Eisenhower would never have failed to provide such support. He said that Khrushchev was "impressed by power," that the Soviet leader wouldn't "start a conflict which would destroy his own country," and said that the United States needed a policy which would "drive communism from this hemisphere and keep it out of the Americas."[5] It is a sign of the Cold War times that there was an official Soviet response to Nixon's appearance with Jack Paar, noting that he "continued to grind out the same old tune for which he was blackballed at the last elections."[6] To be sure, media outlets also covered his appearance on the show, but they didn't comment on the final, and most memorable, part of Nixon's appearance with Paar.

While he talked about serious political issues during his appearance on the *Jack Paar Program*, Nixon's crowning achievement on the show came when he sat down at a piano and played a composition of his own. As Paar explained to the audience, Nixon's wife Pat recorded it ahead of time, allowing the director of his show's band, Jose Melis, to orchestrate the piece so Nixon could play along with the Jose Melis Orchestra. It was a moment in which Nixon was able to appear much less serious, much less angry, and much more fun-loving than ever for such a large audience.

Paar moved Nixon to the piano performance, explaining to the audience that Nixon played the piano and that his wife, Pat, recorded him playing a composition of his own. Paar reported that the leader of his band, Jose Melis, orchestrated Nixon's composition, arranging it as a concerto. As Nixon prepared to perform with Melis and the orchestra, he said to Paar, "You asked a moment ago whether I had any future political plans to run for anything and, uh, if last November didn't finish it, this will because believe me, the Republicans don't want another piano player in the White House."[7] The joke was a reference to Harry S. Truman, who was

Nixon, with wife Pat standing behind, plays the piano for Harry and Bess Truman at the Truman Library in Independence in 1969 (Harry S. Truman Library).

also an accomplished pianist. When he was finished, the audience erupted in applause and Nixon smiled broadly.

Clearly, this successful appearance was memorable to Nixon and those who supported him. The world-famous communication scholar Marshall McLuhan, who had a profound influence on at least some of Nixon's campaign advisers in 1968, wrote about Nixon's 1963 appearance with Paar in his book *Understanding Media*. It was not Nixon's statements about U.S. policy toward Cuba or critiques of JFK that he wrote about. It was Nixon's piano playing. McLuhan wrote that the appearance recreated Nixon into a "suitable TV image," thanks, at least in part, to Paar's guidance and understanding of how TV worked. McLuhan observed that a few moments like this during the 1960 campaign could have changed the outcome, concluding, "TV is a medium that rejects the sharp personality and favors the presentation of processes rather than of products."[8] Writing in 1964, McLuhan was making an observation that Nixon certainly agreed with. Creating a different image for himself was crucial for campaign success.

Given the immense amount of attention McLuhan received in the 1960s, there can be little doubt that his assessment of Nixon's appearance with Paar had a real impact on a variety of audiences. No doubt it made an impression on the several McLuhan devotees who were part of Nixon's political team. If McLuhan wrote that actions like appearing on TV with Jack Paar helped, then key members of Nixon's team believed that they helped. But it is also very clear that Nixo himself saw the value of such shows. The important thing to remember is that the political use of television to *rebuild* an image began with Richard Nixon himself, first in 1952 and then again in 1963. Contrary to public opinion, it most definitely did not begin with Bill Clinton and his saxophone in 1992.

Clinton and His Saxophone Had Nothing on Nixon

Many people may remember that when he was campaigning in 1992, Bill Clinton made a tour of pop culture hotspots attempting to reach out to younger audiences. The first of these was the *Arsenio Hall Show* on June 3, 1992. One of the iconic images of America's first baby boomer president is of him playing "Heartbreak Hotel" on his saxophone along with the show's band, the Dog Pound, at the beginning of the show. He then sat down and spoke with Hall for close to half an hour, talking about a variety of issues, including civil rights, the recent Rodney King–related protests in Los Angeles, and ways to keep young people away from crime.[9] It was a venue in which Clinton could strut his stuff without much fear of harsh questions.

Bill Clinton in the White House music room, January 29, 1996.

Hall was easy on Clinton, gently asking questions about marijuana use and his faults. Clinton could avoid the common charges of adultery and claim that his main fault was being a workaholic, saying, "'I have a lot of shortcomings.... I still sometimes work hard instead of smart.'"[10] Most famously, Clinton took a page straight out of Nixon's playbook by playing a musical instrument. Clinton followed up his appearance on Hall's show with an MTV-sponsored town hall meeting program of about 200 young adults, mostly 18 to 24 years old, on June 16. The 90-minute broadcast covered many issues, including a follow-up on Clinton's marijuana use.[11]

At the time, reporters treated these campaign tactics as though they were new and groundbreaking. Reporter David Maraniss, who became a Clinton biographer, reported in the *Washington Post* after the Hall appearance that it was the season of "newfangled political primaries," meaning the talk show circuit.[12] Two months later, politics and media analyst Howard Kurtz, then with the *Washington Post*, wrote a profile piece about Clinton adviser Mandy Grunwald, who was credited with getting Clinton on shows like Arsenio Hall's. Calling it the "Arsenio strategy," he wrote that her job was to get around the traditional news media to create a more intimate portrait of Clinton.[13]

This was accomplished, Kurtz wrote, by doing things such as getting the Clintons on the cover of *People* in April, quoting Grunwald as saying, "'It's a lot more important to get five pages in *People* magazine than five minutes on 'MacNeil/Lehrer.'"[14] James Carville, already a grizzled political veteran when he ran the Clinton campaign, said of Grunwald, "'She's the one who said we should do all this pop culture stuff. She's definitely post–Beatles. I'm Lawrence Welk. I thought Arsenio was some kind of poison you took.'"[15]

The message in news coverage was that the Clinton campaign was doing something revolutionary in 1992, guided by visionaries such as Grunwald. These Clinton events, along with the appearances by Ross Perot on *The Larry King Show* and by Clinton and Jerry Brown on *The Phil Donahue Show*, were treated by many supposedly expert observers as newfangled media strategies that would forever change presidential campaigns.

This idea has become part of our accepted version of history, and it is reiterated frequently. In a 2012 appearance on CNN, Arsenio Hall and CNN correspondent John King reminisced about Clinton's saxophone playing. Hall asked King if he thought Clinton's appearance on "changed politics forever." King responded that it did permanently change politics. King said that Clinton was facing an unusual field of opponents, such as Ross Perot and Howard Dean, who were bringing new voters into the campaign and Clinton needed to find a way to do the same thing. He said, "Good politicians take a risk and Clinton took one there. And you remember—I was a print reporter covering the campaign at that time—a lot of people criticized, and a lot of people said, 'This is not presidential.' Uh, he won the election so, by definition, it worked."[16]

The problem with this kind of analysis is that it is simply wrong in one major way. It is not wrong to say that these strategies helped Clinton, but it is wrong to say that these strategies were new in 1992. Such statements miss much that went before 1992. They certainly miss events such as Richard Nixon's decision, just four months after the prematurely reported death of his political career, to begin to rebuild it by doing what? By playing a musical instrument on a nighttime entertainment talk show.

Technically, Kennedy beat Nixon to entertainment television, appearing with Jack Paar on *The Tonight Show* in June of 1960. Nixon did not appear until August of 1960. But for Nixon, there was something much more profoundly important about the impact of entertainment television for him and for politicians like him than for Kennedy. Kennedy was the popular kid of American politics. Nixon was not. He needed people to see him in a different light. Nixon understood that television could help him with his image, and unlike JFK, he returned to it several times. It was the *way* he used his appearances on such shows which established the precedent that matters. What was significant about Nixon appearing on *The Tonight Show* and the *Jack Paar Show* was his ability to make political hay out of at least *appearing* to be funny and laid back as a guest on a talk show that was heavy on humor. It was a rather remarkable achievement, given his personality, which simply did not tend toward jovial or funny.

When asked if he ever wrote jokes for Nixon, former Gerald Ford speechwriter and Hollywood comedy writer Bob Orben once observed simply of Nixon, "Nixon was not a joke person. Nixon would never. Nixon tried to avoid the various fun events, the Gridiron dinners and that sort of thing."[17] Orben not only wrote speeches and jokes for Gerald Ford, but he also wrote them for many politicians, including Barry Goldwater. He understood politics and humor innately and he had an accurate handle on Nixon. Nixon was not a man given to humor. This fact means that he was making deliberate strategic choices in doing something like going on with Jack Paar in August 1960 or in March 1963. The fact that Nixon was not at all inclined to be funny—especially in situations that involved making fun of himself—makes it even more remarkable that he was able to be successful in a setting such as the *Jack Paar Show* or, later, with Johnny Carson, Joey Bishop, Mike Douglas, or Merv Griffin.

Prior to Nixon's second appearance with Paar, in 1963 following his loss in California, critic Jack Gould noted sarcastically, "The celebrated 'farewell' of former Vice President Richard M. Nixon has run true to dramatic tradition; he will return to the public eye on March 8 when he will be a guest on the Jack Paar Show. It will be his first since his defeat in the California gubernatorial election."[18] He added, with further sarcasm, though incorrectly, "The program will mark the second time that Mr. Nixon has chatted with Mr. Paar following adversity at the polls. On the last occasion he talked about his defeat in the 1960 presidential campaign."[19] He had spoken with him before the election, not after, though that would've been fascinating had it happened. Gould's criticisms about TV, politics, and Jack Paar notwithstanding, Nixon seemed to understand that success in politics without TV, and without the kind of entertainment TV that Paar specialized in, was not possible for him.

Following the defeat in California, Nixon relocated his family to New York and took a job as a partner in a New York law firm, Mudge, Rose, Guthrie, Alexander, & Mitchell, which became Nixon, Mudge, Rose, Guthrie, & Mitchell when he came on board. In addition to his legal practice, Nixon continued his new, self-appointed role of public commentator on the foreign policy of the Kennedy administration. Following his piano-playing triumph with Paar, Nixon's next big platform came in the form of an address to the American Society of Newspaper Editors on April 20, 1963, in Washington, D.C.

In his run for the White House and then as president, Donald Trump frequently employed a verbal trick, using the phrase "People are saying" or a similar variation that suggested an uncorroborated groundswell of support. Nixon used his own verbal trick to kick off his remarks to the editors. He said: "On such an occasion as this, a battle-scarred political veteran is probably expected to pour it on and let it go at that. If only I were the 'partisan type' what a field day I could have."[20] The trick was to say what a partisan would do, while suggesting that he, of course, was not such a partisan. And then, as soon as he was finished uttering those words, he delivered a very partisan speech, starting with Kennedy's failures in Cuba, which culminated in giving "the Soviets squatters' rights in our back yard."[21] He then critiqued the Kennedy administration on civil rights, relations with Europe, Laos, foreign aid, and deficits.[22]

Taking a break from the discussion of policy, Nixon said, "I appear today before this group in a different role than I have occupied before. For 16 years I have spoken as a candidate, as a party leader, or as an administration official. Today, I appear only as an individual citizen speaking without regard to any effect my words may have on my own, my party's or my administration's political popularity."[23] He then threw Kennedy's own words back at him when he said, "Why speak out at all?" President Kennedy answered that question when speaking as a candidate on September 20, 1960. He said: "'Some people say it is wrong to say we could be stronger. It is dangerous to say we could be more secure. But in times such as this I say it is wrong and dangerous for any American to keep silent about our future if he is not satisfied with what is being done to preserve that future.'"[24] Nixon was, he insisted, not a politician but, rather, just a concerned citizen expressing his views.

The second half of Nixon's speech reads very much like the launch of a campaign. Though he never really was a candidate in 1964, he certainly liked the idea that people thought of him as a potential candidate. With the benefit of hindsight, one can read this speech as a launch of his long campaign for the presidency in 1968. He said that while it was not "fashionable" to talk about defeating communism, he refused to give up on that goal, saying that there was a "responsible strategy" that could avoid either giving up or going to war. Next, as any serious candidate would do, he laid out the details of that three-part strategy, which included rebuilding unity with Western allies, giving more effective support to nations of the developing world facing communist insurgencies, and "developing a new program to extend freedom to match the Communist efforts to extend slavery."[25] It was, Nixon asserted, time for Americans to export their ideas to the world. Only with all Americans working together could the "Communist ideological offensive" be defeated in order to "retain the initiative for the cause of freedom."[26]

Convincing people to work toward this goal, he argued, was partly the job of the president, but, since he was speaking to a room of reporters, he could not help but offer the Fourth Estate some more advice. He ended his speech by telling the journalists that they could be very valuable. Newspaper editors had more power than any other group of people in the country to influence people's opinions, Nixon said. It was okay for them to agree with elected officials, candidates, and political parties, but they should always encourage people to love the country and defend freedom and spread it around the world.[27] The words praised and warned the journalists in the room: with great power comes great responsibility.

Nixon fielded many questions from the editors: whether he was seeking any office in the future; whether he thought Kennedy could be beaten in 1964; which Republican he thought was most capable of beating Kennedy; and so on. He stated flatly that he was not a candidate, nor did he intend to be a candidate for any office in the future. He proclaimed Kennedy was beatable, "on the issues," and while not favoring any particular candidate, he named several frontrunners and predicted that whoever the nominee was, it would not be a "dark horse."

So, after giving the most political of speeches, which he began by saying he was not going to do what everyone expected and give a political speech, Nixon denied any interest in future office. It is difficult, perhaps more difficult than with any major American political figure of the past century, to know exactly what was in Nixon's head, but very little of his behavior, starting with his appearance on Jack Paar's show, then moving to this speech before the editors in Washington, suggested that he was stepping back from elected politics. He was, in many ways, diving head first into elective politics soon after saying he was leaving them.

In 1964, Nixon was a central figure as a leader of the party at the Republican National Convention, where he introduced party nominee Barry Goldwater after he was officially nominated. Nixon said "Mr. Conservative" was now "Mr. Republican" and "he is the man who after the greatest campaign in history will be Mr. President! Barry Goldwater!"[28] During the 1964 election, Nixon campaigned on behalf of Republican candidates in 36 states. Goldwater did not win, but no one said it was Nixon's fault as they did after Republican midterm election losses following his trip to Latin America in 1958. It is unlikely any Republican could have beaten LBJ in 1964 in the wake of the national grief following Kennedy's assassination. In the Republican Party's defeat, Nixon was golden, the ultimate Party Man, doing his very best for Goldwater and Republicans everywhere and banking goodwill for 1968.

In 1966, he similarly campaigned around the country on behalf of candidates and the party, speaking at innumerable venues. In the 1966 midterms, the GOP picked up 47 seats in the House of Representatives and three seats in the Senate. In gubernatorial elections, Republicans won ten states previously held by Democrats and won 23 of 35 elections overall. Nixon ended the election cycle feeling very positive about his party and his role with it as he readied himself for a run for the White House in 1968. For many, especially among Republicans, Nixon had erased the image of an angry loser and replaced it with a new one: happy warrior for the party.

ELEVEN

The Man for All Media

In 1966, the movie *A Man for All Seasons* won the Academy Award for Best Picture. It was about Sir Thomas More, the Lord Chancellor of England who refused to help Henry VIII in his quest to divorce Catherine of Aragon. The movie portrayed More as a man who remained true to his principles against all adversity. In the mid–1960s, Nixon was the man for all media, appearing on every media platform imaginable, telling the country about the principles he believed in, but mostly keeping his name in the public spotlight.

As he did all he could to keep his name prominent with the party and the public, Nixon was happy to give speeches and interviews and utilize as many media outlets as he could, but almost always in ways that allowed him to get his message out in ways that were as unfiltered as possible. What consumers of these media got was pure Nixon. One outlet which he utilized to great effect was *Reader's Digest*, a magazine with a consistently conservative ideological bent. Its publishers, Lila and DeWitt Wallace, were longtime supporters of Nixon, to the point that they became subjects of the Watergate investigation.[1] But in the 1960s, *Reader's Digest* was popular and well read, and Nixon used it as a platform for several statements of his positions on foreign policy.

Reader's Digest

At the end of both 1964 and 1965, Nixon wrote two essays on the topic of foreign policy, the area in which he was working to establish himself as an authority. He wrote a third essay in 1967, as he was launching his campaign for the presidency. In 1964, as Nixon campaigned for Republicans and for the Republican presidential nominee, Barry Goldwater, he positioned himself as the man to bring the liberal and conservative factions of the party together.[2]

But Nixon was never far from thinking about his most important job—promoting Richard Nixon. He did this in detail in the November 1964 issue of *Reader's Digest* published just before the election. "Cuba, Castro, and John F. Kennedy: Some Reflections on United States Foreign Policy" was written before the election but with Nixon's obvious understanding that the Republican nominee, Barry Goldwater, was not going to win. It was Nixon's argument that even though things looked like they were going well for the United States on the world stage, no one should be fooled—they really were not!

The essay began with an introduction by the editors of *Reader's Digest* about the ways in which the fortunes of Cuba and the United States were intertwined. "This timely article," they promised, would explain how Cuba affected the careers of Nixon and JFK. In addition, they promised, Nixon would share his insights on the 1960 presidential campaign and the important issues of 1964. They concluded with a laudatory paragraph about Nixon's extensive experience in foreign policy, arguing that every American should read his reflections.[3] The essay itself is remarkable, for it was a comprehensive critique of the Kennedy administration which included a suggestion that Kennedy was, through incompetence, the architect of his own demise.

Nixon's essay began with his story of his one and only meeting with Castro. He was left, after three and a half hours, with the impression that "Castro is either incredibly naïve about communism or is under communist discipline." He put this opinion in a memo that was distributed to Eisenhower, Secretary of State Christian Herter, and Director of the CIA Allen Dulles. But Nixon laments that most of the officials he addressed did not agree with his take on Castro. They argued that Castro was not a communist and, Nixon is sure to point out, their opinions prevailed over his. The long-term consequence of his opinions being disregarded was, Nixon wrote, that the United States would be faced with continued defeats and with enemies permanently in the Western Hemisphere.[4] Nixon was serving notice: he understood the Soviet threat, he knew how to deal with it, and the consequences of ignoring him were dire.

The next several pages of the essay were dedicated to the Eisenhower administration's handling of Cuba, the campaign of 1960, and the Bay of Pigs invasion. One issue that Nixon addressed repeatedly, in speeches and in his writing, including *Six Crises*, was the notion that Kennedy was the one who looked tougher on Cuba during the 1960 campaign. Nixon's story, explained in detail in this essay, was that planning for an overthrow of Cuba was in the works in the Eisenhower administration while the campaign was ongoing. Kennedy knew about it, thanks to briefings from the CIA, and was able to talk tough about Cuba with a freedom that Nixon did not enjoy.

In *Reader's Digest,* Nixon wrote, "I was faced with a heads-he-wins, tails-I-lose proposition." Had he talked about the preparations to over-throw Castro during the debates, Nixon wrote, he could have neutralized Kennedy, but at the expense of national security. He had no choice but to remain silent. It was, Nixon wrote, right for the country and wrong for the campaign. The damage was clear: Kennedy emerged looking tough on Cuba and Nixon looked weak. It was, Nixon wrote, "the exact opposite of the truth."[5] Nixon concluded this section of the essay with speculation that his decision about how to address the Cuba issue during the debate may have cost him the election, but that he had no regrets about how he had acted. This allowed Nixon to claim high moral ground that Kennedy was not around to dispute.

Following the failure of the Bay of Pigs invasion, Nixon was called on by Kennedy for advice. Nixon wrote that he told Kennedy to find legal cover and invade Cuba. It was imperative, Nixon told Kennedy, to get communism and Castro out of Cuba.[6] He added that he gave Kennedy the same advice about Laos when Kennedy asked him about that country. The meeting ended with Kennedy indicating that American action in either place would be ill-advised.

In the next section of the essay, Nixon wrote of the importance of learning from the mistakes made in Cuba. There were, Nixon argued, two major lessons to be learned from the failure of the Bay of Pigs invasion. The first, he wrote, was that once a decision has been made to act, officials must commit adequate resources to that action, which he clearly felt the Kennedy administration did not do. The second was that the United States must make foreign policy decisions based on its security interests and not worry about "world public opinion." The United States was the strongest nation in the world and had an obligation to lead, not to follow, in defend-ing freedom.[7]

What was the consequence of Kennedy's misstep with the Bay of Pigs as Nixon saw things? It was to embolden Khrushchev, making him believe that Americans did not have the guts to defend their own interests. "As he later said to Robert Frost," Nixon wrote, "'the Americans are too liberal to fight.'"[8]

Nixon wrote about the Cuban Missile Crisis and concluded that it was "the finest hour" of Kennedy's presidency. He wrote that Kennedy calling Khrushchev's bluff made it impossible for the Soviets to conduct diplo-macy through nuclear blackmail going forward. But. There was a big "but" as far as Nixon was concerned. He wrote that while Kennedy prevented the Soviet missiles from being installed in Cuba, he had pulled "defeat from the jaws of victory" with weak and indecisive behavior after the fact. Rather than imposing strong sanctions against the Soviets, Nixon wrote,

Kennedy followed the "incredibly bad advice" of his aides, which included the following actions: (1) failure to insist on on-site inspection of missile sites; (2) adopting a policy to not invade Cuba and banning Cuban exiles from engaging in any further activity against Castro; and (3) allowing a "weak-kneed foreign policy" to encourage America's enemy, the Soviet Union, to "bolder and bolder action."[9] The Cuban missile crisis, Nixon asserted, "turned out to be a net gain for the Kremlin."[10]

Nixon next addressed the assassination of Kennedy, but he did so by making himself the center of the story. He began by telling the story of his own trip to Dallas the day before Kennedy was to arrive. He was visiting a client of his law firm and he spoke to reporters while there. In response to their concerns that there were people in Dallas who might protest the administration while Kennedy was there, Nixon wrote that he called for respect to be shown to Kennedy and Johnson. There was no cause for being discourteous to the president and vice president just because people disagreed with them.[11] The next day, Nixon flew home to New York and Kennedy was assassinated in Dallas.

After a dramatic explanation of how he found out that Kennedy had been shot, he wrote that Lee Harvey Oswald was clearly mentally ill and added that one of the causes of his mental illness was his "contact" with communism, in particular, Castro's "brand of communism."[12] Although he never writes it explicitly, it is almost impossible to read this without concluding that by not more forcefully dealing with the Soviets and Castro, Nixon felt that Kennedy was the architect of his own demise.

Asking where the country was now, Nixon wrote, "This twisted and tragic chain of events brings us to 1964." And in 1964, he asserted, Cuba was a continuing problem and was joined by Vietnam as America's biggest foreign policy concerns in the presidential campaign.[13] Cuba was still a key issue, Nixon asserted, because it symbolized the country's approach to the danger of communism and foreign policy. The bigger issue, Nixon asserted, was how to answer the question of how the United States should deal with communist aggression worldwide.[14]

He wrote that there were some in government who argued that the United States should be more flexible toward communist states, since there were differences and disagreements between communist states such as the Soviet Union and China and that overall the Cold War was "thawing."[15] Nixon did not agree. After relating several troubling situations around the world, he concluded that the Cold War was hotter than ever, writing, "Communism isn't changing; it isn't sleeping; it isn't relaxing; it is, as always, plotting, scheming, working, fighting."[16] The Soviet Union, he asserted, was willing to supply weapons to anyone wanting to create chaos in many places around the world. While the threat of nuclear annihilation was less, he wrote, there was much greater danger of the "subversive and revolutionary" actions of communists which could lead to American defeat without nuclear war.[17]

The United States could not afford to let down its guard, Nixon argued. He reiterated the old Cold War domino theory: if one country falls to communism anywhere in the world, it affects the whole world. Therefore, the United States had to maintain a global approach and must stay concerned about "so-called peripheral areas" like Vietnam and Cuba. Cuba was not important because it was Cuba, Nixon insisted; it was important because it is "at our very doorstep." If Cuba is a foothold for communism, then all Latin America is in danger. If Latin America is in danger, then so too is the United States. The same was true for Vietnam and the far east.

Nixon concluded his essay by writing that the U.S. had to remain vigilant and unmoving in its fight against communism. All of America's recent foreign policy problems came from not standing firm against communist dictators. It was time, Nixon implored, for America to "put an end to this disgraceful, self-defeating behavior." America had to respond to communist aggression everywhere in the world with aggression to defend freedom.[18]

Nixon knew Goldwater was going to lose to Johnson in the upcoming election. He was preaching to the American public, to the Johnson administration, and to the electorate for the next U.S. presidential election in 1968. It was a position paper, a statement of philosophy and action, and an early campaign statement for 1968.

Nixon wrote a second, somewhat shorter, essay for *Reader's Digest* just over a year later in December 1965. Nixon still pressed for victory in Vietnam. The editors' introduction promised Nixon would answer the question many people were asking: why shouldn't the United States negotiate with Vietnam? Nixon began the essay with the premise that things were looking pretty good in Vietnam, arguing that victory was possible, if not imminent.[19] He predicted victory would take two years of hard fighting and, he argued, the greatest danger wasn't the possibility of defeat on the battlefield but, rather, "a diplomatic defeat at the conference table."[20] In other words, he was expecting the Johnson administration to blow it.

Nixon was worried about giving up too much, too easily, much as he argued in his previous essay Kennedy did with the Soviets and Cuba. He wrote, "Just as the military situation has begun to turn in our favor, there is increasing pressure for an immediate negotiated settlement in Vietnam."[21] While American "boys are fighting," Nixon asserted, there were too many Americans at home—students, journalists, celebrities, and Martin Luther King—clamoring for an end to the war. A premature

end. American leaders must not give in to calls for retreat and appeasement because that would just cause more war, not less. Negotiating with
the enemy in Vietnam now, Nixon analogized, would be like negotiating
with Hitler before the German forces were driven from France in World
War II.

Nixon then presented, and knocked down, several arguments he said
were being made in favor of getting out of Vietnam as soon as possible. All
of them boiled down to one core principle, Nixon asserted, which was that
the United States had to decisively win in Vietnam. Anything less would
be appeasement and would give communist powers, such as China, the
momentum they needed to continue taking over parts of the world. Vietnam *was* the global struggle against communism. "Offering rewards for
aggression is like giving a criminal part of his loot in the hope that he will
quit being a criminal."[22]

Nixon argued, essentially, that before the United States entered peace
negotiations with the Vietnamese, three questions demanded answers.
(1) How does the United States get the communists to the negotiating
table? His answer was that the United States had to show them they had
no chance of winning. (2) With whom should the United States negotiate?
Nixon wrote that the only option was to negotiate with the North Vietnamese government, not the Vietcong, because the war was not a civil war
as the communists argued. It was "naked aggression" by North Vietnam.
(3) What, exactly, was to be negotiated? Nixon's answer to this was that, at
a bare minimum, North Vietnam had to stop its aggression against South
Vietnam; South Vietnam's independence had to be guaranteed; and there
could be no gains, no reward, for North Vietnam, "the aggressors."[23]

But none of these considerations, Nixon argued, was the most important. The most important thing was a moral consideration of whether the
United States had the right to negotiate away another country's freedom
after promising to protect it.[24] The United States was not trying to impose
its form of government on the South Vietnamese. It was fighting to protect its —and by extension, every nation's—right to self-determination. He
concluded, "We can hold our heads high in the knowledge that, as was the
case in World War I, World War II and Korea, we are fighting not just in
the interest of the United States but for peace, freedom and progress for all
peoples."[25]

Nixon's best-known essay in *Reader's Digest* was published in October 1967. It is often reprinted in collections read by American history and
American government students. It was part of a public relations blitz, combined with multiple talk show appearances and interviews, Nixon engaged
in to launch his campaign. In this third article, he shifted to domestic politics. It was titled "What Has Happened to America?" and it is a laundry list

of concerns and complaints about the country under the leadership of LBJ and the Democrats.

He began with civil rights. He noted that just a few years before, African Americans were marching toward "full membership in society." Next, however, in the language of law and order many other presidential candidates and presidents, from George Wallace to Donald Trump, would invoke, he asked, "With this star of racial peace and progress before us, how did it happen that last summer saw the United States blazing in an inferno of urban anarchy? In more than 20 cities police and mayors were unable to cope with armed insurrection.... Only the state militia or federal soldiers could regain the city and restore peace." Why and how, Nixon asked, lamenting the current situation, did America become such a lawless society?

There were signs everywhere Nixon looked: drug use on the rise, teenagers being arrested, unrest on campuses, and, lest anyone think Nixon was being racist, he pointed out "the fact that whites looted happily along with Negroes in Detroit is ample proof that the affliction is not confined to one race."[26] There were explanations for this, Nixon wrote. They included, as Nixon put it, authorities who permitted crime because they sympathized with the causes of the crime or because they felt sympathy for "the past grievances of those who have become criminals."[27] In other words, Black Americans and the people who supported their cause were out of control because they were encouraged to act as if the law was the problem, not the people who were breaking the law.

Nixon's words read like a direct response to MLK's "Letter from the Birmingham Jail," which was King's call for civil disobedience. Nixon wrote that teachers, politicians, and *preachers* went too far in encouraging people to decide which laws were just and unjust and, therefore, which laws they would obey and which they would violate.[28] If Vietnam protesters were given too much lenience, civil rights protesters were given too much lenience as well.

Protecting people's rights was all well and good, Nixon argued, but the most important right government was responsible for protecting was each person's right to be safe from "domestic violence." He argued that Americans should "make no mistake": if the country was too lenient on this "anarchy," freedom, society, and the nation itself would be at risk.[29] To ensure that all the problems society faced could be dealt with, the first thing that had to happen was for the riots to end and law and order to be restored the land.

Nixon had a solution: (1) pay and train the police better and (2) increase the number of police. These police had the job of maintaining peace, protecting life, and protecting property. He also argued that Black

Nixon with Barbara Walters and George Romney after the Silent Majority speech in 1969, his desk covered in telegrams.

Americans needed to be protected from themselves, since they were the ones who suffered the most from "radical violence" when police were driven from their neighborhoods, allowing the neighborhoods to be destroyed. Then, quoting Lincoln, Nixon argued that there was no right to revolt or demonstrate outside of the law. Lincoln said, Nixon wrote, there is "no grievance that is a fit object of redress by mob law." It was not permissible, in a "civilized nation," for someone to justify their crimes against others by saying that they were just making up for crimes against themselves. Allowing that was saying yes to anarchy. Every American had to agree and personally commit, Nixon implored, to reestablishing law and order so that the nation's wounds could be healed.[30]

Nixon's presentation of the problem was this: (1) the Blacks were rioting; (2) the Blacks seemed not to know that they were only hurting themselves; and (3) Nixon was offering a solution to that problem. It was for their own good. It was Nixon's pledge to "Make America Great Again." It was not the underlying injustice or unrest and uncertainty about Vietnam that was the problem. Rather, as Nixon saw things, it was how people responded to those legitimate concerns. Not only was Nixon's law and order philosophy his mantra for speaking to what he would come to call the "silent majority," it was a blueprint for many white politicians who wanted to appeal to white voters, some even more overtly than Nixon. In 2020, 53 years after Nixon wrote this essay, Donald Trump spoke of law and order to protect the people living in the suburbs.

TWELVE

Nixon as a Television Guest with a Vengeance

In the middle to late 1960s (1966, 1967 and early 1968), Richard Nixon was a particularly active guest on a variety of television shows, some more clearly entertainment-oriented, such as *The Tonight Show*, and others more public affairs-oriented, such as the public television show *N.E.T. Journal*. He was willing to appear in many different venues, to put himself in front of many different audiences, and to show different sides of himself depending on the audience. It is commonplace for candidates to do this today, but Nixon was key in establishing the model. Each audience was different and each audience needed—and got—a different Richard Nixon. It is not part of the common memory of Nixon, but as he prepared to run for president again, Nixon proved himself adept at several different styles and perceptions of himself.

ABC News Issues and Answers

On November 6, three days before the 1966 midterm elections, Nixon appeared as a guest on the ABC News Sunday show *Issues and Answers*. It was not his first appearance on the show, but this episode was broadcast just before Election Day, after Nixon spent months on the trail campaigning for many Republican candidates, building the political capital he was certainly planning to spend in 1968.

The panelists were ABC News correspondents Bill Lawrence and Bob Clark. The first thing they did was ask Nixon to respond to a "third panelist" and played footage of LBJ at a news conference from November 4, 1966, in which Johnson repeatedly referred to Nixon as a "chronic campaigner." When LBJ was asked about Nixon's comments on a conference Johnson had recently attended regarding Vietnam, Johnson lit into Nixon, saying that he was not about to get into a debate with "chronic campaigner like Mr. Nixon." Johnson said Nixon made it his job every two years, in the month of October, "to find fault with his country" in the name of self-promotion and politics.[1]

It is not difficult to understand LBJ's pique when he was asked about Nixon. The truth was that since the 1940s, Richard Nixon had been promoting himself but had also been promoting the Republican Party. It made him an easy man for Democrats to dislike, but Nixon was also doing something new in the 1960s. He was a roving, highly recognizable politician with access to millions of people's living rooms through television. And he made use of that access in ways no politician before him had done. Historian Irwin Gelman notes, "Nixon's strengths and weaknesses were magnified in the heat of political campaigning. He rallied the GOP faithful from apathy to activism and came to represent their soul.... These relentless efforts to replace Democrats with Republican turned Nixon into the Democrats' chief adversary and their worst nightmare; they characterized him as a liar, a cheat, and a manipulator of partisan bitterness."[2] LBJ, always sensitive to criticism, certainly saw Nixon in these terms.

Asked to respond to Johnson on *Issues and Answers*, Nixon argued that Eisenhower had recently called him the most informed vice president in history and that Johnson's personal attacks were beneath the office of the president. He then invited viewers to consider which president, Eisenhower or Johnson, was the more credible. Nixon argued that Johnson could call what Nixon was doing "chronic campaigning" but the American people were fair-minded and would see through the criticism. He added, condescendingly, that Johnson was overworked and overtired and that he would come to regret his insulting words when he was better rested.

Asked next if his position of supporting the Johnson administration on Vietnam was changed, Nixon said that Republicans still supported the Johnson administration policy of "no reward for aggression" and would continue to do so. He asserted that the Republicans were far more supportive of Johnson than his own party and that Johnson was the first president in history who was unable to unite his own party during a war. He argued unless Johnson got "all the way with LBJ" from everyone, then he wanted nothing to do with them. Nixon said that LBJ's "cheap political demagoguery" would not work on him and that the real problem with LBJ was his complete rejection of bipartisanship. Truman was a reasonable man, Nixon said. LBJ was not. Truman, no doubt, would have scoffed at this, having been the recipient of a great deal of criticism from Nixon over the years, much of it suggesting Truman was a crook or, at the very least, condoned criminal behavior by those around him.

Responding to a question about Secretary of Defense Robert McNamara's promise that the number of troops being drafted would be going down and whether he thought that was just a political ploy for the election, Nixon called McNamara "Lyndon Johnson's Charlie McCarthy, his political stooge" who "loses much of his credibility" and argued the position of secretary of defense should be above politics.

Bill Lawrence asked Nixon about his recent call for a "political pow wow" of Republicans and Democrats after the election to discuss Vietnam. Did he, Lawrence asked, think that Vietnam was a problem that could be solved in the framework of partisan politics? Nixon took the opportunity to criticize Congress as the "most servile" in history. He noted that the Congress voted with LBJ 90 percent of the time and that they should not do that. The purpose of the pow wow, Nixon said, was to get new ideas into everybody's minds.

After roughly two-thirds of the show was spent on Vietnam, the panelists turned to the question of the 1966 elections. Nixon did not argue that Republicans would take control of either the House or the Senate, but he predicted the largest gains by Republicans in a non-presidential election since 1946 and the best gains in 30 years by the opposition in a president's first term.

Bob Clark next asked him about three potential 1968 Republican presidential candidates who were running for other offices in 1966: George Romney for governor in Michigan, Ronald Reagan for governor in California, and Chuck Percy in Illinois for U.S. Senate. He wanted to know what would happen to the presidential campaign in 1968 if all three won their 1966 races. Nixon, with a slight smile and a bit of a scowl, answered that it would leave the party with an "embarrassment of riches," which included several unnamed others. He then carefully reframed the question to talk about some Republican governors who would be great *vice presidential* material, including Governor Jim Rhodes of Ohio and Governor John Volpe in Massachusetts. He did not mention Nelson Rockefeller, the perennial moderate Republican favorite.

Clark asked whether Nixon was worried about his own presidential hopes with so many new Republican stars. Nixon smiled slightly again, nodded, and turned the question to make a point that was never far from his head. Rather than address what the campaign field would look like in 1968, he said, "You're absolutely right. As a matter of fact, the elections of 1966 will be a benefit to the winners. *And the winners are those who run.* You know, somebody has asked me whether or not I'm going to get credit if we gain 30 seats or 40 seats and General Romulo,[3] whom both of you know, used to say to me, 'You know defeat is an orphan and victory has many fathers.' All the winners, there'll be plenty of fathers, and if we lose, I'll get blamed." This was classic Nixon. Who would blame Nixon if Republicans did not do very well in 1966? He was not worried about other

Republicans. What Nixon certainly anticipated was negative commentary in the news media about him and he was taking a preemptive shot at it.

The show ended with Nixon being asked by Bill Lawrence about the 35 states and 70 districts he campaigned in on behalf of 1966 Republican candidates and asked Nixon when he was going to declare his presidential campaign. Nixon smiled broadly and said that he expected that question and he was going to be "quite candid" in answering it. This was politician-speak for, "I'm not really going to give you an honest answer here." Nixon continued, talking about how hard he worked campaigning on behalf of Republicans running in 1966. He said that after all the hard work with just a couple of support staff, he did not have any delegates pledged to him or commitments made on his behalf for the presidency. He also, in Checkers-fashion, said, "I don't have any money. I earn enough, but I don't have any private fortune." Not only did this remind viewers that Nixon was one of them, a man of modest means, it was also a shot at the man many viewed to be Nixon's biggest potential opponent, Nelson Rockefeller.

Nixon continued, somewhat facetiously, saying that he did not have an office or a political base. After the election was over, he was going on vacation and that was the only announcement he was going to make. Beyond that, he claimed, "what the future holds, I don't know." In truth, Nixon was almost certainly decided on running for president. But to do that, he had to remind, and remind often, the members of his party what he spent the last few years doing for them. Nixon continued, insisting that he meant what he said at the start of the 1966 campaign season, which was that he wanted to help rejuvenate and unify the Republican Party. The future after Election Day, 1966, Nixon said, would take care of itself. He added, "That future may have a part for me in it. The probabilities are that it will not, because as Bob pointed out, the big winners are those who actually run."

Bob Clark had never said that. Nixon himself said that the big winners were the people who ran, but it worked well to put a reporter on the record as being ostensibly against Nixon. He continued, saying that he would be happy if the Republican Party did as well in 1966 as he thought it would because that would bode well for the next election, when "we can elect our candidate in 1968."[4] And Nixon, the "chronic campaigner," was very much thinking that candidate should be him.

William F. Buckley, Jr., and Firing Line

One of Nixon's appearances in 1967 was important not for the size of the audience, which was small in comparison to something like *The*

Tonight Show, but for the people who made up its audience and for the insight it gives into what Richard Nixon was thinking in the months before he officially declared his candidacy. The job Nixon had to accomplish with William F. Buckley was to appeal to a very elite group of wonks and party leaders and send a signal to the members of the press who were watching. He needed to demonstrate he was the right candidate for 1968.

The show was *Firing Line with William F. Buckley, Jr.* Buckley was the founder of the conservative publication the *National Review.* His television program moved to PBS in 1971, but from 1966 until 1971, it was produced and syndicated by the independent New York City channel WOR. The show appeared in different markets on different days and at different times, but the audience it attracted was influential, no matter how small it was.

Firing Line, shot before a live audience, was structured as if it would be a debate. Some episodes of the show were indeed very feisty debates which became quite famous, such as those between Buckley and James Baldwin or Buckley and Gore Vidal. This one, with two men of similar minds such as Nixon and Buckley, was really a debate, but they clearly had different opinions about some key issues. It is particularly illuminating because of what both men had to say about the Republican Party, the Democratic Party, voters, and a variety of other key players. For the first few seasons, the show was moderated by a man named C. Dickerman Williams, an attorney with a long record of public service. Williams was in the moderator's chair for Nixon's episode.

The show began with a discussion of the results of the 1966 midterm elections, in which Nixon took a great deal of pride, thanks to the Republican Party's gains in Congress and in gubernatorial elections. Nixon took the opportunity to say that there was a lot of disillusionment with LBJ and his policies and the war, and he suggested that one reason for the Republican success was that the Democrats ran a "bunch of turkeys" who were trying to apply solutions of the 1930s to problems of the 1960s.

Pressing Nixon, Buckley asked if the marginal voters who voted Republican in 1966 were voting affirmatively for Republicans or if it was more of a vote of no confidence in the Democrats. While Nixon wanted to say it was an affirmative choice for Republicans, he also had to reiterate his usual criticism of the Democrats. He said that the Democrats lost the confidence of voters and discussed Ronald Reagan's success in California, saying people voted for him because of disillusionment with the Democrats. Reagan was a particularly delicate subject for Nixon. He could not give Reagan too much credit because Reagan was looming as a possible competitor for the 1968 nomination in the minds of many conservative Republicans.

Buckley asked Nixon if the Republicans were "tilting toward the 1920s" as opposed to having something new to offer. Nixon objected and argued that the new Republican Party advocated change, but that change did not mean being "irresponsible." Changing those things that were wrong did not mean destroying the things that were right, he said. It was far better to do what the Republicans advocated, which was to put more emphasis on the private sector and less on public programs. Nixon argued that advocating for change could mean returning to things that worked well in the past. That, Nixon asserted, also is positive change, not retrogression. It was a classic statement of Republican economic thought, that the government should encourage the people to do what they could do in their private capacities by showing them how much government programs, such as Johnson's Great Society, had failed. Nixon said that while people may have voted for the Great Society's promise, in 1968 they would vote against its performance.

The next area of discussion highlighted the differences between a true party ideologue, Buckley, and a politician who was seeking to do what he needed to do to get elected, Nixon. Buckley asked Nixon, why was 1968 the time—for a Republican president and, ostensibly, for Nixon? Nixon gave a pragmatically political answer, saying that one of the biggest reasons was the difference between two salesmen of Democratic ideas. FDR, Nixon said, was much better at selling the merchandise than LBJ. Almost as an afterthought, sensing what Buckley would say, Nixon added that the merchandise was faulty. A bad salesman most especially cannot sell faulty merchandise.

Nixon expanded on this, saying that in 1964, LBJ's big victory gave a false impression of his vote-getting ability. In 1964, Nixon said, Johnson had peace, prosperity, and low inflation on his side. In a moment of humor, Nixon paused to joke that if he said anything different in the heat of campaigning for Goldwater in 1964, he was now admitting that LBJ had all those good things going for him.

Despite Nixon's effort to anticipate Buckley's response, Buckley still pressed him, asking him if Nixon was saying the future of the Republican party depended on getting a good salesman and not on any real change by voters. Nixon did not back down and simply agree with Buckley. He asserted that the proper sales pitch did, in fact, matter.

He told Buckley that he had great confidence in people but that they need to be informed before they could make the correct decisions. It did, he argued, matter a great deal how the leadership presented choices to the voters. Republicans, Nixon said, meaning those who advocated conservative causes, did well in office but they talked about issues very poorly. And the talk, Nixon insisted, was important. He said, "I'd like to think the people always see the policy that is best," and they were able to reject demagogic appeals, but that was not always true.

Political science then came into the discussion, clearly marking this as a different kind of show from *The Tonight Show* or *The Merv Griffin Show*. Buckley asked Nixon about an interview the political scientist—and presidency expert—Richard Neustadt did with the magazine *Fortune*. In the interview, according to Buckley, Neustadt argued that there was solid reason to believe a new cycle in American history was beginning. Neustadt felt that a Republican such as Nelson Rockefeller, or someone similar, could draw in many young minds and control things for a generation. What, Buckley asked Nixon, was Neustadt talking about?

Nixon began with a joke, saying, "I thought you were the expert on Rockefeller." In 1964, Buckley led a charge of conservatives toward Barry Goldwater and away from Nelson Rockefeller as the Republicans decided who the party's presidential nominee would be. There was no love lost between the two men. Joking aside, Nixon said what he thought Neustadt meant was that the intellectual community was disenchanted with LBJ. They liked JFK, but they did not like LBJ. He did not appeal to them so, Nixon suggested, Neustadt was saying someone like Illinois senator Charles Percy or Rockefeller could appeal to them.

Both Percy and Rockefeller were famously liberal Republicans, so Buckley's next question was to be expected. Buckley pointed out that in the interview, Neustadt argued that the forward progress of the Democratic Party had ended. The reason, as Buckley read Neustadt, was in part because there were some very liberal men, Percy and Rockefeller, positioning themselves as leaders of the Republican Party. But how, Buckley asked Nixon, could the future of the Republican Party be found in imitating the Democratic Party?

Nixon answered that, at least in Neustadt's mind, the kind of candidate who would attract intellectuals must be in the liberal spectrum. He said that he agreed with Neustadt to an extent, noting that the discontent of intellectuals with Johnson's administration "not only runs to style but also to performance. The intellectual is concerned about whether something works and all the fashionable liberal ideas fail in practice and there is a need for new approaches." What was needed, Nixon argued, were candidates who could bring about positive change by solving problems. Someone like that, Nixon argued, would be appealing to the intellectuals Neustadt was talking about, whether they were liberal *or* conservative. Results were what mattered most to intellectuals.

Buckley, himself famously an intellectual, pressed Nixon, asking him if it was not true that intellectuals were better than average people at holding out against reality. How would anything Nixon was saying help the Republican Party? What the Republican Party really needed, Buckley argued, was "a vision." He did not think the party had a vision that would be appealing to a lot of voters. For example, Buckley asked Nixon why it had been necessary to wait for a Democrat to propose the idea of privatizing the post office. He suggested there would have been outrage if Goldwater proposed doing that and asserted, "The other side is picking up conservative ideas and running with them." Nixon agreed with Buckley on this point.

For Nixon, the problem was, once again, much more one of public relations than a dearth of ideas. In Nixon's opinion, Republicans had plenty of good ideas too. Democrats, Nixon said, were co-opting Republican ideas, not coming up with them on their own. Republicans were ideologically consistent but not well presented. Democrats were better at public relations, which allowed them to be less fiscally responsible. Conservatives had better programs and they needed to make them more exciting by showing they would work. What Nixon did not explicitly say yet, but was clearly telegraphing, was that he was the person to make the sales pitch. He undoubtedly wanted the elite audience to take away the same message.

The next topic was another which was aimed at positioning Nixon as a person to lead the party and build on its success from the 1966 midterms. Buckley asked him about critical comments from another liberal New York Republican senator, Jacob Javits, who said Nixon was trying to appeal to both liberal and conservative Republicans and that it simply would not work to do so. The election of 1964, Javits asserted, showed that it was impossible to try to bring disparate parts of the party together and that what needed to happen instead was for the two sides to fight it out and see who won.

Unsurprisingly, Nixon disagreed with this argument and said that, in fact, 1964 was graphic evidence of the negative consequences of a rift in the party, pointing out that "about seven million Republicans deserted the national ticket." It was his objective to avoid that in 1968. He argued—and this was an early argument from Nixon about why he would be the best person to lead the ticket in 1968—that something new needed to be done in 1968. He said he believed in a different philosophy that brought the party together. It was important to come together and support the national ticket. A lack of party unity, he argued, brought the party down in 1964, while more party unity in 1966 helped the Republicans succeed. And, as a person who did a lot of campaigning for the party in 1966, Nixon clearly saw himself as a key ingredient for success.

But Buckley wanted to know how this was possible. How does one keep the different, and opposing, sides of the party from fighting with each other so much that they kill the party? How is it possible to get them to come together to support the nominee, no matter who the nominee is? The solution, as Nixon saw it, was to remind Republicans of recent history. In 1964, they lost, Nixon argued, because they could not come together. The party should remember that lesson and use it to give themselves strength for the coming election. The Democrats would not do this, he argued, "because they don't know what this is like." In other words, the Democrats' success in 1964 would be their undoing in 1968.

Buckley and Nixon then had a discussion that would sound familiar to people thinking about the 2016 election when it became apparent Trump was likely to win the nomination, much to the distress of some leaders of the party. Buckley asked Nixon what could be done by a "responsible party … to enforce its will?" Should sanctions be applied to people who did not support the ultimate winner of the Republican nomination for president? Should people who did not support Goldwater in 1964 be barred from participating in 1968 to get the message of party discipline across?

Again unsurprisingly, Nixon did not agree with this idea. As a person trying to position himself as a leader of all Republicans—as well as disaffected Democrats—he could hardly afford to agree with such an idea. Nixon said that to him, the most important thing was to put forward the strongest possible ticket and that could only happen if everyone participated. Buckley interrupted, asking, "The Nixon doctrine in 1968 is to forgive?" Yes, Nixon agreed. But Buckley was not finished. What, he wondered, if the same sort of party rift occurred in 1968?

This was the crux of the debate on this episode of *Firing Line*. It was the very reason for Nixon doing such a show, hosted by a leader of the conservative wing of the party: to establish his bona fides as the natural leader of the party for 1968. If such a rift happened again, Nixon said, "the Republican Party will be finished." If the party split again, then the party would continue to fragment until there was nothing left. He concluded, "You can't have two decisive defeats and come back from that."

For Nixon, this meant healing old wounds. But Buckley still wondered if the solution was to enforce discipline more harshly. If Nixon was right that division was deadly, why wasn't the real solution, Buckley asked, to exclude people who revolted in 1964 from the process in 1968? Sounding very much like a person who wanted to show how he could lead both liberals and conservatives in the Republican Party, Nixon said that such an action would only create more division for 1968 and would not help. A party leader, Nixon argued, is someone who can hold things together, not encourage division and exclusion. He pledged to support the Republican nominee no matter who it was.

Buckley and Williams pressed Nixon a little more. Should a loyalty oath be required? No. If you, Richard Nixon, a conservative, are the nominee of the party, should you seek a treaty with the liberals? No, that will not be necessary, Nixon argued, because the entire party would be unified in 1968 by the desire to win. The two sides would understand each other, allowing compromise and good sense to win out. Buckley suggested this was too optimistic a vision of the world. Nixon, of course, disagreed. They could heal the rift in the party, and they could appeal to the intellectuals.

Next, Williams asked Buckley if he thought Nixon would have a lot of influence on who won the nomination, even if he did not end up with the nomination himself? Laughing, Buckley said, "That's why I invited him on the show!" While that was not a specific endorsement of Nixon by one of the party's leading conservative voices, it was the next best thing. It was an acknowledgment of the power and influence of Nixon spent the mid–1960s building. He was a person whose opinions mattered.

Williams then introduced the subject of George Wallace and his independent campaign. What would be the impact of such a campaign? Wallace was a huge concern for Nixon throughout the election because while Wallace would undoubtedly appeal to a lot of traditionally Democratic voters in the south, he was also appealing to voters who were starting to turn away from the Democratic Party to the Republican Party. And, more important, the numbers were not on Nixon's side if a Wallace candidacy caused the election to end up in the House of Representatives if no candidate received a majority of Electoral College votes. This was a good, early opportunity to dismiss Wallace without seeming to insult Wallace. And Nixon answered it without even getting close to discussing the great unstated truth of Wallace's campaign—that he was motivated in large measure by opposition to the civil rights movement. Nixon hoped to appeal to some of those same voters.

Nixon was clearly ready for the question and said that third parties usually under-delivered at election time, noting that while they seemed to have support in public opinion polls, most people changed their minds when it was time to vote. He said that he did not mean to underestimate Wallace's appeal but predicted his vote total would be minimal. This would be similar, Nixon suggested, to what happened to Strom Thurmond's third-party candidacy in 1948. Nixon noted that William F. Buckley, who ran a third-party campaign for New York City mayor on the Conservative Party ticket in 1965, was familiar with the fate experienced by third-party candidates.

Williams asked Buckley what impact a third-party candidate on the left might have, such as a "peace candidate." Buckley thought such a candidate would have a lot of appeal, but Nixon was again given the chance to dismiss third-party candidates, which he did, saying that the real issue was whether people wanted four more years of Johnson, which would naturally divide people into two groups. The voters, Nixon argued—if only in the hope that they would appreciate his positive estimation of them— were too smart to throw votes at a candidate who could not win. At least, that was something Nixon fervently hoped was true.

Williams then raised another topic that was never far from Nixon's mind: the viability of Ronald Reagan as compared to Nixon. Since Nixon lost to Pat Brown in 1962 and Reagan beat Brown in 1966, was that evidence that Reagan was a better candidate for the presidency than Nixon? Unsurprisingly, Nixon did not think so. Reagan was certainly a good "vote getter," Nixon said, but the situations in the two elections were very different. Nixon said he was hurt in 1962 by a split with the far right—he got more Democratic voters than a Republican would normally get but he lost on the far right. Reagan did not have to deal with that situation in 1966. If they had not been running out of time on the show, Nixon would no doubt have pointed to this as further evidence of the need to heal party rifts in 1968, not exacerbate them.

Nixon demurred on a question from Williams about what he thought his delegate count would be in 1968. Buckley quickly answered a question from Williams about a split between the Young Republicans and the chairman of the Republican party. Buckley said, "The Young Republicans are the conservative wave of the future, we shouldn't drive them out of the party," and Williams announced they were out of time. He summarized the hour, saying, "Tonight you've seen a discussion of the future of the Republican Party by two of the foremost experts on the subject. I conclude that we will see a party which appeals to young intellectuals and is united for 1968."[5]

Nixon's media strategy was never haphazard. This was an appearance which had a very specific purpose: to unify the party behind him. It was something he lamented frequently in *Six Crises* that he did not have in 1952 during the Fund Crisis or in 1960 against JFK. He needed the full support of the party. He needed to demonstrate to as many Republicans as he could that he was the man to lead them to victory. He wanted to bring liberals along if he could, but he absolutely had to make sure that the conservatives were on his side. Buckley was the leading voice of that crowd and, at least for a while, Buckley was on Nixon's side.

Not Just for Laughs: With the Aid of Entertainment Television Nixon Was Off to the Races in 1968

Nixon's Paar appearances were not his only stints on talk show TV during his years out of office. In 1967 and early 1968, Nixon made the rounds of many of the television talk shows available to him. In 1967, Nixon, who was clearly running for president though he had not yet made a formal announcement, prepared for the primary season to come with an appearance on *The Tonight Show* with Johnny Carson. This was, of all nights, November 22, 1967, the fourth anniversary of the assassination of John F. Kennedy. Nixon once again managed to appear light-hearted, spontaneous, and someone people could relate to. One of the bigger points he made, jokingly—but it was a joke based on his 1960 campaign and therefore reflected a lesson learned—was his opinion that his make-up (or lack thereof) in the first debate lost the election for him in 1960. It was self-deprecating and while Nixon may not have enjoyed self-deprecating humor, it is usually well received by audiences. People like someone who can admit to flaws.

The make-up issue was also something Nixon took very seriously in 1968. In a story about the *Tonight Show* appearance, the *New York Times* reported that Nixon was going to hire the show's makeup director, Roy Voege, to work for him on the campaign. Voege said, "'Nothing's completely settled yet. I've worked with Nixon on some of his filming, and we get along fine. Now we have to wait for the formal announcement.'"[6]

Nixon's exchanges with Carson were often funny, but they also demonstrated, once again, Nixon's keen awareness of the importance of a particular type of image-setting television, such as in an exchange in which Nixon told Carson he thought he sounded a lot like Robert Kennedy. Carson, Nixon said, should run for president. When Carson expressed doubt, Nixon told him he was an expert on running for president, adding that it did not mean he was an expert on winning. Nixon talked Carson through his assets, which were his youth and his effectiveness and charisma on television. Nixon pointed out that he was an expert on how important it was to do well on television. Carson asked him if he would lend him his make-up artist and Nixon got a big laugh by saying, "No, I'm going to lend him to Lyndon Johnson."[7] Nixon's appearance with Carson as an unannounced candidate once again made it clear that Nixon was not new to the idea of going on TV to let America know he could cut loose a little when he wanted to.

In addition to appearing with the "King of Late Night," Johnny Carson, Nixon appeared on several other entertainment shows, with most of the appearances coming in late 1967 and early 1968. These appearances were all essentially announcements of his candidacy for president without Nixon uttering those exact words.

On January 16, 1968, for example, he appeared on the daytime talk show *The Mike Douglas Show*. The show was not just another talk show appearance for Nixon to make himself more appealing to voters. This talk show visit was important to Nixon for another reason. While appearing on the show, Nixon became acquainted with its young executive producer, Roger Ailes, who would go on to join the Nixon campaign as the producer of its television programming.

Merv!

Some of the most interesting appearances Nixon made on an entertainment television before he officially declared his candidacy on February 1, 1968, were on *The Merv Griffin Show,* which was recorded in the heart of Broadway at the Little Theatre (now the Helen Hayes Theater) next door to Sardi's restaurant. Merv Griffin worked his way up in entertainment as a singer, then a game show host, and he eventually became a talk show host, although he made his fortune through the game shows he produced, such as *Jeopardy!* and *Wheel of Fortune.*

During most of the 1960s, Griffin hosted a syndicated show which ran at different times of the day in different markets. Richard Nixon appeared on the show with Griffin about a month after he was on *The Tonight Show.* The date was December 18, 1967. It was the second time he had been on with Griffin. The first time was January 11, 1966. One major difference between the two appearances was that the first time it was broadcast in black and white, while the second was in color. Nixon looked strikingly different in these appearances.

In 1966, the "news" of Nixon's appearance came from questions Griffin asked him about the war in Vietnam. Nixon said that as a leading nation of the world, the United States' role in the world had to be respected, whether that meant in Vietnam or in other countries. Jumping on this, Griffin, who would later have many anti–Vietnam War guests on his show, asked Nixon if he thought that the decision whether to stay involved in Vietnam should be made by Congress.

Nixon's answer to this was no, but he delivered it artfully. He said that while he did not object to Congress debating Vietnam, it needed to be done in a way that did not show division in the United States. This did not mean, he insisted, that everyone in the country, or in the U.S. House and Senate, had to agree, but he worried that if there was too much debate that was blown too far out of proportion, it would send negative signals to the communist world and encourage the enemies of the United States to believe there was division in the country that did not really exist.

Griffin asked Nixon if he feared partisan politics getting involved in the debate and Nixon said no, but then he used it as an opportunity to make a partisan point. It was not Republicans, Nixon said, who were giving Johnson the most trouble. The division about Vietnam, Nixon asserted, was within the Democratic Party, while Republicans supported Johnson. Too much discussion in Congress would put that division on display for the world. Nixon, of course, was pointing that division out to the world with his statements on a nationally broadcast talk show.

Nixon also told Griffin that there should be a "moratorium" on discussion of Vietnam. Nixon said he would not have any comment about Johnson's Vietnam policies. If negotiations were ongoing, it was time for people without full knowledge of what was going on—and he appeared to include himself in that group—to be silent about it.[8] Of course, he said this after making several comments about Vietnam.

His second appearance with Griffin was almost two years later, on December 18, 1967. This time, Nixon was on a kind of pre-announcement tour, refusing to say he was running for president, but saying that he would be announcing his decision after the holidays. Nixon's motivation for doing shows like Paar's, Carson's, and Griffin's was always to demonstrate his likeability, his "regular guy" nature, and this appearance could have tested that, but Nixon held up well.

Griffin's guests stayed on the set for subsequent guests, joining in the conversation with the new guest. The current guest sat in a seat to Griffin's left and the other guests, and Griffin's sidekick, Arthur Treacher, were on the right. One of the previous guests was the host of a talk show who had interviewed Nixon, David Susskind. When Nixon came onstage, he looked at Griffin and said jokingly, "You want me to sit on the *left*?" Griffin teased him for wearing a white shirt and Nixon responded, "Well, I thought this was in color."

With the opening humor out of the way, Griffin thanked Nixon for not imposing any restrictions on the questions he would answer, and Nixon said that it was always his rule not to have any rules because it would not do any good to impose rules. This, of course, was not at all true. Everything about Nixon's media plan as he moved toward the White House was about imposing rules which guided a strategy designed to make him appear open but to give him as much control as possible. Appearing open in a forum such as *The Merv Griffin Show* simply gave him the opportunity to give well-prepared answers while seeming to be spontaneous.

Nixon looked across Griffin at David Susskind and said that he thought Susskind was the one who should be getting into politics, noting that Susskind had nearly as many children as Bobby Kennedy did. After some chuckling about this and a denial of interest in politics from Susskind, Griffin asked Nixon when his "intentions" for 1968 would be made known to the public.

Nixon said he would make the decision in late January. He said that he was being candid in admitting that there seemed to be a lot of factors pointing in the direction of running but no one should make a final decision about such a big thing until the final moment. This was because, he said, as soon as one decided to run for president, his life—and his family's lilfe—would change completely. Running for president, Nixon said, is "war," and a decision to do it should only be made when one was ready to devote his entire life to the contest. This sounded good, but it was not at all true. Nixon was already in the race with both feet.

Griffin asked if Nixon would run in the primaries if he decided to run for president. Nixon said he would and he would announce which ones he would run in when he announced if he was going to run for president. He said that he needed to win a "substantial majority" of the primaries or he would not bother attending the Republican convention. The primaries still were not necessary to win the parties' nominations, as Hubert Humphrey would demonstrate in the Democratic Party, but Nixon was saying that he wanted evidence from the people that they wanted him. He wanted to be called to service by them.

Nixon entered 11 of 15 primaries and won ten of them. The only primary he lost was California. He did not campaign in California and it was won by its governor, Ronald Reagan. Nelson Rockefeller won the Massachusetts primary, and Ohio governor John Rhoades won, unopposed, in Ohio. With each primary he won, Nixon did exactly what he wanted to do—he replaced the image of loser, earned in 1960 and 1962, with the image of winner.

In December of 1967, it was still assumed that Lyndon Johnson was going to run for reelection and that he would be the Democratic nominee in 1968. So, when Merv Griffin asked him about the costs of running for president and pointed out that Nixon was not a rich man, Nixon replied, "Not yet," and added, "I don't own any television stations." This was both an attempt at humor and a shot at Lyndon Johnson, whose wife, Lady Bird, owned several radio and television stations in Texas. It was not a state secret that LBJ regularly used his influence to smooth out licensing by the FCC and other issues.

Griffin then asked Nixon about criticism of Illinois Republican senator Charles Percy for the creation of a "slush fund" to help pay the expenses of serving Illinois in the Senate. The controversy stemmed primarily from an angry accusation from Democratic senator Thomas Dodd of Connecticut. Dodd was censured by the Senate—and publicly criticized by Percy— for converting campaign funds to personal use, which he then used for a variety of things, such as home renovation, liquor bills, and fines for parking violations. When it became public that Percy was organizing a fund, which he contributed to himself, for businesspeople in Illinois to help him defray the costs of running his Senate offices, Dodd was outraged. He saw little difference between his behavior and Percy's.[9] Griffin asked Nixon what he thought about this scandal, especially in relation to his own slush fund scandal in 1952.

Nixon defended Percy, which was also defending himself, of course. He told Griffin that it was important to keep things in perspective. While the salary for senators was higher in 1967 than it was in 1952, it still was not nearly enough to represent a big state such as Illinois or California. He also told Griffin that this should not be a big political issue in 1967 because it *was* a big political issue in 1952. Senators of 1967 should not have to take the heat, Nixon said, because *he* took the heat in 1952. It was, in other words, a dead issue, as Nixon saw it, thanks to Nixon.

It is worth noting that, at this point, Percy was widely thought to be a strong candidate for the Republican nomination in 1968 if he chose to run. He decided not to run. He would have been a very strong choice as a running mate for vice president, but he endorsed Nelson Rockefeller instead of Nixon and was, essentially, a political enemy of Nixon forever. He was, in fact, the first Republican senator to call for an investigation of Watergate and Nixon included the senator on one of his famous enemies lists.[10]

Griffin then asked Nixon what he thought the criteria were for running for president. Did one have to have a winning smile, many children, and be rich? "Can a poor boy be president?" Nixon, getting a laugh from the crowd, responded, "We might find out."

From here, Griffin moved on to the topic of electability, something which Nixon was perpetually asked. He asked Nixon if he was aware of the "undercurrent of people who refer to Nixon as a loser," saying that he carried a stigma of losing two big elections. Was he aware of it? Of course, he was aware of it. Nixon had spent the past six years doing shows like Griffin's, giving speeches around the country, campaigning on behalf of Republicans running for a huge range of offices and raising millions for the party, all to encourage people not to think of Nixon as a loser. "How do you combat that?" Griffin asked.

Calmly, with a slight smile on his face, Nixon responded that it was a perfectly legitimate question that should be raised by anyone trying to find the strongest possible candidate for president. The way you overcome the reputation of being a loser, he said, is by winning something. That was why he planned to run in the primaries. He then pointed out, with no embarrassment, that there were many men who had lost and returned to win. The examples he noted were Abraham Lincoln, Winston Churchill, and FDR. It was an outstanding group of which to make himself a part. He unabashedly evoked a comparison of himself to Abraham Lincoln in the Checkers speech and was happy to continue doing so, as many Republicans since have done many times, including Donald Trump.

Griffin then asked Nixon if he was troubled by the knowledge that, given how experienced he was, he was much more qualified than most people to be president. "Does it," Griffin asked, "drive you crazy when you think how qualified you are?" Nixon took the opportunity to be very presidential and deliver his theory of the presidency. He said, "No, I have a very different view about the presidency."

This was not, he said, a display of false humility. It was, rather, that he had great respect for the office of the president. He said, "What happens here determines whether peace and freedom survive in the world" and the job of the next president was to bring peace to both the United States and abroad. That meant, Nixon said, that it was very important to elect the "most-qualified man" to the presidency, and the people should determine this by watching how a man conducts himself "in battle." There are many with experience, Nixon said. You need to see how they behave in "battle" to see if they have "that extra bit that is needed when great decisions have to be made." Nixon said if people looked at his actions and determined that he was not the strongest and best man, then he should not be the candidate.

Griffin moved on to Vietnam, asking Nixon about comments recently made by former president Eisenhower, who advocated moving ground troops into North Vietnam. This was a tough question, asked by Griffin with an air of naiveté that may or may not have been real. It was tough because it put Nixon in the position with having, potentially, to disagree with the man he served under for eight years and who was regarded by many Americans as the ultimate military expert.

Nixon handled it smoothly. He said that it was important to examine exactly what Eisenhower said, and he proceeded to do so. He said that Eisenhower said that ground forces needed to be used to take out the North Vietnamese artillery. The question that Eisenhower's proposal raised, Nixon asserted, was whether that would widen the war too much by getting the regular North Vietnamese army, as opposed to the Viet Cong, more involved.

Having presented the question in this way, Nixon took the opportunity to disagree with Eisenhower. He said he felt that the country should do all it could to avoid "anything that puts more on our plate" and that going into North Vietnam with ground troops would just bring more enemy troops into the fight. The best strategy, Nixon said, was to use air power against all military targets. But he made clear that he did not favor expanding the ground war into North Vietnam, or Laos, or Cambodia. The war in South Vietnam, he said, could be won without extending the ground war into North Vietnam. Nixon thus nicely separated himself from Ike and won a nice round of applause from the audience.

Griffin then asked a question which had been circulating for a while, both within the Johnson administration and outside of it: should the U.S. stop bombing in Vietnam to bring the North Vietnamese to the negotiating table? Nixon's answer was an emphatic "Not at all." He expanded on this, saying that the track record showed that halting bombing does not have positive effects. He then talked about the troops. He said there were half a million men in Vietnam. He added, "I call them boys. I'd like for some of these demonstrators to go over and look at them." Unless the country backed the boys up with airpower, then they should all be brought back home immediately, Nixon asserted. He repeated that he was not in favor of any action that would widen the war, such as the use of nuclear weapons or a ground war in North Vietnam. But, he said, "we should keep the pressure on and convince the enemy he cannot win politically in the U.S., or militarily. He will quit, but only then."

Nixon was not finished, and Griffin let him continue. He said, "Their objective is different in the world. They want victory. *We* want peace. If they wanted peace, they would come to the table if we stopped bombing. But they want South Vietnam. We can't prove we're for peace by stopping the bombing *because they don't want peace.*"

As they went to a commercial break, Griffin acknowledged David Susskind on his right, saying he knew that Susskind was eager to ask Nixon a question. When they returned from the commercial break, Griffin turned the questioning of Nixon over to Susskind. And Susskind returned, full bore, to the question of Nixon's electability, a question he asked Nixon when he interviewed him in 1960.

Susskind said he had a burning question that he asked with respect. He asserted that statistics showed the country was Democratic by a margin of three to two and, since Nixon was "anathema to Democrats," the math did not give him much chance of winning. This phrase, "anathema to Democrats," was one which would dog Nixon throughout the campaign, all the way up to an interview Nixon did on the second-ever episode of *60 Minutes*, which aired a month before the election.

Nixon did not look especially happy that Griffin turned over the questioning to Susskind and he was not happy with the question Susskind asked, having already handled it once in this appearance. But he gamely answered it, saying, "Well, I did rather well in 1960, if I'm anathema to Democrats." The answer did not satisfy Susskind, who followed up, saying that many Democrats voted for Nixon in 1960 because they were bigoted against the Catholic Kennedy.

Nixon, as partisan as any politician in American history, said, "That's a slander on the Democrats." Susskind retorted that there was academic research to support what he was saying, and Nixon continued to disagree.

Nixon said that Democrats who voted for him in 1960 did so because his views represented their views more accurately. And, he noted, some Republicans voted for Kennedy for the same reason. Yes, there was some religious bigotry, Nixon said, but it was not the main reason for his Democratic support. From the expression on his face, it seems obvious that Nixon was ready to be finished with this line of questioning. Susskind was not done pursuing it, however. He asked, "Why do you think you can receive millions of Democratic votes now if not in two previous elections?"

Nixon, who was certainly more familiar than anyone with the details of his defeats in 1960 and 1962, was ready to disagree with Susskind's presentation of the facts. In 1960, Nixon asserted, the Republican Party was much weaker than at present and yet he ran a virtual dead heat with Kennedy. That did not support the idea that no Democrats voted for him. He also argued that if religious bigotry had been a real factor, he would have done better in Southern states, where the religious bigots were supposed to be concentrated. As for California in 1962, Nixon asserted he won 20 percent of the Democratic vote and felt that polls indicated a similar level of Democratic support for 1968.

Nixon then put forward a new argument, that the country was in a post-partisan age, thanks to the divisive presidency of LBJ. There were so many serious problems at home and abroad, there was clearly something wrong with the nation's policy, leading to violent demonstrations everywhere Johnson travelled. And Nixon wanted the audience to conclude he was the solution to the problem with current policy.

It was a message Nixon stuck to throughout the campaign, and it was a message that was foremost in the minds of the members of his campaign team. In May of 1968, Nixon strategist Harry Treleaven wrote a memo about campaign advertising, arguing that it should emphasize how bad things were under Democratic rule and that Nixon was the only candidate who could bring positive change.[11] It was a sentiment Nixon emphasized with Griffin and consistently carried throughout the campaign: It is broken, and Nixon alone can fix it.

Griffin took control back from Susskind at this point and turned the show fully to Nixon's major goal for doing entertainment television: making him relatable to average folks. Griffin asked Nixon about the fact that his daughter, Julie, was marrying Ike's grandson, David. Nixon joked that he only knew about that from reading the newspapers. He added that he knew it was going to be serious when he heard that they used to hitchhike to meet each other for dates when they were freshmen in college at different schools. Griffin then told the audience that Nixon had to leave for another engagement.

But Nixon took his time leaving, taking time to say that he was happy to see his "old friend from California, Arthur Treacher." Nixon used that as an opportunity for one of his standard talk show jokes about make-up. He said that the same make-up person made up both he and Treacher, so he, Nixon, must be looking pretty good. "Matter of fact," Nixon said, "if I'd had that same girl in 1960, Julie and David would be getting married in the White House, rather than Lynda Bird."

With that bit of humor, he was off. And, thanks to Griffin's change of subject, Nixon avoided having the skeptical Susskind's questions be the last word of his appearance. It was not the most magnificent of Nixon's appearances but, at the same time, he came across with poise in the face of adversity and finished with humor. He walked off the set as someone he was not always able to convince people he was—a good-natured, good-humored fellow. The thing that is important to remember about Nixon's talk show appearances is not that he was great at it but, rather, that he knew he was not very good at it and pushed himself to do them anyway. He knew that anything he did in venues like these was going to show voters a side of him they did not think existed at all. Low expectations always made these ventures successful for Nixon.

Nixon's last entertainment talk show appearance came mid-summer on a short-lived show which was launched to be a competitor to Carson's *Tonight Show*, the *Joey Bishop Show*. A member of Frank Sinatra's famous "Rat Pack," Bishop was a comedian and actor and, for about two years, a talk show host. The *Joey Bishop Show*, not to be confused with the sitcom of the same name from the early 1960s, ran from April of 1967 through December of 1969.

Nixon appeared on the show on July 26, 1968, right before the Republican convention, along with Barbara McNair, Tony Bill, and the singing duo of Guy and David (Guy Hovis and David Blaylock). On the show, Nixon chatted with Bishop and then the studio audience was allowed to ask him some questions. On the same day it was taped, Senator Chuck Percy formally endorsed Nixon's opponent for the nomination, Nelson Rockefeller. This was just a couple of weeks before Republicans gathered in Miami for the national convention. Rockefeller was not a serious competitor with Nixon for the nomination, but it undoubtedly annoyed him to have this happen on the brink of the convention. Nixon, provoked by Percy's announcement, reacted to rumors that Rockefeller offered Percy the vice presidency in return for his endorsement said, "I'm not going to make any deals on the Vice-Presidency to get the nomination."[12]

Following the example of Richard Nixon, Hubert Humphrey, the vice president of the United States and the Democratic nominee for president in 1968, also saw talk shows as a way to press his campaign. He appeared multiple times in 1968 on talk shows such as *The Tonight Show, The Joey*

Bishop Show, and *The Mike Douglas Show,* just as Nixon did. In fact, Humphrey made several talk show appearances in 1966 and 1967 before Lyndon Johnson declared he was not running.

When Humphrey appeared on *The Joey Bishop Show* shortly after Nixon, it prompted one reporter for the *Los Angeles Times,* Hal Humphrey (no relation to the vice president), to write that he thought it was ridiculous for presidential candidates to appear on entertainment shows. He argued that a prime reason they should not be appearing on shows like Bishop's was because they simply were not good at ad-libbing or being funny. He felt that both Humphrey and Nixon looked self-conscious and uncomfortable and that they embarrassed themselves. They were, he wrote, "as out of place as an undertaker at a wedding," and concluded, "it's demeaning to what should be their dignity and puts them in the position of being there just for the plug."[13]

Hal Humphrey's complaints are noteworthy for how different they were from James "Scotty" Reston's concerns in 1960, when he thought talk shows were beneath the office. That was not Humphrey's concern—that ship had already sailed. Richard Nixon and JFK made doing talk shows a fait accompli in 1960, which Humphrey's column acknowledges by critiquing their talent, or lack thereof, as guests, and not whether it befit the presidency. And with specific regard to Nixon being self-conscious or stiff on the Bishop show, it is true that Nixon looked a *little* stiff. But people were accustomed to Nixon looking *extraordinarily* stiff. Anything which allowed him to look even a little bit looser than normal was a win for Nixon. This appearance, along with the other talk show appearances, were all done for one reason: to improve Nixon's chances of winning the presidency. And part of that effort was helping him appear more relatable. In doing that, these appearances succeeded.

THIRTEEN

The Primary Battle and the Road to Miami

"Let me say this. Without television, Richard Nixon would not have a chance. He would not have a prayer of being elected because the press would not let him get through to the people. But because he is so good on television he will get through despite the press. *The press doesn't matter anymore.*"—Frank Shakespeare[1]

Nixon clearly understood the power of television in his political career. This was reflected in the decisions he made throughout his pre-presidential career. The people who worked for Nixon shared his enthusiasm for television. Many of them also approached television with laymen's interest in the work of Marshall McLuhan. The purpose of mentioning McLuhan, who is himself a subject of many scholarly studies, is not to analyze McLuhan but, rather, to point out that Nixon's media people saw McLuhan's work as a guide for the 1968 campaign.

McLuhan was a professor of English from Canada whose work on communication made him one of the most famous academics in the world in the 1960s and 70s. His fame got him a strange cameo in the Woody Allen movie *Annie Hall*, in which Allen criticizes a Columbia professor standing behind him in line at a movie theater for "pontificating" incorrectly about Marshall McLuhan. To prove his point, he pulls McLuhan from behind a movie poster and has McLuhan tell the professor that he knows nothing of McLuhan's work.

Journalist Joe McGinniss, who first became nationally known with his behind-the-scenes chronicle of the Nixon campaign, *The Selling of the President 1968*, wrote that members of the Nixon team were given a summary and excerpts of McLuhan's most influential book, *Understanding Media*, to use in designing the 1968 campaign.[2] Writing his best-known works in the 1960s, McLuhan focused on developing his theory of how we communicate. His best-known line was "The medium is the message," which was also the title of the first chapter of *Understanding Media*, published in 1964.

The most quoted passages of *Understanding Media* come from McLuhan's analysis of television, which he classified as a "cool" medium, as opposed to print or film, which he defined as "hot" mediums. Hot mediums are those which give us everything we need and which we passively consume. Cool mediums, according to McLuhan, such as television or comics, lack in detail and, therefore, prompt us to engage more actively with the media, seeking to fill in the details that are not presented.[3] McLuhan argued, "With TV, the viewer is the screen," making the image in their minds from relatively little data. He wrote, "The TV image requires each instant that we 'close' the spaces in the mesh by a convulsive sensuous participation that is profoundly kinetic and tactile, because tactility is the interplay of the senses, rather than the isolated contact of skin and object."[4]

McLuhan expanded on his ideas in a chapter on TV, writing that a cool medium, such as a book, a speech, or television, is one which requires more work by the consumer than a hot, or high definition, medium such as film. This means, McLuhan wrote, that "because the low definition of TV insures a high degree of audience involvement, the most effective programs are those that present situations which consist of some process to be completed."[5]

In 1968, Nixon's team, inspired by McLuhan, saw television as a medium that allowed their candidate to give as much, or as little, as he wanted to give to audiences, while letting his supporters fill in the gaps (detractors could do the same, of course) without the authoritative, interpretative words of journalists doing it for them. This was ideal for Richard Nixon, who wanted more than anything to avoid the reporters he did not trust. It would be interesting to know what McLuhan would think of the 21st-century version of the medium that allowed a candidate to give as much, or as little, as he wanted to give audiences while letting his supporters fill in the gaps: Twitter.

One of Nixon's campaign aides, who later became one of Nixon's speechwriters in the White House, was William Gavin. Gavin joined the Nixon campaign in the summer of 1967. Gavin gained the attention of Nixon's law firm colleague Len Garment with a letter urging Nixon to run for president. In it, he made many suggestions, including several about the use of television. He urged Nixon to give live press conferences during the campaign. He said Nixon would be using television instead of television using him. He wrote that doing so would show viewers Nixon was authentic, not a "glamor boy" or someone hiding behind rhetoric. He concluded,

"The real Nixon can revolutionize the use of television by dynamically going 'live' and answering everything, the loaded and the unloaded question."[6] Nixon didn't make a campaign of live press conferences in front of reporters the way Gavin urged, because reporters were people he saw as enemies, but he did utilize television in a way that it hadn't been before, taking questions from real life people and largely barring the news media from the opportunity to question him.

Before Gavin joined the campaign, he was first a high school English teacher and then a master teacher, analyzing the performance of student teachers at the University of Pennsylvania. In a memo written after some of the work of McLuhan was distributed to the campaign staff, Gavin offered McLuhan-related advice, first noting the appeal of a candidate like Robert Kennedy in the television era, who projected an emotional appeal without any apparent "reasoned analysis." He was not saying Kennedy had no substance but, rather, that he was able to appear on television with less substance. This allowed viewers to make what they wanted of Kennedy. He could be many things to many people.

This was something, Gavin argued, LBJ was not able to do. LBJ wanted to convince people, to make logical arguments. And on television, logic got in the way. His advice to Nixon was to leave as much unsaid as possible and let his audiences fill in the gaps, making Nixon into the candidate they wanted him to be. The more said, the less ability audiences had to fill in the gaps for themselves. He also urged Nixon to make a film about himself to be shown to New Hampshire voters on television, editing the footage to allow voters to take away the best possible impression of Nixon. The most important thing for campaigning to the television audience, Gavin asserted, was making them like the candidate. Logic and rational arguments got in the way. The less of that done by Nixon, the better. Rather, Nixon should appeal to viewers' emotions. Gavin concluded, "get the voters to like the guy, and the battle's two-thirds won."[7]

The Nixon campaign of 1968 was largely focused on portraying an image of Nixon that people could feel comfortable with. They wanted to get voters to like the guy. The fact that many people seemed to *not* feel comfortable with Nixon was largely perceived by his team and others, including many in the news media, as his major problem in his losses in the presidential election of 1960 and the California gubernatorial race of 1962. One of Nixon's key advisors, Bob Haldeman, came from the world of advertising. Before coming to work for Nixon, he was in advertising, working at the advertising giant J. Walter Thompson in Los Angeles. Haldeman was a strong advocate of using television as the campaign's prime tool for reaching voters. But not through television journalists. They wanted television that the campaign could control.

In a memo written by Haldeman to Nixon in 1967, he laid out a plan for the coming campaign. Haldeman's memo has become quite famous as the blueprint not only for Nixon's 1968 campaign but for all presidential campaigns since. This assessment is not wrong, but it is important to understand that the candidate had to agree to it and the candidate did so based on the lessons he, himself, learned in his failures and *crises* of the past. In the memo, Haldeman called for political campaigns to "move out of the dark ages and into the brave new world of the omnipresent 'eye,'" which was television.[8] Nixon, of course, began that process in 1952 when he went on national television to defend himself, without reporters interrupting, to the people of the nation.

Haldeman continued, "A candidate for any city-wide, state-wide or national office can't afford the old tried and true' methods of campaigning," which meant giving many speeches, standing around shaking hands, and "a soul-crushing travel schedule." Haldeman added, "Just because it has always been this way doesn't mean it always has to be."[9] He recommended a nationalized campaign, writing, "How many stories per day will any newspaper or radio or television station carry about a single candidate? Answer: one—if he is really lucky, important, or controversial. So, what is the use of roaring around making six, eight or ten stories every day? Obviously, it is to get localized coverage in each area of the constituency. But isn't the wire story, the commentator or the syndicated columnist what really counts? It sure is!"[10]

What was the solution? It did not imply, Haldeman wrote, returning to the front porch campaigns of old, à la William McKinley. Rather, "You plan a campaign that is designed to cover the important localities, provide excitement and stimulation for your supporters, generate major news every day, generate intensive coverage in depth by commentators and columnists, develop a meaningful dialogue (even if one-sided), and still offer a reasonable chance of the candidate's survival."[11]

The main goal, Haldeman wrote, was to program the "candidate's time, energy and thinking ... for maximum possible benefit. *And maximum benefit is defined as reaching the most people most effectively. And this does* not *necessarily mean in the flesh.*"[12] The solution? Haldeman wrote, "He has to take maximum advantage of the media of mass communications, with emphasis on that or those which reach the most people and present him most favorably and believably. Television will undoubtedly be pre-eminent—but radio, newspapers and magazines should not be overlooked."[13]

Haldeman called for one or, at the most, two major news leads a day, and he believed no day should pass without a major news lead planned. "The whole approach should be one of initiation and attack, rather than reaction and counterattack. The timing and approach should <u>not</u> be dictated by the opposition," though Haldeman did acknowledge that it would sometimes be necessary to "counterattack."[14]

Public appearances should be calculated for maximum media impact and should be decided upon based on the overall campaign strategy, not in kneejerk reaction to the demands of local campaign organizations. And most important, every appearance should be controlled by the campaign for its media message.

Fitting with Nixon's appearances on entertainment television, Haldeman wrote of the role in the campaign for what he called "offbeat activity." He wrote, "The offbeat 'color' activity should be planned for particular effects, generally in the 'image-building' area. In many cases these would *appear* to be unscheduled and spontaneous," but Haldeman added, "they would always be an integral part of the overall plan."[15] Undoubtedly, appearing on talk shows or on the hit program *Laugh-In* would count as "offbeat activity" which was, in fact, planned with precision.

If there were to be meetings with small groups, they should be with "people who will in turn reach large numbers of other people. Concentration is on TV and radio commentators, columnists, syndicate feature writers, publishers, station owners, major civic leaders, party leaders, specific issue spokesman."[16] Haldeman, expecting a critique, added that while some might say this approach wouldn't reach enough cities physically, that wasn't the point. He wrote, "The answer is that the important thing is not the one city where the candidate is, but the coverage of his activities that goes into all cities. Only a minute fraction of the people in a city where the candidate appears actually see him in the flesh. The vast majority just watch on TV or read about it in the newspapers. To these people, what difference does it make if he's in their city, the neighboring one, or one clear across the country?"[17]

Anticipating today's social media, Haldeman counseled using the social media of the day, telephone and snail mail, to keep regular contact with supporters, both of which avoided the filter of the media. He also urged using daily radio messages, broadcast on national radio networks, to do the same. Haldeman suggested a daily routine that included at least an hour and a half for television taping.

Haldeman's memo began with a cover letter that argued, "I am firmly convinced that the whole basic approach to campaigns <u>must</u> be revised— and you are in an especially good position to do this in 1968."[18] If Nixon was in an especially good position to revise campaigning, it was because he had been doing so in many very significant ways for much of his career. Haldeman added, "A great deal of truly creative thinking is needed in the development of ways to use TV, and this is especially important if this general approach is used. I have not tried to develop these in the attached draft."[19] But, of course, Nixon had already been working on the development of ways to use TV. Nixon biographer Stephen Ambrose writes that "Nixon originally had resisted the Haldeman approach.... But the staff convinced him to give it a try,"[20] and after a while he was sold on it. But the truth is, no matter how Nixon might have gruffly reacted, he was implementing Haldeman's ideas long before Haldeman had them.

As political writer James "Scotty" Reston wrote after Nixon's 1962 defeat in California, no one then in public life had spent so much time studying reporters while understanding them so poorly. Reston argued that Nixon felt as though reporters were supposed to be transmission devices, dutifully recording and reporting what Nixon said and not trying to interpret what it meant or why he said it. Nixon resented reporters who did not play that simple role because he did not accept that there was a difference between news and truth. Reston wrote, "To him what he said was 'news' and should be left there. Maybe he was right. It could be that the 'real Nixon' was the one on stage, but that is beyond journalism now and will have to be left to the historians and the psychological novelists."[21] Reston's analysis of Nixon is not wrong, but it misses Nixon's point. What Nixon certainly understood was that he needed to be the one presenting Nixon to the world, not the reporters covering Nixon, and so he did his best to control their access to him and their ability to interpret him to the world. The task facing Nixon's team in 1968 was not to decide *whether* to use television; it was to devise a plan for *how* to use television.

In a second memo, William Gavin offered many ideas, covering a great deal of territory, still suggesting that the campaign was to be won, or lost, on television because it was now part of the daily lives of voters. He suggested that it was important to offer many different impressions and attitudes and offer a kind of three-dimensional view to voters, writing, "This may be the key: enveloping the audience, bringing it in, entwining it. It's this three-dimensionality we've got to construct."

Gavin took issue with some of what McLuhan wrote, but he stuck to the main idea—that positive impressions of Nixon could best be built on television. He wrote derisively of voters that they were too lazy and uninterested to follow logical, directional arguments. Instead, Nixon should use a scattered, shotgun approach, firing many pellets in many different directions. It was not just the age of television, but an age in which people are conditioned by television, in which thought patterns are "undirected or multidirectional.... Thus a simple directional logic won't do." The election of 1968 was not winnable with the techniques of the election of 1952.

One solution to the problem, Gavin wrote, was the use of humor, which shows a human side and could help people find a common experience like a laugh. He added that it also helped cut through "the veils of logic." Logic is for the written word, not for the spoken, televised word, according to Gavin's interpretation of McLuhan.

Gavin suggested that the great power of television, over print, or even film, was that it had become an everyday part of life for so many people. Television gave the campaign the opportunity to create a sense of community and to replace old, negative images with new, positive ones. The idea was to get out of the 1950s and old images of Nixon and point toward the future and to invite viewers to be part of the participatory process of the campaign. He concluded, "What we're talking about here isn't so much a new image as it is a new use of the medium, a use better attuned to its own shortcomings and advantages and, more particularly, to the peculiar ways in which it gets to the people watching."[22]

The notion among his advisers, including Haldeman and Gavin, was that Nixon was not a very good TV politician. By 1968, the Checkers speech was largely regarded as an embarrassment, even though it saved his career at the time he made the speech. Ambrose wrote of the dilemma campaign staffers saw about television and Nixon, arguing that he had some "devastating" television images in his past which suggested Nixon should be kept off television as much as possible. But rather than doing this, the staff understood that Nixon simply had to be given television opportunities that avoided trouble and played to his strengths. Ambrose wrote, "if Nixon was not all that good by himself, or one-on-one, or with reporters, there were times when he was outstanding," such as speaking to large audiences or to small groups.[23] So, one solution the team arrived at was to develop a series of town hall meetings in which Nixon could appear before small panels of regular folks asking him questions.

Nixon's team of media specialists featured people such as advertising executive Harry Treleaven; CBS executive Frank Shakespeare; the executive producer of the nationally syndicated *Mike Douglas Show*, Roger Ailes; and the head writer of *Rowan and Martin's Laugh-In*, Paul Keyes. When the team prepared the 1968 campaign to elect Nixon, it did so understanding his problems with, and resentments of, the news media. They worked to eliminate as many of them as possible by finding ways to avoid the press and let him speak directly to the people.

After all, appealing directly to the people and deliberately ignoring the news media outlets that he felt were criticizing him unfairly worked for Nixon in 1952 with the Checkers speech, much as it worked for FDR on radio in 1933. Nixon hated the fact that people called it the "Checkers speech," but he always knew the key role it played in his political life. Even if people in the Republican Party were embarrassed by his long, sometimes rambling, Checkers performance by 1968, it undoubtedly saved his political career in 1952 and his advisers in 1968 knew that the right TV style could push him over the top to the White House. Having control of the camera was the priority for Nixon and his team.

Nixon's longtime adviser Herb Klein said there were two consequences of the Checkers speech. One was that people working on the 1952 campaign understood they could have some independence from Eisenhower's people. Klein observed that they realized "they were strong on their own and that they didn't have to bow to everything they said on the Eisenhower train." More important for Nixon's future career, however, was that Nixon "learned something about television for sure that night," which was that it gave him a power to speak to the people, directly and unfiltered, that no other medium did.[24]

The cornerstone of Nixon's media strategy for 1968 was a series of infomercials, or what are now referred to as "town hall meetings," in which Nixon appeared before a friendly crowd and answered questions from a handpicked panel of "average citizens" meant to represent all walks of life, genders, and ethnicities. Nixon aide Frank Shakespeare, a vice president of CBS who took a leave of absence during the campaign, said there were basically two ways to make use of television in a political campaign. The first way was with 30- or 60-second spots. The purpose of a spot, he said, was to promote a slogan or concept. Short ads did not give a full picture of the candidate. You did that, Shakespeare argued, with the town hall meetings, a way people could feel as if they were sitting down with Nixon in their own living rooms and getting to know him.[25]

The Primaries: "Nixon's the One!"

In 1968, primary elections were still not as common as they are now. In 2016, 34 states had primaries in the Republican nomination process, while the other states held caucuses. In 1968, there were 15 primaries and Nixon entered 11 of them. While he did some campaigning in the states with primaries, it was nothing like the nearly four-year-long experience the build-up to the primaries is today. It was still truly possible in 1968 that a candidate could win the nomination without entering in the primaries. In fact, on the Democratic side, the eventual nominee of the party, Vice President Hubert Humphrey, did not participate in any of the 14 Democratic primaries. On the Republican side, not doing much active campaigning in the primaries was the strategy of both the governor of California, Ronald Reagan, and the governor of New York, Nelson Rockefeller.

Nixon, on the other hand, was much more fully engaged in the primary season, as he promised Merv Griffin. After spending much of 1967 unofficially announcing his campaign, he used the occasion of the upcoming New Hampshire primary to make his candidacy official, in a letter to the people of New Hampshire, dated January 31 and released on February 1. In it he told the voters of New Hampshire how important they and their primary were. The nation faced many problems and needed new leadership, Nixon wrote, and he explained how someone who had been around as long as he had could be new leadership. He wrote of lessons learned in 14 years serving in Washington and of eight years out of Washington, when he "had a chance to reflect on the lessons of public office, to measure the nation's tasks and its problems from a fresh perspective." He promised voters he would apply those lessons to the problems of the last third of the 20th century.[26]

As Nixon's "debate" with William F. Buckley, Jr., demonstrated, Nixon was trying to pull the party—left, right, and center—together while also attracting some Democrats to build a winning coalition. There were some candidates with higher national profiles who appealed to the left and right elements of the party: Ronald Reagan on the right and George Romney and Nelson Rockefeller on the left. Romney formally declared his campaign. Rockefeller first said he would not be running for the presidency, then changed his mind and announced his candidacy. Reagan never formally announced but allowed surrogates to campaign on his behalf in the primary states. He was the only candidate on the ballot in California.

For more than a year before the New Hampshire primary, which was held on March 12, Michigan governor George Romney worked on mounting a challenge to Nixon. However, he had trouble overcoming controversial remarks he made in late August 1967 about the Vietnam War, in which he told a reporter that he had been "brainwashed" to support the war in Vietnam and had, subsequently, come to regret that support. He was ridiculed on both sides of the aisle for those remarks but still declared his official candidacy for the presidency in the fall of 1967. He stayed in the race for months after those remarks, but he withdrew from the race two weeks prior to the New Hampshire primary after his campaign team told him that he was trailing Nixon by a margin of roughly 70 percent to 11 percent.[27]

Romney's decision to drop out ensured an overwhelming victory for Nixon in the Granite State, where his campaign spent around half a million dollars and Nixon engaged in the retail politics New Hampshire demands. Chester et al. summed up the victory this way: "He rolled up 79 percent of the Republican vote in the primary, but did this really mean that he had shed his loser's image? He was, after all, without opposition."[28]

Easy victory or not, Nixon's New Hampshire campaign has an

enduring legacy. Out of the New Hampshire campaign came the development of a new campaign tactic that Nixon and his staffers would use and evolve throughout the rest of campaign '68: the television town hall. Nixon was certainly a competent speaker in front of big audiences. He had been doing this for many years. As the lessons of *Six Crises* demonstrate, he did not like interacting with reporters, but groups of supporters were just fine. In a small group, he was able to appear spontaneous and original, even if he was responding to a question for the umpteenth time.[29] He seemed warm, engaging, and interested in the people in the room with him and that naturally made people like him. The key remaining ingredient was taking these intimate audiences with Nixon and delivering them to the broader public.

The solution was the town halls, which were filmed and broadcast. The first, conducted in Hillsboro, New Hampshire, gave birth to what the campaign referred to as "the Hillsboro approach."[30] And thus, born from an idea of Bob Haldeman and implemented by Shakespeare and Treleaven, came a new and enduring form of campaigning invented by the Nixon campaign. It was all done as part of allowing Nixon to build and control an image different from the one voters might remember from 1960 of 1962.

Following Gavin's suggestion, a documentary was produced for the Nixon campaign by John Donaldson Productions about the New Hampshire campaign. The film, *A Time to Begin*, featured what seemed like a

Nixon on the campaign trail in 1968.

behind-the-scenes look at the Nixon campaign, with interviews with staffers like John Ehrlichman and Pat Buchanan. In it, Nixon's director of information, Arch McKinlay, talked about the panel shows. "You notice that in the television material that's been put together an effort has been made to put Mr. Nixon in front of a panel of people. Now, he's never met these people before. He walks on cold. He's meeting them for the first time. The panels are heterogenous. Some are Republicans, some are Democrats, some are independents. One panel is an agricultural group. Another panel is a youth group, another panel is a business group." The narrator of the documentary explained, as had many aides of Nixon, that "Richard Nixon prefers informal, no holds barred discussions." He also preferred them without reporters.

In an interview while driving from one campaign stop to another, Nixon spoke from the front seat to the camera in the back seat. He talked about his preference for tough questions. It was a line right out of one of William Gavin's memos. He said, "I have a rule about press conferences that some of the professionals on my staff don't agree with: I never plant questions. And I know that most people do. I say most. Many do. I'm not sure that most do. The reason I don't plant them, however, is that the answer then is contrived. Nobody's going to get away with a question where you say, 'Now I'd like to have this question asked.' The other thing is this: I also have a feeling that, generally feeling, where the question is hard and strong and tough, not belligerent, but strong and tough, it gets a better answer. Always save me from what I call the easy questions, where someone's trying to help me. Because the average viewer, or listener, to that kind of a question says, 'Uh uh, that's a patsy. That's one of his friends.'" It may be that Nixon preferred tough questions to easy questions, but only when he wanted any questions at all. As president, Nixon participated in far fewer press conferences per year than any of his predecessors going back to Calvin Coolidge.[31]

The documentary contained a telling line, delivered by the narrator, about the Nixon philosophy for 1968: "Television is a vital political meeting place. To be successful, a candidate must use the medium and use it well." Nixon knew better than anyone how important television was. In the interview from the front seat, Nixon spoke about his personal media philosophy. He said he was his own media consultant, and he was uninterested in being handled. He said, "I'm really the most difficult man in the world when it comes to a so-called public relations firm. Nobody's going to package me. Nobody's going to make me put on an act for television. I'm not going to engage in any gimmicks or any stunts, wear any silly hats, do something for the purpose of getting a publicity picture, or the rest. I am not an actor, I'm not a good actor." This was a not-too-subtle reference to one of the presidential nomination threats still lurking out on the horizon, Ronald Reagan.

Nixon was no actor; he was just Nixon. He continued, "I'm just gonna be myself. And so, when people say to me that I've got to change myself, take lessons about how to stand, how to talk, how to act, look in the mirror, listen to my voice on the radio, look at myself on television; the answer is I never have and I'm not gonna start now. If there is anything I do have to offer to the American people and to leadership, as far as our role in the world is concerned, it's the fact that I believe deeply in what I say and that I am myself. And I'm going to continue to play that role. If the people, looking at me, say 'That's a new Nixon,' then all that I can say is, 'Well, maybe you didn't know the old Nixon.'"[32] Once again, the message was Nixon is Nixon. What was new was that Nixon's time had finally come.

Romney's decision to drop out left New York governor Nelson Rockefeller as the prominent left-to-moderate candidate with national standing. However, on March 21, just after Spiro Agnew, then-governor of Maryland, helped to open a Rockefeller presidential campaign headquarters in Maryland, Rockefeller announced that he was not a candidate for the presidency. However, he did say that if he were drafted to be the nominee of the party at the convention in Miami, he would accept.[33] Rockefeller was not the only one who thought, at least for a while, that he could have leverage at the convention as a "favorite son" candidate.

On April 30, the day of the Massachusetts campaign, Nelson Rockefeller changed course and announced he was officially a candidate for president. During the time Rockefeller was officially *not* a candidate, LBJ withdrew abruptly from the race, Martin Luther King, Jr., was assassinated, and race riots erupted in cities across the country. When he officially entered the race, Rockefeller said, "My purpose in doing this is to give our party a choice of candidates and of programs. I have become convinced that the party wishes to have a choice. I have become convinced that I can present it with a framework of party unity. This I pledge to do."[34] Rockefeller won the Massachusetts primary. It was the only one he won, but Rockefeller remained in the campaign as a declared candidate all the way to the convention in Miami in August. Nixon felt Rockefeller was working in concert with Reagan to prevent Nixon from winning the nomination.

Ronald Reagan was in the first half of his first term as governor of California and he feared it was unseemly—something which would probably not be seen as a limitation today—for a newly elected governor to actively campaign for the presidency. Instead, an indirect campaign was organized by his very enthusiastic supporters. Reagan did no campaigning in primaries and his name was put on the ballots by a variety of surrogates.

The supporters of Reagan got him to allow filming of a fundraising speech he was giving in Oakland, California, and it was added to a Reagan documentary which compiled footage of Reagan from throughout his life. The movie was central to his non-campaign campaign and it was aired six times during the Oregon primary campaign.[35] This was just part of the Reagan-less Reagan for president campaign effort in Oregon, where "the media budget was virtually open-ended (Reagan's rivals claim he must have spent two hundred thousand dollars in the state), and the 'biography' ... won critical acclaim as well as good ratings."[36]

The Oregon primary, held on May 28, was widely viewed as a last hurrah for possible competitors of Nixon such as Reagan. Nixon declared before the election that he thought a decisive victory in Oregon would put a bow on the nomination for him. Nixon, using language that sounded like language used by Donald Trump nearly fifty years later about "Never Trumpers," said, "If I come out of Tuesday's primary with a vote greater than the other Republicans combined, I think the stop-Nixon drive will have suffered a heavy blow. Rockefeller and Reagan are, of course, the ones who have combined forces against me. I believe my triumphs in all the primaries I entered will prove once and for all there is no truth in the statement that 'Nixon can't win.'"[37]

Prior to what he viewed as the decisive primary, Nixon purchased network time and broadcast a statewide telethon in Oregon. It had elements like the campaign town halls that happened earlier in New Hampshire and to *The Nixon Answer* shows that would follow in the general election. But rather than have a panel of semi-autonomous people from the community asking the questions, in this format they came over the phone. It was a telethon in a very real sense of the word. People's calls were answered by receptionists such as Nixon's daughters, Tricia and Julie, and the questions—carefully curated—were read to Nixon by Bud Wilkinson, the former University of Oklahoma football coach. Nixon bought an hour and a half of television time for this reporter-free exercise on May 27, 1968, the night before the decisive Oregon primary, which Nixon handily won.

Reagan won the uncontested California primary after the Oregon primary, but Reagan's campaign was essentially over without Reagan ever participating it. As three British journalists who covered the campaign for the *Times of London* and who wrote a book about it in 1969, Chester et al. observe, "Short of making Reagan an open candidate, everything that could be done was done.... Over-all the grassroots operation had been sound but had failed to yield sensational results."[38] Reagan's largest vote total was in California, where he got 100 percent of the vote, but Nixon wisely chose not to oppose him there.

In the nine states where Reagan and Nixon appeared on the ballot together, Reagan got the most votes in Nebraska and Oregon, with 21 per-cent and 20 percent of the vote. Because Reagan won California, he ended up with approximately 20,000 more popular votes than Nixon, but Nixon won the lion's share of delegates and went to the convention only 20 votes shy of the total he needed to secure the nomination. As David Broder noted in a column written at the end of the convention, "In Oregon on May 28 Nixon won 73 per cent of the vote against full-scale campaigns by supporters of his two absentee rivals. 'I actually believed,' Nixon said this morning, 'that the nomination was won on the night of the Oregon pri-mary,' and that proved to be the case."[39]

On to Miami: The Convention

It wasn't until the convention began that Reagan formally announced himself to be a candidate, disingenuously saying of a draft message from the California delegation, "Gosh, I was surprised. It came out of the clear blue sky."[40] When Reagan joined the race, Rockefeller and his supporters hoped that conservative delegates might split over Reagan and Nixon and find a path for Rockefeller to the nomination.

Both Reagan and Rockefeller were late in jumping formally into the race and Nixon was privately furious, believing that the two men were col-luding with each other to derail his nomination. Even if it was true, in retrospect it was a fool's errand. Nixon simply was too careful and had worked too hard to be beaten at the last moment. As Chester et al. point out, "Compared with his rivals, Nixon possessed assets that seemed almost impregnable."[41] He had the support of all the people who worked for him in the primaries and the support of all the party leaders he cultivated not just for the months of the campaig but in the years that preceded it. That was the point, after all, of all the speeches, campaign events, and television appearances he made between 1962 and 1968.

Chester et al. wrote that the leaders of the party, the work horses, were on Nixon's side. He also had many of the big leaders on both the lib-eral and conservative sides of the party, such as Mark Hatfield and Strom Thurmond, on his side. And finally, they noted, Nixon had an excellent operation for recruiting and holding on to delegates at the convention.[42] It was simply not a fight Nixon was going to lose.

Nixon had allies like Goldwater and Thurmond working on Southern conservatives to eliminate any possibility of Reagan staging a last-minute coup. If Nixon was concerned, he never let it show. On Tuesday, the second day of the convention, Nixon held a long press conference and then seven meetings with different groups of delegates. In all these meetings, Nixon behaved like he was the nominee and left no doubt about it. But he held the meetings to make sure there was no doubt about it. As the *Washington Post* reported, "Still, if the accounts of delegates are to be believed, there were subtle differences in the tenor and pitch of the Nixon appeal, depending on whether he was speaking to Southerners or Northerners. On the minds of the Southerners were the selection of a vice presidential running mate, the Supreme Court, the war in Vietnam, and the space program," and, of course, civil rights.[43]

When he was asked specifically about Ronald Reagan as a running mate, to which the room responded with applause, Nixon demurred, saying, "Whomever I select, I can assure you I will not select a name who will not be acceptable to all."[44] When he was asked about the Supreme Court and LBJ's nomination of Abe Fortas to be the chief justice, Nixon said, "I assure you I will select men who will interpret the Constitution strictly.... I am a strict constructionist."[45] On the civil rights issues of education and open housing, Nixon told the delegates that judges were not "qualified to be a local school district and to make the decision as your local school board" and that open housing should be decided by the local and state governments. The only reason, he assured Southern delegates, that he supported a federal open housing bill was to avoid splitting the Republican Party.[46]

As for Vietnam, he said, "How do you bring a war to a conclusion? I'll tell you how Korea was ended. We got in there and had this messy war on our hands. Eisenhower let the word go out ... to the Chinese and the North Koreans that we would not tolerate this continual ground war of attrition. And within a matter of months, they negotiated.... Well, as far as negotiation is concerned that should be our position. We'll be militarily strong and diplomatically strong. Think we've got to change our position regarding training the Vietnamese."[47]

An assessment published in the *Washington Post* considered how Nixon shored up needed Southern support to keep delegates from turning to Ronald Reagan. There were, according to the analysis, three reasons for Nixon's success. (1) Southerners wanted a "solid, practical candidate who had a good chance to become President." Because they were stung by Goldwater and his performance as an "erratic charmer" in 1964, many Southerners had trouble seeing Reagan as president. (2) Nixon very effectively lined up the support of nearly all of the "important" Southerners influential in the Republican Party. (3) He promised the South he would choose an "acceptable" running mate and "sounded a conservative civil rights theme."[48] It is true that Nixon and his supporters simply outworked and out-convinced Southern delegates, a job no doubt made easier by the fact that Reagan refused to officially declare his candidacy until the convention began.

The vote for the nomination took place on Wednesday, August 7. While there were moments of concern among the Nixon people, he won the nomination on the first ballot. He got 692 delegates to Rockefeller's 277 and Reagan's 182. A few favorite sons also had some votes on the first ballot. After Nixon won the nomination, most delegates switched their votes to him, and Nixon ended up with a final tally of 1238 delegates.

On the question of a vice president, Nixon chose Spiro Agnew as his running mate, after Agnew switched his support to Nixon. Nixon wrote in his memoir that he made a tentative choice of Agnew shortly before the convention, in consultation with his future attorney general, John Mitchell. Nixon wrote, "But like most important decisions, this one would not be final until it was announced. I still wanted to test it, to weigh alternatives, to hear other views. It was a tentative choice, and still reversible."[49] Nixon made quite a show of seeking the input of people from different factions of the party but in truth he never really wavered from Agnew once he decided from a short list which had included John Volpe, Howard Baker, John Tower, and a few others.[50]

That does not mean, however, that the press or all the delegates were friendly in their assessment of the choice. The *Washington Post* editorial page, for example, featured an analysis titled "…And His First Decision," which questioned how Agnew, who had no foreign policy experience, could possibly fulfill what Nixon said was his number one criterion for vice presidency: someone who could step in immediately as president if needed. The *Post* editors concluded, "In making his first major decision as a presidential candidate Mr. Nixon appears to have acted hastily, without full assessment of the national interest."[51]

The delegates were not universally thrilled with the choice of Agnew either. Agnew was seen as a political opportunist by many, changing his stripes to appeal to Nixon. For a while it appeared some states were going to try to lead revolts in favor of candidates such as Nelson Rockefeller, Ronald Reagan, George Romney, or New York mayor John Lindsay. In the end order was restored and Agnew was nominated with nearly as many delegate votes as Nixon. However, there was one serious consequence of the protests and attempts to supplant Agnew: Nixon's acceptance speech to the nation was bumped out of primetime.

Before considering Nixon's convention address, it is important to consider some other Nixon campaign communication from before the convention. In his speech at the convention, Nixon harkened back to speeches from the stump and to a nationally-broadcast radio address he delivered on May 16. In mid–May, Nixon was still in the middle of the primary campaign, but he clearly believed that he would be campaigning as the Republican nominee in the fall. In that speech, he called for a "new alignment" of American voters, whose glue would be a group he called "the silent center," which Nixon would later famously change to "the silent majority."[52]

May 16: The "New Alignment" and "the Silent Center"

On May 16, Richard Nixon stopped in Chicago to record the speech that he broadcast on the CBS Radio Network. In the speech, "A New Alignment for America," Nixon did what he told William F. Buckley, Jr., he would do—he tried to appeal to all the elements of the Republican Party and to Democrats too. He suggested the time was ripe for a new American realignment, a shift from the Republican-Democratic order to something new. It was not television, but still, it was Nixon buying broadcast time to make his point without the interference of the press. In tone, it was not dissimilar to one of FDR's calming fireside chats.

Quoting Alexis de Tocqueville and Victor Hugo, Nixon suggested an electoral coalition for himself, if not an actual new political party. Nixon was clearly looking ahead to the general election with this speech. Nixon told listeners of something they might not have known was coming but should welcome. He said, "Most Americans have not been aware that this new alignment has been gathering together. Yet it has happened, and it is an exciting, healthy development."[53] The new alignment, Nixon said, was ready to be a new majority. "Men and women of all backgrounds, of all ages, of all parties, are coming to the same conclusions. Many of these men and women belong to the same blocs that formed the new coalitions. But now, thinking independently, they have all reached a new conclusion about the direction of our nation. Their very diversity of background provides a basis for a new unity for America."[54]

The new alignment consisted, Nixon argued, of a variety of "political elements" which was "comparable in importance to the formation under Franklin D. Roosevelt 35 years ago of the Democratic coalition of organized labor, minority groups and the solid South."[55] First, Nixon spoke of Republicans who, he said, call for a government "to do for people what they cannot do for themselves: to open up new opportunities, to mobilize private energies to meet public needs, to protect and defend every citizen, to create a climate that enables every person to fulfill himself to the utmost."[56] Nixon called this "the Republican voice" of both liberal and conservative Republicans. And, he asserted, it was a voice that was attracting independents and Democrats. He said, "The traditionally Republican thinking is the well-spring of the new alignment."[57]

Next in the new coalition were what Nixon called "new liberals," who were more like the classic liberals of old or the Libertarians of today and not the liberals versus conservatives of modern political parlance. The new liberal, Nixon wrote, wanted a more responsive, less intrusive government and more personal freedom. The new liberal wanted a government that promoted social responsibility and free enterprise. Nixon promised, "In that context, liberals and conservatives will find themselves coming closer together, rather than splitting apart."[58] In explaining himself, Nixon argued that there was a crucial difference between the "new liberal" and the "new left." New liberals are good. New leftists are dangerous radicals who fight against gradual change and want to tear down society. He said, "The New Left has a passion, while the New Liberal has a program."[59] Nixon concluded his discussion of this part of the coalition saying that he thought there were more young people who were new liberals than new leftists. They want to make change, not just shout from the rooftops.

The next part of the coalition were the people of what he called "the New South." These were, he hoped, not blindly-voting Democrats of the old Solid South. The New South was a place where racism was no longer appealing and people were no longer fighting the Civil War. He concluded, "Politically, the new South is in ferment. It is breaking the shackles of one-party rule. Its new voices are interpreting the old doctrines of states' rights in new ways—those of making state and local governments responsive to state and local needs."[60] Nixon had many reasons to try to pull the South into his coalition. He worried about a challenge for conservative support from both Ronald Reagan and from the independent presidential campaign of Alabama governor George Wallace.[61]

The next new members of the coalition were what Nixon referred to as the "Black Militants." There was, Nixon argued, a growing call for self-sufficiency among Black Americans. Some would certainly argue it was language aimed mostly at white voters, not Black. He said there was an increasing divide between Black leaders and "the doctrinaire welfarist." He argued that Black leaders did not want handouts, saying, "The message of giveaway, of handout, of permanent welfare is no longer of interest to people who want dignity and self-respect." The time of handouts was over.

At the same time, Nixon made an argument for a kind of civil rights, saying, "What we can and should do immediately, is respond to their demands for a share of American opportunity, for a legitimate role in private enterprise."[62] Nixon was regarded by many Black leaders as a racist who was hostile to the Civil Rights Movement. But if one gives him the benefit of the doubt that his words *might* be sincerely expressing his feelings, then this part of the speech sounds like a call for moderation in the name of real, sustainable progress. One Black leader, Roy Innis, the associate national director of the Congress of Racial Equality (CORE), was reported to have said that "Mr. Nixon was the only Presidential candidate who understood black aspirations."[63]

Many critics did not give him that benefit of the doubt, however. *St. Louis Post-Dispatch* Washington correspondent Marquis Childs wrote, for example, that while Nixon's call for Black capitalism won him the applause of "militant Negro leaders, where his strength is weakest," Nixon failed to explain how that Black capitalism would be achieved. Childs argued Nixon was deceiving people by trying to convince them it was possible without extensive intervention by the federal government, which Nixon himself said was impossible in the same speech. He would not support pouring "additional billions into the cities."[64]

In another critique, Tom Wicker of the *New York Times* addressed Nixon's rhetoric on urban issues and race, both in this radio speech and in his campaigning in Oregon. He argued that Nixon called for an anti-crime bill and drew applause by blaming the Supreme Court as having "gone too far in weakening the peace forces against the crime forces in this country."[65] Wicker criticized Nixon's platitudes and pandering, but he didn't blame Nixon alone. Nixon, and other candidates, used such lines because that was what the audiences responded to. Nixon was, Wicker noted, adept at coming up with "facile" lines that appealed to different segments of his audience.[66] So, while Wicker did not accept Nixon's message on race as sincere, seeing it only as self-serving campaign rhetoric, he grudgingly respected his messaging ability.

The final part of the new coalition Nixon spoke of, "the fifth element," was the "Silent Center." He called this group the "non-voice" of "millions of people in the middle of the American political spectrum who do not demonstrate, who do not picket or protest loudly." That did mean they were apathetic or uninterested. They, Nixon argued, "are willing to listen to new ideas, and they are willing to think them through." It was an argument against the New Deal Coalition of FDR. He said, "We must remember that all the center is not silent, and all who are silent are not center. But a great many 'quiet Americans' have become committed to answers to social problems that preserve personal freedom. They have rejected the answers of the Thirties to the problems of today." It was, once again, an appeal to a new liberalism, which was a new name for classic liberalism. The Silent Center was crucial to making this change to dismantle the New Deal, Nixon argued, because with the Silent Center becoming part of the New Alignment, the alignment would become a new majority. And that, Nixon argued, "is why we are witnessing a significant breakthrough toward what America needs: peaceful, orderly progress."[67]

Nixon did not cite Plato or Aristotle here, but he was clearly hearkening back to the Greeks in this passage of the speech which refers to the Silent Center as the "Fifth Element." The four terrestrial elements identified by Plato are earth, water, fire, and air. To this list, Aristotle added a celestial element that others later dubbed "aether" or ether. It refers to a binding material that fills the universe above the world, the terrestrial. The metaphor seems apt here. For Nixon, the Silent Center was the large group of people at the core that could bind the other elements together.

The rest of the speech was Nixon's promise of what he would do if he were elected president. Just because the elements existed did not mean that they naturally saw eye to eye as a functioning alignment. They had that promise, but not the reality, Nixon argued. He said, "Tomorrow, as we focus on the new movement more clearly, Americans will gain a new unity. We will not seek the false unity of consensus, of the glossing over of fundamental differences, of the enforced sameness of government regimentation." And, he argued, this was something more than simply pushing to form a new party made up of component parts like the big tent Republican and Democratic parties. He said, "We will forge a unity of goals, recognized by men who also recognize and value their own diversity. *That is the great advantage of an alignment of ideas over the coalition of power blocs.*"

It was a message of classic liberalism and an updated version of Rousseau's Social Contract. Nixon said, "The new alignment speaks in many accents, and approaches its point from many directions. But the common message is there: People come first, and government is their servant. The best government is closest to the people, and most involved with people's lives. Government is formed to protect the individual's life, property, and rights, and to help the helpless—not to dominate a person's life or rob of him of his self-respect. The concept is great not because it is new, but because it is right and it is relevant."[68]

In an impressive rhetorical flourish, Nixon suggested to people that they didn't need to take any action to become part of the New Alignment because "if you believe that people do come first; if you believe that dignity must replace the dole; if you believe that order and progress go hand in hand; if you are idealistic about personal freedom; then you don't have to worry about where to go to join the new alignment. You are already a part of it." If you are part of it and Richard Nixon is talking about it, then you should vote for Richard Nixon.

It was not a great speech for the Republican Party. Nixon knew he was running for president in a time of Democratic dominance. But the presidency, as held by Democrats, showed signs of weakness, maybe not for all the reasons Nixon pointed out, but certainly because of the Vietnam War. And he knew that if he were going to win, he would need a coalition. The Democrats did, in fact, have majority support in the country at the time.

In this speech, broadcast to the nation, he did not call for people to vote Republican. He invited them to vote for Nixon—and the New Alignment.

Nixon concluded, "No man can predict the ultimate shape of the alignment that is happening in America today. But I know this: It is alive, it is moving forward, it is rooted in reality, and it calls out for you to come aboard. In the years to come, I believe that historians will record this: That in the watershed year of 1968, America, in a time of crisis, responded as it has responded before—with new ideas, with great traditions, with a new alignment and with the fresh hope that comes from a new unity."[69] And Nixon was ready to be the man to lead that new unity, or so he wanted people to believe. The speech was not one delivered by a man worried about the competition in the primary season. It was a speech aimed directly at the heart of the general election competition for 1968 which, at that point, could have been any of several Democratic primary contenders such as Eugene McCarthy and Robert Kennedy or convention contenders like George McGovern and the eventual nominee, Hubert Humphrey.

There were many critics of this and other Nixon campaign speeches. He was regularly accused of not offering specifics and of dealing only in platitudes and generalities. In response to his campaign style, Marquis Childs called Nixon the most homogenized of all the presidential candidates whose broadly general rhetoric was specifically designed to play to "all the fears and frustrations of the moment" and said Nixon was the one who could "bring unity at home and peace abroad."[70]

Of Nixon's positions on the urban crisis and other issues, columnist Tom Wicker wrote, "Even Richard Nixon ... gets more audience response from his quips ... and his well-targeted slogans ('Let's have fewer millions on the welfare rolls and more millions on the payrolls') than from any serious talk about the problems of the cities or the races."[71] These criticisms do not ring hollow. They point to very real problems with the kind of campaign rhetoric Nixon was spouting in the effort to present the new Nixon to the country and to appeal to as many voters as possible. That was what Nixon cared about. And it is a model most candidates have followed since.

The Convention Speech: "The Forgotten Americans"

The job to be done in the acceptance speech at the convention was the same as the nationally-broadcast address on May 16. It was to demonstrate to the nation that Nixon really was "The One." And to do that, he wanted to do everything he could to show he was both a new man from the person

Nixon speaks at the Republican National Convention in 1968.

voters might remember from eight years before and to remind them that he was an important part of the greatness of the 1950s.

Nixon's speech began with an emotional appeal for the health of Dwight Eisenhower who was hospitalized the week before the convention after suffering his seventh heart attack. Telling the audience that things were going to be different in 1968 because he was going to win, Nixon cited Eisenhower as reason number one, saying that people would give the ailing former president a boost by voting for Nixon. To cheers, Nixon said emphatically, "I say let's win this one for Ike!" There was no bigger hero in the country than Eisenhower, especially among the people most likely to vote for Nixon, so it could certainly not hurt to invoke his name and lay claim to his support.

As he continued his acceptance speech, Nixon said he was giving voice to the "great majority of Americans, the forgotten Americans—the non-shouters; the non-demonstrators." These were the members of the Silent Center from his May 16 speech. He listed the people who fit this category: they were *not* racists or criminals; they *were* Black, white, natives, immigrants, blue collar, white collar, old, and young. They were, in other words, everyone. He said, "They are good people, they are decent people; they work, and they save, and they pay their taxes, and they care. Like Theodore Roosevelt, they know that this country will not be a good place for any of us to live in unless it is a good place for all of us to live in."

He told the crowd, "Let's never forget that despite her faults, America is a great nation. And America is great because her people are great.... America is in trouble today not because her people have failed but because her leaders have failed. And what America needs are leaders to match the greatness of her people." He then listed all the things that were, as he saw them, wrong with the country. First and foremost was the war in Vietnam, but he added economic troubles, lawlessness, and racial violence.

It was time for new leadership in America and Nixon announced to the delegates and the nation that he was the man to provide that new leadership. It was time to do away with "big promises and little action." Nixon said the country was worse off in virtually every measurable way since Eisenhower left office and then went into detail explaining how the nation was worse off in each area of policy.

Donald Trump would, 48 years later, crib big parts of the spirit of Nixon's message, if not his actual words, in his own nomination acceptance speech. Nixon's speech included lines such as "And I say the time has come for other nations in the Free World to bear their fair share of the burden of defending peace and freedom around this world. What I call for is not a new isolationism. It is a new internationalism in which America enlists its allies and its friends around the world in those struggles in which their interest is as great as ours." He promised that the American people would "restore the strength of America so that we shall always negotiate from strength and never from weakness." When Nixon hit these lines, they received the applause they were no doubt calculated to inspire, as Willard Edwards of the *Chicago Tribune* noted, "Nixon's pledge that he would restore respect for the American flag around the world caused the crowd to jump to its feet in such display of cheering that he was forced to suspend for a minute."[72]

When Warren Harding ran for president in 1920, he called for a "return to normalcy," which involved pulling back from the international stage the country was thrust upon by World War I. Nixon's version of a call for a return to normalcy was a return to what he saw as America's lost standing as the world's greatest power. He said, "And it is time we started to act like a great nation around the world. It is ironic to note when we were a small nation—weak militarily and poor economically—America was respected. And the reason was that America stood for something more powerful than military strength or economic wealth.... Today, too often, America is an example to be avoided and not followed." Nixon promised to restore international respect for the United States.

Nixon also called for a restoration of order and justice for all Americans. He said, "And to those who say that law and order is the code word for racism, there and here is a reply: Our goal is justice for every American. If we are to have respect for law in America, we must have laws that deserve respect." But it was not possible to have order without progress or progress without order. They were, Nixon argued, necessary for each other. When he told the crowd that "the right to be free from violence in the streets" was "the first civil right," it drew speech-stopping applause.

As for poverty, government programs were not the solution, Nixon argued. The war on poverty did not begin during the Johnson administration. It dated back to the beginning of the nation and it was the most successful war on poverty in global history. He argued that there was more wealth, broadly shared, in the United States than any other nation. And this was not because of any actions of government, "but because of what people did for themselves over a hundred-ninety years in this country." Using a line he used in his radio address and on the stump, he called not for more welfare rolls but for more payrolls. Putting more people to work was the solution for America's ills. And this was true for both Black and white.

Nixon then went through a list of things he predicted for the nation—assuming people voted for him and allowed him to put his program into place—by the time the bicentennial and, presumably, the last year of his second term in office came around. As Chester et al. noted in their analysis of his speech, "Where policies are difficult to adumbrate, pipe dreams can be a useful device. And Nixon used them."[73]

Nixon predicted a country that was strong, proud, prosperous, and racially harmonious. Nixon said, "Tonight, I see the face of a child. He lives in a great city. He is black. Or he is white. He is Mexican, Italian, Polish. None of that matters. What matters, he's an American child. That child in that great city is more important than any politician's promise. He is America. He is a poet. He is a scientist, he is a great teacher, he is a proud craftsman. He is everything we ever hoped to be and everything we dare to dream to be."

"But wait!" Nixon seemed to shout. That's the dream. That is not reality unless things change. The reality is, Nixon said, "he sleeps the sleep of childhood and he dreams the dreams of a child. And yet when he awakens, he awakens to a living nightmare of poverty, neglect and despair. He fails in school. He ends up on welfare. For him the American system is one that feeds his stomach and starves his soul. It breaks his heart. And in the end, it may take his life on some distant battlefield."

But that was the fault of the Democratic regime and Nixon wanted the audience to know it did not have to be that way. With autobiographical flourishes, Nixon talked of the greatness of America and the American dream. "And," he said, "what I ask you to do tonight is to help me make that dream come true for millions to whom it's an impossible dream today." And, like all good Republicans aspiring to the presidency, Nixon once again invoked the image of Abraham Lincoln. He said, "One hundred and eight years ago, the newly elected President of the United States, Abraham Lincoln, left Springfield, Illinois, never to return again.... Abraham Lincoln lost his life, but he did not fail."

Nixon said with God's help and the help of the American people, he and they would succeed. They would, thinking forward 48 years, make America great again. He promised, "My fellow Americans, the long dark night for America is about to end. The time has come for us to leave the valley of despair and climb the mountain so that we may see the glory of the dawn—a new day for America, and a new dawn for peace and freedom in the world."

The final line is haunting with the benefit of hindsight, of course, for when Gerald Ford took the oath of office to become president when Nixon resigned, he used a very similar line, pronouncing that "our long national nightmare is over." But in August of 1968, the speech was generally well received and there were, of course, no thoughts that Nixon would resign from the presidency a year into his second term. The *New York Times* commented on both Nixon's speech and Agnew's speech accepting the vice presidency, saying that both had appealed to "basic, old-fashioned American values."[74] One report about the speech in the *Chicago Tribune* stated, "The new Republican nominee set the tone of his acceptance speech with the phrase 'new leadership' and said he accepted the challenge and commitment to prove it."[75]

A separate analysis of the speech in the *Chicago Tribune* noted, "He gained the true reward of great oratory—the rapt attention of a vast audience in between outbursts of sound." Comparing Nixon's 1968 speech to the one he gave in Chicago accepting the 1960 nomination, the *Tribune* observed that he had not changed much over the years. He still possessed "blazing eloquence" and he had effectively both ensured Republicans he (and they) would win in 1968 and warned them that there were many challenges to be faced after the election.[76]

As he got ready to deliver it, Nixon called this the most important speech of his career. And, arguably, it was the most important speech of his life. But only after the Checkers speech was the most important speech of his life and after the 1960 convention speech was the most important speech of his life. Chester et al. characterized Nixon's goal for the speech as wanting to inspire the country, not specific segments of the population as he did during the primary campaign.[77] Inspiring the country was what Nixon wanted to do with many of the speeches he gave in the 1960s, including the television appearances and the May 16 radio address. But in this case, there was one specific thing he wanted to inspire Americans to do: believe in him, at least enough to vote for him.

It was not possible for Nixon to turn himself into Kennedy. But what he could do, and what he *did do* for enough people to catapult him to the nomination and, ultimately, to win the election, was to turn himself into a *new* Nixon. Chester et al. gave a lukewarm analysis of the success of the speech, writing, "If it did not inspire, the fault was not entirely Nixon's.... Nixon is not a man who naturally expresses himself in inspiration terms. His greatest flights often are reminiscent of something one has heard someone else do better before. All orators borrow rhetorical tricks from one another, but the best ones have a way of transmuting them and making them own. With Nixon, the scars of the grafting operation still show."[78] However, there is an advantage to be gained from low expectations, which Nixon no doubt understood. And if the ultimate test of any campaign tactic's success is winning, it is hard to say Nixon failed.

No one thought of Nixon in the same terms as William Jennings Bryan, or JFK, or MLK. So, if he could do a job that appeared at least a little charismatic, he was doing the job well. And Chester et al. add, "This is not to say Nixon is a bad speaker. It is simply a surprise to find that, after so many years on the stump, he is not better than good."[79] But this standard applies to most people who live public lives. If "great" were not a true superlative, we would call everyone great. But many people toil on golf courses, football fields, soccer pitches, and baseball diamonds for years to never be better than good. In fact, most are never better than average. What Nixon needed to do was change the image of himself that people had from November 1960 and November 1962 of a sulky, angry loser. And in that, the convention speech was part of a successful formula.

Nixon entered the primaries for the reasons he told Merv Griffin. He wanted to win some elections and he won many. Those victories were responsible, in part, for winning the nomination of his party for the second time in his political career, both because they helped him secure delegates and because they showed the party and voters he was not a loser. His second nomination was separated from the first by eight years, two bruising defeats, and an enormous amount of work on building a new image. Nixon engaged in six years of framing a new narrative, in building a new vision of himself for the people to see.

Coda

An important coda to the primary and nomination campaign of 1968 is how journalists felt about the new style of campaigning candidates like Nixon and Reagan were engaging in—campaigning which minimized the need of reporters. It is important because their response was a kind of self-fulfilling prophecy for Nixon, who believed the press was out to get him no matter what he did. It created a vicious cycle that continues unabated to the present day.

One such critical reporter, who covered the campaign for the *Washington Post*, was Ward S. Just, who went on to a distinguished career as a novelist. Just correctly observed that the Nixon campaign style was designed to avoid the press as much as possible. On the day of the Oregon primary, Just wrote a whimsical, sarcastic column that critiqued Nixon's campaign tactics and treatment of the press. He wrote that members of the press were confined to a campaign hotel, briefed by campaign advance men, and then left to hang out in the hotel bar while Nixon went to rallies and campaign events without them.

Suggesting there was an oppressive presence to keep the press in line, Just wrote that when they were invited to events, reporters were escorted to a bus, kept together in a group on the outskirts of the crowd, and talked amongst themselves as Nixon talked about his family and asserted that the country was not doing very well. Neither, as Just saw it, was the press. He wrote that being sidelined, the reporters spent their time at such events people watching and arguing among themselves about trivial matters. In the same way Nixon argued the country was having a bad year, Just asserted, "It was a bad year for journalism."

Just was only 33 years old and one of the younger reporters there. But he saw a campaign designed to keep the press at arm's length and, if possible, dazzle them into seeing the Richard Nixon the campaign wanted them to see. The older journalists who knew Nixon from before, Just wrote, were not fooled. Just asserted that the Nixon campaign forum was not only designed to deny journalists a role but was openly hostile to them. When reporters were considering whether to go cover Nixon's Oregon telethon, Just wrote, many argued facetiously that they were in danger from the adoring crowd. But the bigger message is that the only image the Nixon campaign cared about was the adoration of the crowd. Journalists only got in the way of that message and many of the older, more experienced reporters opted to skip the telethon.

Just wrote that the younger journalists like himself attended only to return from the event feeling as the older journalists felt—relegated to the back bench. Just's column was titled "Covering Oregon Can Be a Killer."[80] Just felt journalism was being killed by the kind of campaigning Nixon was conducting as well as teaching generations of future politicians. More than 50 years later, Just has been proven correct many times over.

FOURTEEN

Campaign '68:
The Nixon Answer

Once Nixon won the nomination, it was time to win the election. As a major part of the strategy for accomplishing that goal, Nixon and his campaign decided to continue the format of the town hall which they invented during the New Hampshire campaign, but with some changes, such as adding a live studio audience. Frank Shakespeare explained that live audiences gave the shows an air of "genuineness" and "luster." What they wanted was a live, applauding audience that would keep the viewers at home focused.[1] The shows were also expanded to an hour from the half-hour format they used during the primaries.

The panels were picked by Garment, Ailes, and Shakespeare. This should raise suspicion that the panelists were ringers. Many accused Nixon of rigging the panels but his staffers maintained that the panelists were not all Nixon allies. They said they wanted some hostile questions because the staffers felt Nixon did well with hostile questions, as Ambrose noted about the panels first used in New Hampshire.[2] This was also asserted in the Nixon campaign documentary *A Time to Begin*. Nixon did well in these small group formats, responding to tough questions and even a little hostility.

Nevertheless, the panelists were chosen from a list suggested by friends of the campaign, the Republican Party, and other sources in each locality. Shakespeare said, "It is impossible to get a microcosm of a region, but we try to get a cross-section."[3] Whether or not the panels contained members who were not fans of Nixon, the audience was always full of Nixon supporters, ready to applaud their candidate. The shows allowed Nixon to do what every presidential candidate wants to do—speak to the people on his terms, without the interference of the press. It also allowed the Nixon team to use segments on specific topics in other media efforts.

Getting Nixon to try the format was the tricky part, but once he did it, he was a fan. Nixon was, according to Ambrose, still of the opinion that he won the 1960 election and was, therefore, hesitant to change campaign styles. However, before the first town hall in New Hampshire, Nixon's staff was able to convince him based on two things: (1) reporters would not be present for the taping and (2) staffers such as Treleaven and Shakespeare would have the ability to edit the shows before the press or voters saw them. Understanding this, "Nixon quickly relaxed" and enjoyed himself for more than the planned two hours.[4] These New Hampshire events were taped without a studio audience and then broadcast as half-hour shows.[5] In reality, they served as pilots for *The Nixon Answer* during the general election campaign.

While Bob Haldeman is frequently given credit for the original idea in New Hampshire, devising how the panel shows in the fall would operate was the work of several campaign aides, including Harry Treleaven, Frank Shakespeare, Leonard Garment, and Roger Ailes. A memo by Harry Treleaven explained the basic concept of the shorter infomercials used in New Hampshire (as well as in Oregon) which were the inspiration for *The Nixon Answer* shows during the fall campaign. Treleaven gave a very elaborate description, ending with a line that critics of Nixon assumed was true about all of these shows: "Questions would be planted to make sure that the issues we want discussed would be brought up."[6] The implementation evolved from Treleaven's description, but regardless of the details, the main point never changed, and that was to allow Nixon to present an image of himself to the audience that he and his staff curated.

Much of the work of producing the longer *The Nixon Answer* panel shows was done by Ailes. But he followed a model laid out by the campaign's core group of advisers. The basic idea was explained in a memo by Treleaven. He wrote that following Labor Day the campaign would have two main objectives: (1) to present Nixon in a way that emphasized his sincerity and dispelled "negative feelings about his personality" and (2) to present Nixon's positions on the issues in "provocative and compelling ways." This would be accomplished, Treleaven wrote, in large measure with what came to be known as *The Nixon Answer*. The campaign would record shows in key states. They would open with a campaign rally atmosphere, followed by a short monologue by Nixon. The bulk of the shows would be Nixon answering questions from the panel and then there would be five or ten minutes of closing ceremonies. Treleaven wrote, "Although the programs will, of course, deal with issues, their principal objective will be to present Nixon the Man, and to surround his candidacy with excitement and enthusiasm."[7]

Roger Ailes, famous for his involvement with Fox News, was a TV producer and a political media consultant before Fox News, working for three successful presidential candidates—Richard Nixon, Ronald Reagan, and George Herbert Walker Bush. In 1968 Ailes, who was then just 28 years old, left *The Mike Douglas Show* to produce *The Nixon Answer*. There were ten scheduled panel shows to be aired in specific local markets, such as Chicago, Los Angeles, Cleveland, Detroit, Philadelphia, Boston, and New York. There was also a show produced in Atlanta that was broadcast to several Southern states. The first was done in Chicago on September 4, just a week after the tumultuous Democratic National Convention was held in that city.

The hour-long panel shows were part of a continuing revolution in campaign communication that was born of the Nixon campaign in 1968. They featured Nixon standing on a low, circular platform, with a simple background and taking questions from a panel of local people. The panelists were chosen in each city from lists of 50 to 60 names given to the Nixon campaign by local Nixon advisers.[8] They were, in each case, "a group of regional panelists of varying age, ethnic background, economic interest and political complexion."[9]

An internal campaign memo gives insight into how the panels were put together. For the Illinois *Nixon Answer*, the criteria for recruiting a group of panelists were to have six Illinois residents with no more than three from the Chicago area. They wanted three younger members, between 25 and 35, and three older members, but not much older, between 35 and 50. They wanted a mix of men and women, and they were all supposed to be "reasonably attractive," white, and middle class. The most important criteria were "they should be intelligent, articulate, well informed, and interested in current affairs." Specifically, they wanted panelists who knew something about crime and rioting, "the race problem," inflation, taxes, and the war in Vietnam.[10]

According to the Nixon campaign, the panels included Democrats and independents, as well as Republicans, and each member was "free to ask Mr. Nixon questions—not submitted in advance—on any subject."[11] A Nixon campaign memo emphasized the point that the panelists didn't have to be fans of Nixon, as long as they weren't "actually hostile." They also wanted panelists who were extroverts who would not find the television studio or cameras intimidating. They did not want anyone to freeze up. And finally, they could not be politicians or associated with the Nixon campaign.[12]

The panelists sat at small desks in front of Nixon and the audience sat in bleachers behind the panelists. There was no grievous incident of freezing up and, while there were plenty of people who clearly supported Nixon on the panels, there were also, just as clearly, people on the panels who were not Nixon fans. But that was the beauty of this set-up. It created the impression of spontaneity, but the truth was that the number of issues was limited and Nixon was able to easily turn campaign rhetoric into what seemed like easy, open answers to tough questions. There were two important characteristics of the panelists which made them different from journalists in a scrum at a campaign event: (1) the panelists were almost all worried about being polite even if they disagreed with Nixon and (2) even in situations where someone might want to press an issue, the format made it easy for Nixon to move on.

Some who have written about these panels observe that there was one group of people notably not given a role in the events: reporters. This is not completely accurate. It is true that there was no pool of press reporters in the studios shouting questions at Nixon. Reporters did not have control of the process of questioning the candidate the way they were accustomed to having it. But journalists were included on the panels. In the Southern town hall, for example, the editorial page editor of the *Atlanta Constitution*, J. Reginald "Reg" Murphy, was on the panel. Murphy was notable for his opposition to the Vietnam War, and in 1974, he was kidnapped by a man who characterized himself as a right-wing activist. *Detroit Free Press* columnist Judd Arnett was on the Detroit panel show, along with Stanley Krajewski, the editor of a Polish-language newspaper, *The Polish Daily News*. There were also two journalists on the first panel broadcast from Chicago. These were the editor of *The Moline Dispatch*, Jack Sundine, and Jack Mabley of *The Chicago American* newspaper.

As was the case with the telethon at the end of the Oregon campaign, Nixon's events were nominally moderated by Bud Wilkinson, former head coach of the Oklahoma Sooners football team and a commentator for ABC college football broadcasts, but in truth Nixon did nearly all the moderating. Nixon was introduced by Wilkinson and took it from there. Wilkinson was not really heard from again until the very end, when he would ask Nixon a question that made some sort of sports analogy. At the end of the Detroit *Nixon Answer*, for example, Wilkinson told Nixon that it was often a challenge, as a football coach, to keep his team motivated if they went into halftime with a lead. Since he had the lead in the polls, Wilkinson asked Nixon, how did he plan to keep up the energy of the campaign until Election Day? In each show, as Nixon answered Wilkinson's final question, his words served as parting remarks while patriotic music slowly swelled in the background.

McGinniss noted that Nixon's aides were troubled by Wilkinson's deficiencies as a moderator. One exchange reported by McGinniss was between Roger Ailes and the director of the show. The conversation centered on the complaint both men shared that Wilkinson was too much of a cheerleader on camera for Nixon. The show's director told Ailes that if Wilkinson was going to remain the moderator, he needed to stop applauding everything. Ailes agreed, lamenting that Wilkinson had been told this several times.[13]

Before the first *Nixon Answer* aired, several Nixon staffers were talking about a recent fundraiser broadcast by the McCarthy campaign, which raised $125,000. McCarthy was joined onscreen by actor Paul Newman. Nixon aide Ruth Jones, who was the campaign's advertising time buyer,[14] said, "It was a personal involvement pitch. Dick Goodwin wrote it for him." Frank Shakespeare responded, "We'll use the same pitch, but we don't have as strong a man." Jones asked who Nixon had. Shakespeare responded, "Bud Wilkinson."[15]

But if Wilkinson had deficiencies in the eyes of some Nixon staffers, he was chosen for his crucial role for a reason, because he was a calm, reassuring presence, there to introduce his friend, Richard Nixon, a man who he reminded the audience was respected by world leaders and millions of his fellow Americans alike.[16] Wilkinson was part of the carefully crafted image Nixon and his team wanted to portray. If Wilkinson was *too* supportive at times, in the eyes of some of the more cynical Nixon staffers, that did not matter. They were not the target audience. The audience that mattered were the people at home, watching from their living rooms. It is hard to imagine that they really would have wanted someone of a different demeanor in the role or that they would they have liked having someone with more star power than Wilkinson brought to bear on *The Nixon Answer*. Nixon had to be the star of his own show and Wilkinson facilitated that.

One characteristic of the shows which reflected Nixon's belief learned from his "crises" was that while journalists could be on the panels, the press should not be allowed to cover them. Prior to the first *Nixon Answer*, Nixon staffers debated the wisdom of excluding the press from the studio. Herb Klein was responsible for press relations for the campaign and urged that they allow a small group of perhaps three reporters to be in the studio. This idea was not well received. As McGinniss reported, Frank Shakespeare did not want any reporters interfering with his television show. Roger Ailes was even more adamant, reiterating that *The Nixon Answer* shows were not press conferences but, rather, television shows. McGinniss related a conversation between Ailes and Treleaven in which Ailes explained that 1968 was the first electronic election in history and he did not want Nixon campaign staffers to treat reporters arrogantly or rudely, perhaps by suggesting that they were not needed anymore, and cause the reporters to "get pissed and go out of their way to rap anything they consider staged for TV." Ailes felt that the surest way to generate negative press coverage was to let them attend the tapings.[17]

Each show began with an explanation from an announcer. All of them went something like this: "Tonight Richard Nixon, in person, is going to face a panel of citizens asking questions they want answered." The announcer introduced Bud Wilkinson, who explained the ground rules and introduced Nixon. In the Southern *Nixon Answer*, Wilkinson said: "Thank you and good evening. I'm pleased to play a part in this unusual television event: Richard Nixon, in a live telecast, answering questions put to him by a panel of Georgia citizens. I'd like to stress the point that the program *is* live. No one has any idea what questions will be asked. Mr. Nixon cannot possibly know. His answers must be immediate and direct, and our panel *is* representative. It includes a dairy operator, an editor, a farmer, a grocer, a lawyer, a minister and a garment textile worker. Some are Democrats, some Republicans, and some supporters of the third party. And now it is my pleasure to introduce a man that I have known, respected, and admired for many years, Richard Nixon."[18] The Southern show was produced in Atlanta but broadcast in several Southern states.

The panelists on the shows were told to ask tough questions, and some of them did, but the truth is that the environment was always highly controlled by Nixon's team. While there were different questions asked in each of the panel shows, they were frequently very similar to questions from other panels, and they allowed Nixon to simply restate parts of stump speeches he'd been giving on the campaign trail for months. For example, one subject which popped up on multiple occasions was some variation of this question from the Chicago broadcast: "Would you comment on the accusation which was made from time to time that your views (on the issues) have shifted and that they are based on expediencies?" This time, and every time he was asked a variant of this question, Nixon restated it, saying something such as "I suppose what you are referring to is: Is there a new Nixon or is there an old Nixon?" This allowed him to do something he did frequently on the stump and in these broadcasts, which was to say that Humphrey changed his positions frequently, sometimes in the same speech. Nixon would then explain that he had changed as he grew older, learning from life experience.[19]

Nixon's habit of rephrasing questions to fit prepared answers was challenged by a panelist on the Philadelphia show, a talk show host named Jack McKinney. McKinney began by asking Nixon why he was reluctant to make comments about the war in Vietnam since, during the 1952 campaign, he was very willing to make partisan comments about the war in Korea. It was a Vietnam question which Nixon was normally well prepared for. He answered that it would be inappropriate for him to say anything that could harm the ongoing negotiations of the Johnson administration. But McKinney phrased his question in a way that made it difficult for him to simply repeat a stock campaign line about the war. The question was designed to throw Nixon off his game and make him address a contradiction from his past. It was, McGinniss argued, a way of questioning Nixon that put Nixon's strategy at risk.[20] That is not to say, however, that Nixon was in any way defeated by McKinney. Nixon simply forged ahead and turned the question to answer what he wanted to answer.

When McKinney got another chance at Nixon, he did more statement *making* than question *asking*. Frustrated, he said that Nixon was asking voters to choose him without giving them real information about his views on the issues, especially the Vietnam war. What Nixon was providing instead was "nothing but a wink and a smile." Nixon again repeated the same basic non-specific statement on Vietnam he made before and the audience loved it. McGinniss wrote, "Outnumbered, two hundred forty-one to one, McKinney could do nothing but smile and shake his head."[21]

After the show, McKinney complained to reporters, saying that the show was "very slick." "I don't think you can finalize a question with an applause-getting technique. You just dissipate the questions." As McKinney complained, he referred to William Shakespeare, saying that Nixon was "splitting the ears of the groundlings."[22] The groundlings, in Shakespeare's day, when his plays were performed in the famous Globe Theatre, were the people who paid the lowest admission to stand in front of the stage, while the wealthier theatergoers sat in the seats. McKinney was, in a literary way, accusing Nixon of pandering to the gullible masses.

One reporter, E.W. Kenworthy, noted that when McKinney pointed out to Nixon, and to viewers, that Nixon simply restated campaign talking points rather than answering questions and did not allow panelists to ask follow-up questions, Nixon responded by letting McKinney ask follow-up questions. And Nixon, Kenworthy wrote, "proceeded to ride him down on every question."[23]

The basic complaint of McKinney was reasonable. Nixon gave adaptations of parts of campaign speeches as answers to the questions. Unlike reporters, most of the panelists simply did not press for the opportunity to follow up. McKinney was an extremely rare exception. It was exactly what Nixon and his team wanted: a forum where they controlled inherently unpredictable human beings as much as they could be controlled.

They were not able to control *everything*, of course. During *The Nixon Answer* program from Cleveland, Nixon found himself in a debate with a panelist who was married to a mail carrier about postal salaries, the intelligence of mail carriers, and what Nixon argued was the inefficiency of the postal service.[24] His answers did nothing to satisfy the woman, and this was not the only awkward Cleveland moment. A Black panelist said to Nixon than many Blacks were afraid of him. Struggling with a response, Nixon said, "'Well, I am not afraid of Negroes.'"[25]

But despite the occasional misstep, this candidate town hall concept was a unique and shiny object in 1968, distracting and new for voters and media alike. That largely kept it from being condemned too much. Some journalists covering the campaign praised them, even though they were designed to cut them out. One reporter for the *Washington Post*, Tom Littlewood, wrote that the shows were professionally produced and interesting. He also noted the most important thing to the Nixon team (and what would be important to future presidential candidates) was that the ratings for each show were high.[26] This kind of event has become part and parcel of political campaigning now, as candidates strive to take any chance of genuine spontaneity and unpredictability out of the process. The appearance of spontaneity is desired, but actual spontaneity, not so much. In his story about the Cleveland *Nixon Answer*, Littlewood noted that the bit of trouble Nixon got into with the postal spouse and the Black panelist reiterated for Nixon and his staff that there was nothing to be gained from the unpredictability of participating in debates with Humphrey.[27]

Nixon was good at speaking in this forum, perhaps to the surprise of many. He was at ease onstage by himself and he was often witty and engaging in repartee with members of the audience, the panelists, and the moderator Bud Wilkinson. One person who was oddly critical, perhaps trying to take more credit for the success of the forum at the expense of Nixon himself, was Roger Ailes. Speaking about the programs and Nixon, Ailes said, "Nixon is not a child of TV and he may be the only candidate who couldn't make it on the Johnny Carson show who could make it in an election."[28] Ailes's comment is both factually and substantively incorrect. Nixon could be the most stiff, uncomfortable person on earth, but he was a pioneer in the use of entertainment television such as *The Tonight Show*. He *did make it* on the Johnny Carson show. His career was, in a very real sense, reborn thanks to his ability to make it on the Johnny Carson show. Nixon may not have been "a child of TV," in the sense that he was born before the technology became a reality of modern life, but he was among the very first to adapt it for use in politics with the Checkers speech. For all his faults, Nixon often succeeded on television, both in his life as a private citizen and in several elections.

The *New York Times*' James "Scotty" Reston saw Nixon's performance on these panel shows much differently than Ailes did. He begrudgingly admired Nixon's ability in this format. In an editorial, he wrote about Nixon's media strategy during the campaign, including the panel shows. He wrote that Nixon was the most willing of all candidates to meet with reporters and speak freely but only off the record. On television, Nixon was a master at "contrived candor," as Reston saw it. He wrote that Nixon's television style was the appearance of "reckless sincerity" which was, in fact, highly controlled.[29] The panel shows exposed viewers to a relaxed, happy, and confident Nixon. Changing his image to frame a new Nixon was the plan and it succeeded greatly with *The Nixon Answer.*

FIFTEEN

Laughing-in to the White House: Comedy and the Nixon Campaign

When the television show *Laugh-In* was a hit in the late 1960s, it was seen by many critics as TV at its most McLuhan. For a few years, the rapid-fire variety show was one of the most popular television shows in the United States. The show was inspired primarily by the old traditions of vaudeville. It also was heavily influenced by the play and its movie adaptation *Hellzapoppin'*, which took great delight in breaking the "fourth wall" and allowing characters to speak directly to the audience, just as *Laugh-In*'s players would do. *Laugh-In* was on the air from 1967 through 1973, and during its second and third seasons, it was the number one show in the ratings.

The pace of each episode was very fast, moving from bit to bit so quickly that detail was impossible. In a story about the show in October of 1968, after Nixon appeared on it, producer George Schlatter called the blazing pace of the show "energy film." A review of the show described its impact on viewers. Each hour-long episode, the reviewer noted, had as many as 350 video clips, moving at such a fast pace that its effect was "almost subliminal."[1]

This left the audience to fill in the gaps, to come up with whatever meaning there might be, on their own. It was, therefore, a very "cool" show on a very "cool" medium, at least as McLuhan defined things. Again, whether McLuhan's characterization of television was correct is less important than the fact that Nixon's team *thought* he was right and were influenced by his scholarship. Key members of the Nixon team fancied themselves experts on his work and designed the campaign with it in mind.

Politically speaking, the most important thing about *Laugh-In* was the relationship between one of its staffers, Paul Keyes, and Richard

Nixon. Keyes was with the show for most of its run, first as its head writer and later as its producer. McGinniss described him, writing, "He was a big man with gray hair and rimless glasses. The kind of Republican who thought John Wayne was good for the show."[2] While playing these key roles at *Laugh-In*, Keyes frequently visited and vacationed with Nixon. The apparent closeness of their relationship was unusual for Nixon, who had few close friends.

Keyes met Nixon when Nixon appeared on *The Jack Paar Show* in 1963. Keyes was a writer and producer for Paar on the *Tonight Show* and on Paar's subsequent program, *The Jack Paar Show*, both of which played key roles in Nixon's career. When Keyes died in 2004, the obituary in the *Los Angeles Times* reported that Keyes was with Nixon watching election returns when his victory was announced in 1968 and that Keyes said he was the first person to call Nixon "Mr. President."[3] Their relationship adds even more significance to Nixon's brief but very important appearance on *Laugh-In*.

When Nixon moved to New York in 1963 to begin work as a partner in the law firm of Nixon, Mudge, Rose, Guthrie, Alexander & Mitchell, many stories were written about him and his relocation. Nixon was a fascinating character, and many wondered what he would do with the stage provided by living in New York City. Frequently mentioned in stories about Nixon in New York was Paul Keyes. One story, published shortly after Nixon moved to New York, noted a list of Nixon friends who also lived in New York, many of whom worked in the Eisenhower administration: Thomas Dewey, quarterback Frank Gifford, and Paul Keyes, Jack Paar's producer.[4]

In a piece written by journalist Robert J. Donovan[5] in the *New York Times*, it was noted that "old associates often write him suggestions for gags in speeches, and Paul Keyes, a friend and writer for the Jack Paar show, sometimes helps him put punch in these gags."[6] Donovan argued that Nixon was working on building a political base beyond California. He noted that Nixon had a humorous response to questions about his base, no doubt one that he worked on with Keyes: "'Someone suggested that I get a house trailer and move around from state to state establishing residence. Then I could pick the best one as my base for 1968. Why not? I've tried everything else.'"[7] The joke is funny, number one, and, number two, it has Nixon, in 1965, making no bones about his intentions for 1968.

The friendship of Nixon and Keyes is also reflected in brief stories that popped up in the press throughout Nixon's time in the Oval Office; in letters one of the titular characters of the show, Dan Rowan, wrote to the thriller writer John D. McDonald; and in anecdotes from a variety of other sources. For instance, in the opening chapter of his book *The Selling of the President,* Joe McGinniss described a session to make several campaign commercials in the studio where the *Merv Griffin Show* was taped. It is a story that is revealing about their relationship. Paul Keyes was a person who could help make Nixon relatable to the rest of the world.

When leaving the studio, McGinniss related, Nixon ran into an employee of the *Merv Griffin Show.* Nixon shook his hand and asked if the woman with the funny voice was still on the show. The employee was confused and Keyes, acting as Nixon whisperer, jumped in and told Nixon he was referring to Tiny Tim, a man. Everyone, including Nixon, laughed and the awkward moment was neutralized.[8] Keyes was someone who could help Nixon interact with the "regular folks" and help the "regular folks" relate to Nixon. Richard Nixon was not a man of natural humor, or warmth, or anything that might make him seem like a natural born politician. But he *knew* that about himself and he worked on it for most of his career. In Paul Keyes he found someone who could help him work on it.

Such friendships come with many benefits, and throughout Nixon's presidency, Keyes was often Nixon's guest and adviser. The obituary for Keyes in *Variety* reported that Keyes was often called on to consult with Nixon about state dinners and White House celebrations. He travelled with Nixon and Nixon friend Bebe Rebozo and was even present for an event that caught press attention when Nixon, cruising in a borrowed yacht, and his Coast Guard escort came upon a sinking sailboat in Santa Catalina harbor.[9] In describing a 1973 Nixon vacation in the Bahamas, the *New York Times* reported that Keyes travelled with Nixon and Rebozo and that Keyes was working on producing the entertainment for Nixon's White House celebration for returning POWs from Vietnam and their families.[10]

The idea for the Vietnam POW event, held as the Watergate crisis reached its crescendo, began as a suggestion from Sammy Davis, Jr., who headlined. Nixon responded with great enthusiasm, writing a lengthy memo about it.[11] But it was Keyes who took the lead role in organizing the May 23, 1973, event. Nixon wrote about it nostalgically in *RN*, noting the role that his wife Pat Nixon played in setting the theme for the night and the role that Keyes played in bringing it off, with many celebrities such as Davis and Bob Hope. Nixon concluded, "The result was a beautifully produced, tasteful, and deeply moving program that everyone who saw it will always remember."[12]

In truth, it probably was not one of Nixon's greatest nights. In describing the event in his autobiography, Nixon includes an entry from his daughter Tricia's diary that lamented what she saw as the press's unwillingness to focus on the POWs because of the ongoing Watergate scandal. But notably, even this lament included praise for Keyes. Tricia wrote that even while complaining to his family that the press covered the POW event negatively, Nixon took time to call Paul Keyes and thank him for organizing the event.[13]

Neither the event nor the call with Keyes distracted Nixon from his funk about Watergate. Tricia wrote, "After he hung up, we were all silent for a moment and then, very simply, he said to Julie and me, 'Do you think I should resign?'"[14] Although it took a few more months, Nixon did, of course, resign. By the time of the POW event at the White House, *Laugh-In* had finished its run on NBC and Nixon's political career came to end about a year later in August of 1974.

But through it all, Keyes was both a friend and an extremely valuable unpaid asset to Nixon. Bringing in help from Hollywood was not a Nixon innovation. He and his advisors had a ready example from Nixon's days in the Eisenhower administration, when actor Robert Montgomery was an asset, also unpaid, to Dwight Eisenhower for most of his presidency as a media adviser. Montgomery became involved originally at the suggestion of his fellow actor George Murphy, who went on to represent California as a Republican in the U.S. Senate.[15]

At the time of the 1952 campaign, Montgomery was the host of an anthology drama show on NBC titled *Robert Montgomery Presents*. He appeared on the campaign trail endorsing Eisenhower. He also offered advice for Eisenhower's public appearances. When Eisenhower took office, Montgomery came to the White House as an unpaid media consultant with an office in the Executive Office Building next door to the White House. Historian Craig Allen describes his contributions upon joining the administration in a voluntary capacity, noting that the actor made a strong contribution on how to produce televised FDR-style fireside chats, teaching Eisenhower and his team how make-up, lighting, and direction could vastly improve the final product. He also consulted on the building of state-of-the-art broadcast facilities at the White House.[16]

The Montgomery-Eisenhower experience proved one thing for sure: there were lessons Hollywood had to teach politicians in this new age of television. But Montgomery taught Eisenhower the basics of presenting himself for the camera. Keyes's contribution to Nixon was much more profound. Eisenhower never had a warmth problem. Nearly the entire country, almost without regard for partisan politics, regarded Eisenhower as the nation's grandfather. No one saw Nixon in such terms. Teaching camera technique is one thing. Teaching human interaction is entirely different.

Nixon's advisers in the 1968 campaign understood that one way of humanizing Nixon was with humor because it had worked well for him in the past. But Harry Treleaven knew that Nixon needed professional help coming up with material.[17] Nixon was not an improv guy. One of the pros that the campaign leaned on was Paul Keyes, Nixon's old friend from *The Jack Paar Show.*

Even if Nixon never became a natural on television, he always understood how important it was to his political fortunes. Unhappy with a television appearance early in his presidency, Nixon wrote a long memo to his chief of staff, Bob Haldeman, and demanded a full-time media adviser he could meet with before every television appearance to talk about every detail of the event and what Nixon should do.[18] Paul Keyes never became a full-time staffer, but he remained loyal to Nixon throughout his presidency, and he was as professional an adviser for television as Nixon could find.

One of the reasons that Keyes always worked for Nixon in the background was because Nixon and his staff were hesitant to have the fact that he had television advisers be public knowledge. He had many staffers and advisers who came from the media world and from advertising, but many of them only worked with Nixon if their involvement didn't become well known, including Keyes.[19]

Paul Keyes's particular knowledge and skills came into play at various crucial times in Nixon's career when he needed them most. Not the least of these was times was during the 1968 campaign. Today, when people mention *Laugh-In*, it is often about the perceived politics of the show. If polling data were available on this topic, it is likely that most people, including those who are old enough to have watched it, as well as younger people who seen clips on YouTube or on Netflix, would say that the show was quite liberal. But much of the show was not political at all. There were naughty allusions to sex and drugs that made it seem liberal, but allusions to actual politics were rare, especially when Keyes was in charge. It was an incredibly fast-paced updating and recycling of some very old vaudeville material and one of its frequently appearing guest stars was one of the country's staunchest Republicans, John Wayne.

Paul Keyes's close association with Richard Nixon and his integral role at *Laugh-In* also belies the conclusion that *Laugh-In* was a bastion of liberal comedy. It was not. Certainly, it was not liberal in the same way that *The Smothers Brothers Comedy Hour* was a liberal, anti–Vietnam War vehicle.[20] Richard Nixon's two-second appearance on *Laugh-In* during the 1968 presidential campaign is the single most famous segment from the show's five-year run and is certainly its single most impactful segment, and it was in no way liberal. But the beauty of the misperception of *Laugh-in* for Nixon is that it further expanded the impact of his appearance on the show. Not only did he look like a fun-loving guy willing to have a little humor at his own expense, but he was willing to do it on an alleged bastion of liberal politics.

The key guiding hands of any television show are always its head writer and its producer. For much of the run of *Laugh-In,* Paul Keyes was either the head writer or the producer of the show. So close was the relationship with Nixon that Keyes temporarily left the show in 1969 because he felt that there were too many Nixon jokes being made thanks to the influence of George Schlatter, the show's producer. Keyes was also frustrated with what he saw as overbearing behavior by Schlatter, with whom Rowan and Martin also frequently clashed.

Dan Rowan related Keyes's temporary resignation in a letter to novelist John D. MacDonald, writing Keyes was unhappy with the direction the show was taking. He noted that Keyes was "a very strong Nixon man" and part of the Nixon inner circle. He wrote, "For whatever humor is in that campaign, Paul is the guy who wrote it. He was the first man into the suite on election night. President Nixon calls him four or five times a week and when he's in San Clemente, Paul's always there, etc. etc." While Rowan was not a fan of Nixon, he admired Keyes's professionalism and told MacDonald than Keyes was very funny and affable and his personal views never interfered with the show.[21]

From Rowan's perspective, the show suffered—both in terms of material and in the ratings—not from Keyes's politics but from his absence. He pushed for Keyes to return. Keyes came back for the 1971 season and Rowan wrote to MacDonald that the show was getting much better because executive producer George Schlatter was being much more hands off and leaving the details to Keyes.[22] About a week later, Rowan again wrote glowingly of Keyes and the positive influence his return was having on the show's ratings.[23]

Not everyone was quite so sanguine as Rowan about Paul Keyes's politics and the effect they had on the show. Particularly outspoken was comedian Lily Tomlin who left the show because of Keyes and his relationship with Nixon and other conservatives. She was unhappy, for instance, with the number of times John Wayne was invited to appear on the show.[24] In an interview after leaving *Laugh-In,* she said, "'He's very tight with Nixon.... Paul's a nice man, but when a person's head is in a certain place, he just produces a certain result, right?'"[25] Lorne Michaels, now famous for more than 45 years of producing *Saturday Night Live,* was a writer on *Laugh-In* and he noted Keyes's relationship with Nixon as a major factor in his resignation from the show.[26] In one interview, Michaels commented on what he saw as the profound impact of having Nixon on *Laugh-In,* arguing that it changed Nixon's image, making him "a less dark figure."[27]

"Sock it to me?"

"Sock it to me" was a classic vaudeville bit. *Laugh-In* cast members and guest stars would utter the line "Sock it to me!" and they would be doused with water, or fall through a hole in the floor, or get hit in the face a pie, or something equally unpleasant. Sometimes multiple things happened after saying the line. The idea Keyes had was for Nixon to say the line on the show but with a twist.

Nixon's two-second appearance on *Laugh-In* was broadcast on September 16, 1968. Nixon did not appear in-studio. He was recorded uttering his famous lines backstage before a speech delivered in the Los Angeles area. On the show, just before Nixon appears, cast member Judy Carne gets it "socked" to her several times. On many episodes, Carne was "tricked" into uttering the famous phrase and always suffered abuse consequently. On this episode, Carne got hit by a clock, dropped through a trapdoor, squirted by a skunk, hit by dozens of ping pong balls, her dress ripped off leaving her in a slip, hit on the head with scenery, and doused with water. She then crawled over to a buzzing telephone switchboard and answered a call. Carne said, "NBC. Beautiful downtown Burbank. Oh! Hello, Mr. Rockefeller! Oh no, I don't think we could get Mr. Nixon to stand still for a 'Sock it to me.'"

At this point, Nixon appeared on screen, looking to the right. He turned his head to face the camera and said, with a look of surprise, "Sock it to *me*?" Turning it into a skeptical question instead of making a demand, Nixon created the most famous moment of the entire five-year run of *Laugh-In*. The moment is famous because of the sheer number of times it has been viewed and because of the popular perception that the appearance made a difference in the outcome of the election. Anyone can watch it on demand on YouTube today, but one of the first replays came notably as a re-run of Nixon's episode, broadcast on the night of his inauguration on January 20, 1969.[28]

Reporter Joan Barthel, in a long *New York Times Magazine* piece about *Laugh-In*, wrote that Nixon's appearance got the show's new season off to a "spectacular, perhaps even a historic start."[29] Foremost in the minds of many, including the reporter Barthel, was whether it was appropriate for Nixon to appear on the show. Barthel quoted co-host Dick Martin as saying, "The network said, 'But what if he becomes *President*?' Martin recalls. They were scared to death. We said, 'So what?'" The inherent concern was not about unintentionally helping Nixon win the presidency, but that it would be unseemly for a president of the United States, or even a candidate for that office, to appear on a nationally broadcast comedy show. But being shocked about such a thing, Barthel argued, meant being out of touch with modern society.[30] She noted that the fact that Nixon appeared on the show was merely a testament to how strong its ratings were and how far its pop culture reach was. No other primetime show had attracted a presidential candidate before because no other show had the same reach.[31]

It has become conventional wisdom today that the appearance helped Nixon but, curiously, in the two most famous books written about the 1968 campaign, McGinniss's *The Selling of the President 1968* and Theodore White's *The Making of the President 1968*, there is no direct reference to the *Laugh-In* appearance, although Keyes's role in the Nixon campaign is frequently discussed. Neither Nixon's, nor Humphrey's, autobiographies make any mention of the show or Nixon's appearance on it, although Humphrey is widely reported to have said that he felt, in retrospect, that his refusal to appear on *Laugh-In* cost him the election.

In a documentary, Dick Martin and producer George Schlatter recollected Nixon's appearance and Paul Keyes's role in it:

MARTIN: Nixon loved to be funny.

SCHLATTER: He would do anything to get elected and Paul Keyes convinced him that it was good for his image to appear in the midst of this kind of avalanche, this kind of, uh, tsunami of youth and vitality.

MARTIN: He is not president of the United States yet. He is running for president. That's what he was doing there.

SCHLATTER: His press people were saying, "No, you can't do this, you can't do that." In the meantime, we went over and I said, "Just say 'Sock it to me.'" "Yeah, all right, ready, ready? Okay. Sock it to me." "No, no, Mr. Nixon, that sounds too intense." "Yes, yes. I'm new at this comedy business." We did six takes 'til we finally got the one that we used on the air.... It shook up everybody."[32]

Reporter Elizabeth Kolbert, upon seeing the Nixon *Laugh-In* clip at the Museum of Television and Radio, contacted George Schlatter to discuss it. He made similar comments to her as those he made for the documentary. Schlatter told Kolbert that despite the urging of Keyes and multiple requests from *Laugh-In* producers, Nixon and the rest of his aides were very reluctant to have Nixon do the show. But Schlatter and Keyes showed up at one of Nixon's appearances in Los Angeles with a camera crew and got Nixon to utter the four-word phrase, convincing him in the moment that it would be crucial to furthering his career. Schlatter said it took six takes because they all sounded angry. That is hard to verify, of course, and Schlatter made it very clear in many interviews that he was no fan of Nixon. Schlatter added that they left quickly before Nixon could change his mind.[33]

In another interview, Schlatter said that the NBC Standards and

Practices officials, those charged with censoring material that could get the show in trouble, were worried that having Nixon appear would trigger the equal time rule. Schlatter said they successfully argued that it was a non-political appearance that last less than five seconds.[34] In addition, Humphrey was also invited to appear on the show but refused.

From Schlatter's description in multiple interviews, Nixon's appearance on *Laugh-In* was the consequence of a kind of guerrilla filmmaking driven by Paul Keyes's feeling that it would be a good thing for Nixon to do.[35] They came in, they shot Nixon saying the line, and they got out before anyone could get Nixon to reconsider. Nixon may well have reconsidered. It could explain why he did not refer to it in his autobiography. But he used the line "Sock it to me" repeatedly during the rest of the campaign, making it clear that he understood the importance of his appearance on the show.[36]

Even if he and his aides were too embarrassed to talk about it, Nixon clearly understood its resonance with the public. Another famous observer of culture who saw the importance of Nixon's appearance was Dan Rowan's friend John D. MacDonald. In a letter to Rowan to ask him for a contribution to the Senate campaign of another friend, written a week after Nixon's appearance, author MacDonald wrote, "I mean, man, if you got Nixon elected by accident, how about helping me get Collins into the Senate for 6 years on purpose?"[37]

The most important question about Nixon's appearance on *Laugh-In* is "Did it make a difference in the election?" Polling from the time fails us in that no questions were asked about Nixon's appearance on the show, making it impossible to empirically test the notion. But, in a very close election, decided by about 512,000 votes, the appearance could well have helped Nixon. It is impossible to say it was a decision maker, but it is also not implausible to argue that a small but decisive percentage of voters were influenced to vote for Nixon because of his appearance and the coverage and discussion it generated. After all, 512,000 votes are only .7 percent of the total 73 million votes cast in the election. It is not unreasonable to think that less than 1 percent of voters might have been influenced to reassess their view of Nixon by such a high-profile event.

Hubert Humphrey never appeared on the show, though Schlatter wanted him to. As entertainment reporter Army Archerd related in a story about his interview with Schlatter, the producers of *Laugh-In* not only invited Humphrey multiple times to appear on the show, but they also invited him to be on the same show as Nixon, responding to Nixon's "Sock it to me" with "What a good idea!"[38] Humphrey declined and this was, apparently, a matter of regret for both Humphrey and Schlatter.

In her chronicling of the Nixon *Laugh-In* experience, Elizabeth

Kolbert writes that Schlatter said that after Nixon appeared, they continued to pursue Humphrey, trying to get him to say, "I'll sock it to you, Dick!" for the cameras. Kolbert quoted Schlatter who said, "'And Humphrey later said that not doing it may have cost him the election. We didn't realize how effective it was going to be. But there were other factors in the election, too—I can't take all the blame.'"[39] It is intriguing to think that Humphrey may have said what Schlatter claims, but we have only Schlatter's word on that at this point—again, Humphrey certainly made no mention of it in his memoir.

Nevertheless, the story of Humphrey's lament persists. It was Schlatter's claims about Humphrey's regret about not appearing on *Laugh-In* that journalist Rick Perlstein used in his recent book *Nixonland* as his source for his assertion that Humphrey regretted not appearing on the show. He noted that as soon as Nixon's aides saw the show, they realized it allowed Nixon to grab some of Humphrey's claim to being the cheerful candidate, the "Happy Warrior." Perlstein wrote, "Not going on *Laugh-In* himself was one of the things Humphrey lamented cost him the election."[40]

In a way, the importance of Nixon's appearance on *Laugh-In* is self-fulfilling prophecy. So many people *think* it made a difference that it now continues to make a difference in the behavior of many political candidates in election after election. Whether or not the appearance prompted many people to vote for Nixon who might not otherwise have voted for him, most politicians making a serious run for the presidency and other offices now do what Nixon did because they *believe* it makes a difference.

They appear on late night talk shows and they appear on comedy programs to seem relatable and to tell jokes, often jokes at their own expense. Gerald Ford and his press secretary Ron Nessen went on the then-brand-new *Saturday Night Live* in large measure because Nixon did *Laugh-In*.[41] And the rest is history. The list of politicians who have appeared on *Saturday Night Live* alone would fill this page. In 2016, Donald Trump, who hosted *SNL* twice (once during the 2016 campaign), took a reputation built almost entirely in entertainment media all the way to the White House. So, regardless of whether Nixon's two-second appearance affected the outcome of the 1968 election—and it truly is credible to think that it affected some votes—it undoubtedly affected the behavior of many politicians since Nixon.

Nixon clearly believed in the importance of controlling his media image, and the lessons learned from the Checkers speech and his visits to entertainment TV encouraged this belief. Appearing on *Laugh-In* may not have been Richard Nixon's idea. But he ultimately made the decision to do it. No one forced him to stare at the camera and ask, quizzically, "Sock it to *me*?" No matter how much of it was consciously done, Nixon's performance was brilliant. The way he says the famous line, uttered by many other famous people by that point, was unique and funny. By making the line a question that dared them to even consider doing it, rather than the usual request to "Sock it to me," Nixon made the line his own. It was a difference maker because of the discussion it generated about Nixon being something other than the robot many thought him to be. It changed the campaign, and it did what Nixon had been working to do for more than 20 years: it helped him frame a particular image of himself and control the message.

Nixon's appearance on *Laugh-In* wasn't the final moment in the campaign. He did not appear on the show on the eve of the election. In fact, Nixon's appearance on *Laugh-In* was not even the last time *Laugh-In* played a role in the campaign. Not only did Keyes invite Nixon onto the show for his very famous two seconds, giving him a line to use on the stump for the rest of the campaign, but Rowan and Martin also campaigned for him. At a rally in Burbank, California, held at the local high school, Nixon was introduced to the crowd by none other than Dick Martin and Dan Rowan, laughing it up as Nixon took the stage. Nixon's remarks at the rally included this *Laugh-In* reference: "We're going to

Nixon socks it to them on the campaign trail in 1968.

sock it to 'em all over America!" It was a line Nixon used frequently in his speeches and television appearances.[42]

In addition, one of the most infamous campaign commercials in the era of televised commercials debuted and died during *Laugh-In*. Eight days before the election, on Monday, October 28, 1968, the Nixon campaign bought ad time during *Laugh-In* for a spot titled "Convention." The ad was made by a documentary filmmaker, Eugene S. Jones, who became famous in 1968 for a movie that took an unflinching look at the war in Vietnam called *A Face of War*. From that success, Jones and his company, ESJ Productions, Inc., went on to work for the Nixon campaign, making several documentary-style campaign ads.

Targeting the youthful demographic that watched *Laugh-In*, the ad was a mash-up of photographs and a soundtrack that featured an instrumental version of the song "Hot Time in the Old Town Tonight." It is a jarring juxtaposition of photos of people at the Democratic convention and of Hubert Humphrey happily accepting the nomination, with photos of bloody rioters in the streets, wounded soldiers and aspects of war, and victims of abject poverty. As the scene switches from the convention to the more shocking images, the music seems to get stuck, like a record needle caught in a groove. There is no narration, and it ends with a black screen and the words "This Time Vote Like Your Whole World Depended on It" and "Nixon." It was the television equivalent of portraying Humphrey as Nero fiddling while Rome burned. When it aired, NBC reported receiving roughly 200 calls complaining about it.[43]

Just as Barry Goldwater was outraged by the "Daisy" ad produced by the Johnson campaign in 1964, this ad sparked outrage from some in the press, the Humphrey campaign, and the Democratic Party.[44] For its part, the Democratic Party issued a statement condemning the ad and trashing the "dying" Nixon campaign as a distortion of Humphrey and his positions that was "beneath contempt." Noting that the ad ran during *Laugh-In*, the statement made the network, NBC, a kind of co-conspirator in modern dirty politics with Nixon. It read, "N.B.C. brought politics to its lowest depth in many years.... It is a smear in keeping with Nixon's below-the-belt reputation in politics and unworthy of a man running for the Nation's highest office."[45]

Speaking for the Nixon campaign, John Mitchell said that the ad was meant to show Humphrey's "politics of joy in contrast to the serious politics of our time" and added that it did not serve the Democrats to complain about a Nixon-Agnew campaign ad when the Humphrey campaign was showing so many "distorted spots."[46] Mitchell said, "It ill behooves the Democratic National Committee to complain about this spot when compared with its media attempts to relate Richard Nixon to the atomic bomb and the vilification the Humphrey campaign has heaped on Governor Agnew."[47]

The Humphrey ad that annoyed the Nixon campaign the most was one called "Laughter," which featured a man laughing until he sputters out in a cough at the end. The visual consists of a television screen with the word "Agnew for Vice President?" Nevertheless, the Nixon campaign pulled the "Convention" ad, prompting NBC to issue a statement that read, "It is not NBC's decision whether to run the commercial or not, but the Nixon-Agnew campaign committee has decided to withdraw that particular commercial from all future broadcasts."[48]

An editorial in the *Washington Post* took very clear note of the fact that the spot aired during *Laugh-In*. In the column titled "A Very Sick Joke," the editors picked up on a *Time Magazine* cover story about *Laugh-In* published on October 11, 1968, in which George Schlatter called the show's style an "energy film." The editors wrote, "The way the Nixon-Agnew crowd handle 'energy film' we doubt that anything went over anybody's head or that anybody was left saying 'Humph.'"[49]

The editorial continued, arguing that the Humphrey side was also guilty of being "increasingly blunt," and that it was "not always easy for either side to draw the line," but that it was easy to see that the Nixon "Convention" ad had crossed the line. They argued that NBC had an obligation to show more discretion in what they aired and, if the law and the First Amendment did not allow them to show that discretion, then something needed to be changed with the law. The editorial concluded with a return to the place in which it started, noting that the ad aired during *Laugh-In*: "In the meantime, the Nixon-Agnew ad men need to strike a somewhat finer line between what is fair comment, whether funny or unfunny, and what is sick."[50] The unwritten implication is "*Laugh-In* they aren't."

The Nixon campaign's ad people certainly knew what they were doing when they bought time for the spot during the number one show in the nation, which just happened to appeal to a young demographic and which just happened to have some very solid ties to the Nixon campaign. It is also noteworthy that the style of the ad is similar in style and pace, if not humor, to *Laugh-In*. It is a fast-paced ad with many cuts, going from photo to photo quickly, with the pace slowing several times to linger on shots of the war in Vietnam and photos of desperate poverty, all interwoven with a photo of a smiling Humphrey.

In the aftermath of the controversy created by the ad, there was an incident of blame shifting that pointed directly at how much the ad was inspired by the ties to *Laugh-In*. In an interview, Richard Depew, an executive from the Nixon campaign's ad firm, Fuller & Smith & Ross, said that people at his firm thought it was a terrible ad. As Depew put it, the Nixon campaign simply tried to fight fire with fire against negative Democratic ads and failed. He said, "They just plain goofed it and made a booboo. They tried a smear and it didn't work."[51] Depew asserted they tried to talk the campaign out of using it and it was the decision of Harry Treleaven, "the Nixon organization's creative consultant," to run the ad.[52] The Nixon inner-circle, of which Keyes was a key player, along with Treleaven and others, made the decision. The ad did not just run, it ran during *Laugh-In*. And *Laugh-In*, thanks to Nixon, revolutionized American politics.

There are some who write of Nixon's two-second appearance on the number one entertainment show in the country as if it were nothing more than an oddity, a curiosity. But it was much more than that. It was strategy aimed at making Nixon appear to be the things he had trouble being, namely, relatable, warm, and fun. Nothing has been the same in American politics since. Now we deal with candidates for office in every imaginable nonpolitical setting. That began with Richard Nixon in the Checkers speech and on *The Tonight Show, The Jack Paar Show, The Merv Griffin Show, Rowan and Martin's Laugh-In* and many other outlets. Nixon was not a natural entertainer. He was not a warm and fuzzy person. He was not loveable. But he knew these things about himself and worked to counteract his natural self. He also believed that the news media were not his friends, and that if he were going to change the public's perception of him, he would have to do it himself.

SIXTEEN

Working the Refs

Making use of non-traditional forms of media was not the only tactic Nixon employed in his campaign to take control of his image. Nixon also made it a practice throughout his political career to work the refs, in the form of complaining about, lecturing to, and hectoring the press *about* the press. He did it with the Checkers speech and stepped up his game with *Six Crises*, his "final" press conferences, appearances on talk shows, and in many speeches throughout the 1960s. This continued apace during the 1968 campaign. It was another part of the effort by Nixon to frame an image of himself that was acceptable to him. He did not let the news media frame him; he made his own frame, and part of that included knocking the news media down a peg or two.

Nixon Talks to the News Media About *the News Media*

Many historians and reporters have written about the fact that Nixon talked to a lot of reporters during the campaign in 1968, but when he did so, it was frequently under the condition of being off the record. At the end of the campaign, however, Nixon made three very high-profile media appearances, and in all three, he made complaining *about* the news media a major part of the agenda.

60 Minutes

The news magazine show which invented the news magazine format is *60 Minutes*. It has been on the air for more than 50 seasons. It premiered in October of 1968 and Richard Nixon was on the second episode (Humphrey was on the third). Nixon, interviewed by Mike Wallace in Nixon's New York apartment, spoke about nothing as explicitly as he did the news media. Wallace's questions, in fact, opened the door for Nixon to reiterate many of the things he wrote about in *Six Crises*.

The story began with an introduction of Nixon by Mike Wallace. Wallace said that no one, especially a politician, likes to admit errors, but that Nixon candidly admitted many errors made during the 1960 campaign, including debating with Kennedy; pledging to campaign in all 50 states; delegating too much control of his own campaign to others; and allowing a "wall of suspicion" to grow between him and the news media in which he came to fear and avoid them. The *60 Minutes* interview, Wallace promised, would cover Nixon's relations with the press and other things he rarely spoke about on the campaign trail.

There is a lot to consider in this introduction. Wallace said Nixon feared and hid from the press in 1960, but the reality is that he was *still* avoiding the press in 1968. The thing that was different was that he managed to find ways to make it *appear* that he was open to the press, while managing to impose as much control over that exposure as he could. The interview with Wallace was a case in point, and he had a very clear agenda in mind when he did so.

The first subject Nixon addressed in the story was the press. Nixon began with Wallace's promised assessment of his faults, saying he was not as effective handling the press in 1960 as he should have been and admitting Kennedy did a better job. He added that in 1968 he discovered the tougher the questions were, the better he did. His bad answers came in response to "one of those patsies" people asked to try to help him. He concluded, "So, as far as I'm concerned, I think that the best answer to the handling of the press is not to withdraw, but the answer is, 'Well, come on, fellas, give it to me. Sock it to me! And see what I can do in return.'"

Nixon *did* speak to a lot of reporters during the campaign but, again, it was frequently on an off-the-record basis. Second, it is easy to see here how much Nixon thought his appearance on *Laugh-In* mattered. This was not an interview on a nighttime talk show, but Nixon was sure to get the punch line across anyway. Third, the toughest questioning Nixon endured during the campaign was about his own personality, which was exactly why he did television shows such as *The Tonight Show* and *Laugh-In*.

Next, Mike Wallace did the same thing David Susskind did nearly a year before, asking Nixon how he could get elected if people did not really like him. He began with a question that made Nixon relive the 1960 campaign, asking him if he had been overwhelmed by Kennedy's glamour. Nixon, with an expression of vague annoyance, denied being overwhelmed by glamour. He said, "I think everyone tries to rewrite history in terms of what the book should read, but while I do not have money and, perhaps while I am not blessed with particular social grace, I have a confidence that comes from a different source. I fought my way up all the way." Nixon said pointedly that he did not mean to imply that someone who did not have to struggle could not be a success but having to struggle builds character and when you must struggle, you are not in awe of anyone—or their glamour.

The answer was partly Nixon's attempt to do what he did 16 years before in the Checkers speech when he tried to put the picture of Abraham Lincoln in people's minds next to their image of Nixon: to show that he was a fighter of humble means who pulled himself up by his own bootstraps. But the *first* thing Nixon said in response to Wallace's question was that the people who wrote the story of *his* campaign against JFK—both the press and historians—had their own, not necessarily accurate, version of history. It was less angry, but substantively the same as what he said in his "final" press conference in 1962. And he, Richard Nixon, was going to set the record straight, just as he did when he wrote *Six Crises*.

Then Wallace got to the question of Nixon's personality. He told Nixon that neither Nixon nor Humphrey had much charisma and asked, "Have you given no thought to this aspect of campaigning and of leading?" Nixon did not try a laugh line here. Instead, he suggested that the country did not need a showman but a real leader. Being loved is not the same as being what the country really needs. His allusions to Kennedy were not at all subtle. He said, "Well, when style and charisma connote the idea of, uh, contriving, of public relations, I don't buy it at all."

Looking back through history, Nixon said, many of the people we think of as great leaders would be terrible television personalities. That did not keep them from being excellent presidents. They were excellent because of their beliefs, character, and courage. He told Wallace that he wanted to win the election, and if he did, he was going to be president in a way that earned the respect of the American people which would give him the tools he needed to lead. Some leaders are destined to be loved and others are destined to be disliked, Nixon said. And then, Nixon uttered one of his most famous lines. It is a clip that is played over and over because of Watergate.

Having a lot of charisma, looking like a matinee idol, and being good with public relations did not make a person a leader. If people wanted a showman, Nixon was not their guy. He said, "But the most important thing about a public man is not whether he's loved, or disliked, but whether he is respected. And I hope to restore respect to the presidency, at all levels, by my conduct." It is certainly true that, with the benefit of hindsight, Nixon's argument that he would bring respect back to the presidency dramatically missed the mark. But Watergate was in the future and he wanted viewers to see what he saw: the substance-less glamour of the Kennedy White

House and the corruption and chaos of the Johnson administration. To what he believed was a silent segment of the population that was simply exhausted and looking for something calmer, it was a perfectly rational and effective line to utter. He was saying, "You've had the show biz and the agent of chaos, now let's get down to business."

Wallace next drew from the David Susskind playbook, using the very same word Susskind used, telling Nixon that his name was anathema to millions of people who saw him merely as an unprincipled political opportunist. He admitted there were some who considered him anathema because of his 22-year "hard political career." But Nixon asserted he had the leadership ability to earn the respect, if not the love, of those who "have a very bad picture of Richard Nixon." Once again, Nixon is saying something like "Well, we've had the popular boy and look where it's gotten us. How about if we try someone who is a little more serious about hard work now?" For Nixon, as always, this interview was about framing himself to the American people. In this forum, the frame was of an experienced problem-solver, not a rah-rah pretty boy. In the same answer, Nixon also dismissed another commonly raised issue, mentioned by Mike Wallace: the possibility that the presence of George Wallace in the race would prevent Nixon from getting a majority of Electoral College votes and sending the election to the House of Representatives where Humphrey had an advantage.

Still working on the idea that there were plenty of Americans who did not like or trust Nixon, Wallace opened the door to another chapter from *Six Crises* when he asked Nixon if there was anything he would change if he could do his career over again, especially from the late 1940s or early 1950s, when he built his career as a hawk against communism and communists. Nixon shook his head and responded first by saying that he wasn't going to worry about the past and address the critics from the '40s, '50s, or even the '60s. He was able to take the criticism, he asserted, and he respected the right of people to have different views from his. After dismissing the question, Nixon then reframed it entirely.

If Wallace intended for him to talk about possible excesses in the days of the Red Scare, Nixon was not going to cooperate. He reframed the question to a broader analysis of his full career in politics. Nixon said that he insisted he be judged on issues, not personality. A politician should be judged by what they have done and said in their public career. Opponents have the right to attack anything someone has done in that career. Nixon had attacked and been attacked, he said, and he made no apologies for presenting his case as well as he could. If you do not like me, Nixon seemed to suggest, it is perhaps because I am not as smooth a talker as some people. But you should not hate the message because the messenger is not a smooth talker. Again, he was framing the image of someone who is focused on results, not on *image*. Of course, creating an image of not worrying about image *was* an exercise in building an image.

Mike Wallace asked again if Nixon was sure he had no regrets. If he was fishing for Red Scare regrets, Nixon did not take the bait. Instead, he took the question as one about campaign style and gave an answer about his first campaign for the presidency without admitting he made mistakes. Nixon told Wallace he was a good self-critic and that he certainly *must* have made many mistakes over the years. The key was learning from mistakes because that helps you become a better person. And that meant, Nixon said, "I think, for example, I'm a much better candidate in 1968 than I was in 1960." Wallace interrupted with a one-word question: "Why?" Nixon gave an answer he used many times during the campaign, including during his appearance on *The Merv Griffin Show*. He said that he was physically older, with less hair and bigger jowls, but he was a new answer to the problems of the world. If he did not have new solutions to the problems of the world and the country, then he was not a worthy candidate. Of course, he did feel he had solutions to offer. Nixon did a lot here. First, he gave viewers a little bit of the self-effacing humor that people love in their leaders, making fun of his jowls and his hairline. He was working on the image of the everyman. Then, once again, Nixon said people like Mike Wallace can say he is anathema if they want, but let's vote and see if that is true. He was the one with the blueprint for restoring American greatness. It was up to the voters to realize that.

Although Nixon had already addressed the 1960 campaign in his own way, raising the issue when he did not want to talk about the Red Scare, Wallace still had another question to ask about the 1960 campaign. Did Nixon think, Wallace asked, that he was too successful, too soon in his political career, having only served in Congress for six years before running for vice president at the age of 39? The implication was that too much success had somehow harmed Nixon when he ran for president. But it ignored the fact that Nixon had served eight years as vice president and that Kennedy's rise was just as sudden as Nixon's. It was a strange question, but Nixon adeptly used it remind America how long he had been a prominent national leader and to once again explain why he was the right man for 1968. Wallace began the story about Nixon suggesting that Nixon was a man who realized and learned from his mistakes. However, the main takeaway is that Nixon wanted America to know that it was now ready for him. He had not really changed; America had. And now, he was saying that this time of chaos and upheaval, this time of little success in Vietnam and unrest in the streets, was Nixon's time.

It was not a confrontational interview. It was not classic Mike Wallace–*60 Minutes* ambush style. But there was an edge to Nixon that was easy for viewers to spot, and he used it to make several points he thought were important. He was ahead in the polls when he did this interview and he was determined to make sure that the people he thought were his voters got the message: there would be a new boss in town, laying down the law for the press, the protesters in the streets, and the North Vietnamese, if America voted for him. This was about framing the image. Even if you did not think Nixon was a guy you wanted to drink a beer with, he was a guy you wanted minding the store. It was exactly the kind of framing Druckman and Jacobs found Nixon and his aides tried to do while he was in office as president.

Sunday Talk Shows

In the last days of the campaign Nixon made an appearance on both *Face the Nation* and *Meet the Press* as well as a final paid TV appearance on his election eve "telethon." The news program appearances gave Nixon a chance to reiterate many of the themes of his campaign, to burnish the image of himself he crafted, and to restate, once again, his complaints about the way the news media covered him and his campaign. It was yet another airing of grievances.

On *Face the Nation*, Nixon was asked first about earlier comments on the possibility of a Johnson administration bombing halt and a cease fire in the Vietnam War as a part of ongoing negotiations in Paris to bring the war to an end. He was pressed by all the members of the panel, which included David Broder of the *Washington Post* and Martin Agronsky and John Hart of CBS News, about whether his comments, made on the campaign stump, could be seen as pulling the rug out from under LBJ in his attempts to negotiate an end to the war. Nixon denied this and pointed out that any comments he made about the possibility of a bombing halt or a cease fire were based on things he read and saw reported in the news media. In other words, he was arguing, if I am saying something wrong, it is because you are reporting it wrong.

After several minutes of back and forth on Vietnam, Martin Agronsky served up a golden opportunity for Nixon to rail against one institution of the press which has remained a target for politicians ever since: the *New York Times*. On October 20, the *Times* editorial board published a column that was both an endorsement of Edmund Muskie for vice president and a denunciation of Spiro Agnew. It compared the men, pointing out that neither was well-known before being nominated, both came from immigrant families, both worked their way up from humble means, and both succeeded as opposition party governors who successfully advocated for progressive legislation. But that, the editorial continued, was where the similarities ended. Agnew, it asserted, abandoned his liberal Maryland image to become a "law and order" man who "cracked down hard on civil rights demonstrators," whereas Muskie was "one of the Senate's most skillful legislators, a pragmatist who worked quietly and persistently for liberal goals."[1]

The editorial called Agnew "rash, maladroit, insensitive to the deeper problems afflicting the nation and quick to exploit public prejudices for political gain."[2] Muskie, on the other hand, was "a leader of moderation, taste and sensitivity, a man of character who attacks problems, not people."[3] The final judgment issued in the editorial was that Muskie's behavior showed he was ready to be president and Agnew's did not.[4] The conclusion was unambiguous: Agnew was not fit for a position a heartbeat away from the Oval Office.

Then, on October 26, the day before Nixon's appearance on *Face the Nation*, the *New York Times* published another negative editorial about Agnew. On *Face the Nation,* Martin Agronsky asked Nixon about the second editorial. The editorial, titled "Mr. Agnew's Fitness," was short and to the point. It raised questions about Agnew's actions as the chief executive of Baltimore County, as a member of the Baltimore zoning board, and as the governor of Maryland, suggesting that Agnew benefited financially in return for helping business interests.

Hubert Humphrey (left) and Edmund Muskie at the 1968 Democratic Convention.

The editorial argued that Agnew approved the route for a new road after a group he was part of bought the land the route would be built on. It also asserted that Agnew was involved with a Maryland bank that raised many conflicts of interest since Agnew was ultimately in charge of the enforcement of state banking laws. The editorial further argued that Agnew lied about how he acquired his interest in this bank. But it was not just corruption that disqualified him, according to the editorial. It concluded, "In his obtuse behavior as a public official in Maryland as well as in his egregious comments in this campaign, Mr. Agnew has demonstrated that he is not fit to stand one step away from the Presidency."[5]

Nixon took the opportunity on *Face the Nation* to unload on the *New York Times* and, indirectly, on the assembled journalists for raising the issue. After saying he would not need long to refute the *Times*, he proceeded to spend several minutes on the issue. First, he called the *New York Times* a great newspaper and pointed out that panelist David Broder once worked for the *Times*. Niceties delivered, he reminded viewers of the *Times'* top of the page motto, "All the News that's fit to print," and called the paper's reporting about Agnew "the lowest kind of gutter politics that a great newspaper could possibly engage in. It is not news that's fit to print, and I'll tell you why." The allegations were old and disproven, Nixon said, and he wondered aloud if there was any communication between the newspaper's editorial and reportorial staffs. He said his campaign would be officially demanding a retraction from the *New York Times*.

But, Nixon asserted, even if the *Times* printed a retraction, it would be placed in "back with the corset ads or the classifieds, toward the end of the week when nobody will pay any attention." He continued, asking why, since the *Times* had the largest, best-paid team of reporters of any newspaper in America, it took them until the last week of the campaign to make such charges against Agnew. Nixon's implication was that they waited until the last week in the hope of affecting the outcome of the election. Nixon said that the *Times* owed the people of the United States an apology, noting that this editorial was not worthy of such a great newspaper.[6]

Nixon then launched into a defense of Agnew. He said he agreed with Agnew's approach to the "crime problem," which was a central element of Nixon's campaign. He applauded Agnew's stance in saving Baltimore from riots and agreed with Agnew's assertion that cities did not have to be burned down to rebuild them, regardless of what criticism Agnew received from civil rights advocates. Nixon said Agnew may have made some mistakes during the campaign, but all candidates made mistakes. The nation needed Agnew's strength and firmness, Nixon asserted, and "this kind of libel by the *New York Times* doesn't help the American decision-making process."

When David Broder tried to press Nixon on the details of Agnew's relationship with the Maryland bank, Nixon avoided specifics and more forcefully insisted on a retraction from the *Times*. He began with a phrase he used hundreds, maybe thousands, of times during his career, "Let me make one thing very clear," and continued, "a retraction will be demanded *legally* tomorrow, and I think it will speak for itself."[7] This launched a back and forth between Nixon, Agnew and the *Times* which lasted until the election. In 2020, Donald Trump's campaign starting threatening legal action against television stations broadcasting anti–Trump ads during the campaign. Many people responded with shock at what they characterized as an unprecedented attempt of the Trump campaign to tear apart the First Amendment. But there was nothing new about it.

Following the broadcast, the *New York Times* editors responded by reprinting the Agnew editorial, adding an introduction which stated that Richard Nixon had made serious charges against the *Times* and had demanded a retraction but that his allegations were "so imprecise" it was impossible to tell what he wanted the newspaper to retract. The introduction continued, noting that Agnew also responded to the editorial and that his statement would be published in the *Times* along with a response to Agnew's response. The editorial then offered a response to Nixon's charge that the editorial staff of the *Times* apparently paid no attention to the work of the *Times* news staff with a statement which read that the *Times* editorial was based on *Times* reporting from four days before the editorial was published. The story was, indeed, published in the *New York Times* on October 22. It was not an accusatory piece of newswriting but, rather, one which suggested that there were several unanswered questions about Agnew and his business dealings.[8]

Following the reprinted material, the new editorial reported that the newspaper was contacted by attorneys for Nixon and Agnew. The attorneys offered an objection to just one sentence in the editorial. The editorial stated that Nixon's objection was related to the timing of Agnew's selling of his land. The editorial refuted Nixon's claims and, finally, refuted Nixon's accusation that the charges offered by the *Times* were "stale." They had been reported before, the editorial read, but concluded, "that fact makes them not one whit the less valid, nor less pertinent to a judgment on Mr. Agnew's fitness to be Vice President of the United States."[9]

James "Scotty" Reston, then serving as the executive editor of the *Times*, wrote a column which appeared in the paper on October 30. In it, Reston wrote of Nixon's longstanding attitude toward reporters, feeling that they should merely be transcribers of what politicians said and never offer interpretations of what they said, suffering from the "illusion that the press is a kind of inanimate transmission belt which should pass along anything he chooses to dump on to it."[10] Reston went on, drawing the connection inextricably between Nixon and Lyndon Johnson. He wrote that presidents have three options when dealing with the press. Best is to tell all; second best is to tell nothing; and third best was, as Reston saw it, what LBJ and Nixon did, the worst way. He wrote that their way of dealing with reporters was to "try to manipulate them, to pretend to be candid in private conversation, but to use every trick in the book to get them to fill the headlines and front pages with calculated trash."[11] Reston was wrong in his comparison of LBJ to Nixon. LBJ, as previously discussed, took a much more personal approach. Nixon tried the personal approach, but he also tried many new methods designed to close reporters out completely. But he was not wrong to criticize Nixon, who took his case to the public, over the heads of reporters, repeatedly. And there was a ready audience for it.

It is easy to close one's eyes after reading this and think not of the politics of 1968 but, rather, of the politics and tweets of 2016 and beyond. Reston observed, concluding his column, "It is easy to say that this is not a model of democratic discussion, but it is hard to say it has failed. It takes a natural, confident, experienced, and even wise man to grapple with the hard and often unfair questions of the press in public and he is apparently doing all right. Yet it is fairly clear at the end that more people are going to vote for him than believe in him, and more newspaper editors than newspaper reporters are going to endorse him." This is a scathing indictment from Reston. Nixon was successful, he argued, in putting together what seemed to be a winning electoral effort, but he did so by eschewing traditional democratic values. He had done so by attacking the press as an enemy and he had worked to convince people that they should not vote for him so much as they should vote against the other guy. He created the appearance of openness to questions but controlled every aspect of the environment in which the questions were asked.

Scotty Reston was more than experienced with churlish politicians. He had dealt with the slings and arrows of LBJ from the White House for five years at this point. But LBJ's attacks were more personal and less systematic. Reston's words "not a model of democratic discussion" were both descriptive and prophetic. They described what Nixon had done and they were prophetic in that Nixon created a blueprint for those who came after him. And so many have followed it.

John Mitchell, the manager of Nixon's campaign, responded to Reston's column, complaining that Reston was making "another demonstrably false charge against the Republican ticket" and demanded another retraction. Reston did not back down in the face of this criticism. To Mitchell, he responded, referring to Nixon's panel show, "I think Mr. Mitchell has a fair but limited point. My column gave the impression that all questions put to Mr. Nixon on television were carefully selected. That is not true. On television, his aides select the questioners.... But the main point I was trying to make was that he usually operates in a controlled situation, giving the impression of complete candor which, in my view, is misleading."[12]

The *Times* editorial responding to Nixon's attack from the set of *Face the Nation* created a firestorm of reaction from both Nixon and Agnew and their supporters. Agnew's campaign chief of staff, George W. White, said he would recommend that the campaign file a lawsuit against the newspaper. Agnew said he would wait to see how planned meetings between campaign attorneys and the *Times* went before he decided if his chief of staff was correct, adding, "I'm not the kind of person who goes around looking for every imagined grievance."[13] When the Nixon administration began, this would turn out to be as false a statement as one could imagine. Nixon had already established a clear strategy of never letting any grievance, real or imagined, go unanswered.

The *Times* editorial prompted other newspapers and journalists to weigh in with their own opinions. One appeared in the *Washington Post* which questioned the *Times*' editorial, and the Nixon campaign jumped on it, with Agnew suggesting that it gave him even further grounds for suing the *Times* for libel. Agnew said that the *Post*'s editors "make me think I ought to look at the possibilities of a lawsuit." But while the *Post* criticized the *Times*' journalistic methods, the *Post* editorial was far from complimentary, or vindicating, of Agnew. The editorial concluded that it was poor timing so late in the campaign for the *Times* to raise these charges and that the charges did not raise serious questions about Agnew's fitness for office. And this, the *Post* editorial asserted, was unfortunate because they distracted from other, more serious, aspects of Agnew's record which could be disqualifying. The *Post* editorial promised that the *Post* would be focusing on these more serious things in the coming days.[14]

Washington Post columnist Joseph Kraft concluded of Nixon's attack on the *Times* that it was understandable Nixon would want to refute the *Times*' accusations. However, Kraft found it disturbing that Nixon used such over-the-top terms as "gutter politics" to describe the reporting and that he seemed to take great personal joy in attacking the *New York Times*.[15] But publicly attacking organs of the press had been part of Nixon's pioneering strategy for years and would only evolve as he became president, escalating to an all-out war on the press, characterizing journalists as purveyors of mistruth in the name of taking down the president.

Agnew stepped up his criticism of the *Times* after the newspaper reprinted the editorial as part of its response to Nixon's comments. In a speech in Virginia on October 29, Agnew said the *Times* was responsible for "the major blooper in the campaign." He complained that the news media want politicians to admit when they made mistakes. Agnew said he was happy to admit his errors. But it was not fair, Agnew argued, that newspapers did not admit when they made mistakes. He concluded, "I say to the editorial board of the *Times*: Act with decency, act like men, act with intellectual honesty, let in the fresh air."[16]

In addition, the Nixon campaign issued a statement which reiterated the accusation that the *Times* was engaging in gutter politics by first printing and then reprinting its "false and libelous editorial" rather than correcting the record as its editors promised. Instead, the Nixon statement read, "they have now published two separate and distinct libels." The statement questioned the intelligence of the editorial staff and asserted that all the charges listed against Agnew were incorrect and uncorroborated by any evidence. The paper was, the campaign asserted, acting with "wanton, reckless disregard" for Agnew's reputation. It accused the *Times* of arrogance. It asserted that the newspaper was in violation of the journalistic code of ethics by refusing to report the news fairly and impartially. Instead, it was acting in a partisan way, supporting its favored candidate, Hubert Humphrey. The *Times* had many fine reporters, the statement lamented, who must be very disturbed by the recklessness of the editorial staff.[17]

The *Times* responded to the aggression of the Nixon-Agnew campaign with another editorial, this time titled "Mr. Agnew's Unfitness." In it, the editorial board rejected the charge that it was being libelous and argued that Agnew's own statement, published in full by the *Times*, did nothing to vindicate him and only highlighted his inability to understand the ethical demands of a position of public trust. After reviewing what they saw as many conflicts of interest, the authors of the editorial concluded, "unequivocally," that it would be very unfortunate for someone of lax ethical standards like Agnew to become vice president. Agnew's self-defense and denials of undeniable conflicts of interest only showed more clearly that he was not qualified to be "one step away from the Presidency of the United States."[18]

The *Washington Post* kept its promise and published an Agnew editorial in the November 1 issue. The editorial took Nixon to task for choosing Agnew as his running mate. They quoted Nixon's criteria for choosing Agnew: "'(1) qualified to be President, (2) an effective campaigner, (3) an administrator who could assume new responsibilities for the office of Vice President.'" After assessing Agnew to be a "competent state official, no more and no less," the editorial addressed Agnew's record as a vice presidential candidate and concluded that Agnew completely failed to meet the first criterion, which was that he was ready to assume the presidency at a moment's notice. The *Post*'s editorial argued that Agnew's campaign had been almost nothing but lies and innuendo about Hubert Humphrey and "grotesque failures of judgment." They also criticized his policy proposals on issues like law and order as ineffective because they did nothing to address the factors which cause crime.[19] This added up, as the *Post* editors saw it, to someone who was not ready to be president if that became necessary. Nothing Agnew had done, the *Post*'s editors concluded, should make voters comfortable he was ready to be president.[20]

Because it is a well-accepted bit of political wisdom that very few people base their voting decisions on the vice-presidential nominee, the *Post* added a couple of final paragraphs, suggesting that the choice of Agnew, such an unqualified man, as his running mate should be a reason to question Nixon's decision making "under heavy pressure." This should be something voters kept in mind when deciding whether to vote for Nixon.[21] If Nixon flubbed this decision so badly, the *Post* asked, what else might he do from the Oval Office?

On November 2, the *Times* published a lengthy column rebutting the accusations made against the paper by Agnew and his supporters. The column offered a review, point by point, of what were characterized as several "unclear" points in the "dispute" between the newspaper and Agnew. In each of the three points, the column noted clarifications of the record but concluded in each case with the judgment that Agnew had, in some way, still misstated the true record. It also suggested that Agnew's campaign should go ahead and file a libel suit against the paper if they felt justified, rather than simply talking about it, as Agnew's chief of staff, George White, continued to do.[22] Agnew did not file a libel suit against the *New York Times*. What he did instead was to take out a full-page ad, paid for by the Nixon-Agnew campaign, in the *Times* the day before the election. The ad was titled with a play on words, "The Truth Hurts at *Times*," and took the newspaper to task for its criticism of him. It was paid for by the Nixon-Agnew campaign committee.[23] The ad was arranged in three columns. The first column repeatedly used the phrase "the truth," in bold print to show how the *Times* got the facts about Agnew wrong. The middle column contained quotes from four newspapers, the *St. Louis Globe-Democrat*; the *Washington Post*; the *Baltimore Sun*; and the *Washington Evening Star*, which the ad claimed were critical of the *Times*' statements about Agnew. The third column argued that "even Democrats" found the *Times*' position on Agnew offensive and reiterated earlier arguments made by Agnew that the *Times* previously endorsed him for governor and that now the *Times* was "trying to twist the old facts to give them new meaning."[24] The ad's final line was "In their search for truth, men must rise above the *Times*."[25]

The *New York Times* responded with an editorial published the same day as the ad. It began with a line that could have easily been published in the political climate of 2016 or 2020. But it was not. It was published in 1968, about a campaign that is, in many ways, the prototype for the campaigns that followed, right up to 2016 and 2020. It read:

> In an advertisement attacking *The Times* today, the forces behind Gov. Spiro T. Agnew carry to its climax in this campaign one of the oldest of political strategies: When criticized, deny everything, cry "Foul," capitalize on a posture of injured innocence and denounce your critic in the wildest terms.[26]

The editors wrote that Nixon set this course for the campaign and Agnew continued, posturing as an "innocent victim" of an aggressive, unfair attack by the press. The editorial asserted that it had been forced to return, continually, to questions of Agnew's fitness for the vice presidency due to the Nixon-Agnew campaign's continued statements about the editorial. Thanks to the advertisement, which the *Times* referred to as "renewed misrepresentations," the newspaper was obliged to "discuss this distasteful subject once again." The editorial then detailed several "misrepresentations" made by Agnew about his record, following each with "the facts."

After dissecting three examples, the *Times* concluded that there were several other questionable things in Agnew's advertisement, but they felt enough had been done to expose "the misleading character of Mr. Agnew's denials, which have been fully published in *The Times*." The editorial was unrelenting in its assertion that Agnew was not fit to be vice president, arguing that Agnew's continued denial of wrongdoing and an apparent lack of understanding that he did anything wrong proved him inadequate to the job of vice president and to being one step away from the presidency.[27]

The Nixon campaign made a deliberate decision to pick a fight with the *Times*, drawing national attention, on television, to something most people would never see. And then they carried that fight on for days. It can only be understood as a rational choice if it is seen as a deliberate decision to make the press an opponent in the election. This motive was clear in the comments made by Harry Treleaven to Len Garment on the day the ad ran in the *Times*. The ad was put together by Treleaven. Of it, he said, "It was something Nixon himself wanted done. And even if it doesn't get us any votes, it's worth it just for the fun of hitting those guys."[28] But Nixon *did believe* it would get him votes. In the television age, Nixon used an attack, begun on television, to carry a fight with the press all the way to Election Day.

Meet the Press

The week after the *Face the Nation* appearance, Nixon was on *Meet the Press*. It was to be the last time he exposed himself to reporters, something

he did infrequently during this campaign, and it was hoped to go even bet
ter than the *Face the Nation* appearance. His staffers thought the Agnew
stuff went just fine. What they *did* care about from the appearance on CBS
was image related. They were unhappy with was how Nixon was situated
on the *Face the Nation* set. Nixon aide Al Scott said, "The camera height
was wrong. I didn't like the chair, and there was a bad shot of the back of
his head which made it look like he had a point there."[29]

With *Meet the Press*, the team hoped for a better set-up. Al Scott
promised it would be better, saying he had connections at NBC and he
could get things set up with the producer of the show.[30] The arrangement
on-set was much more to their liking. In addition, most of the questions
asked were easy for Nixon to answer.

As with *Face the Nation*, the topic of the first segment of the program
was the bombing pause in Vietnam, which LBJ announced in a speech
to the nation on October 31. The bombing pause took effect on Friday,
November 1. Nixon was asked by panelist Herb Kaplow if he thought the
bombing pause had been made to assist the Humphrey campaign. Nixon
rather artfully took advantage of this opportunity with a classic "people
are saying" response that did not actually refer to anyone who was saying
it. It is a tactic that became an almost everyday occurrence in the Donald
Trump presidency.

Nixon said that he personally did not believe that was true but added
that many people did think it was done to help Humphrey. Kaplow followed up, asking Nixon about his supporters who continued to argue
the bombing pause was a political stunt. Nixon reiterated that he did not
agree, while also suggesting he was not sure the pause was a great idea and
concluding that all that really mattered was getting all sides to the peace
negotiations.

Pressing, Kaplow asked Nixon if the statements made by Nixon supporters were contrary to the "spirit of cooperation" Nixon was personally
expressing. Nixon took this question as an opportunity to criticize the
Humphrey campaign as being "gleeful" about the bombing pause. He took
care to exempt Humphrey himself, but despite his previously uttered faith
in LBJ, he said, "We have made it clear that the bombing halt was politically motivated."

After a commercial break, panelist Vermont Royster, the editorial
page editor of the *Wall St. Journal*, took over the questioning and served
up a softball for Nixon, mentioning that Nixon spoke on the campaign
trail, and on *60 Minutes*, about the need to restore people's respect in government. Royster wanted to know why Nixon was the man for that job.

Nixon, a man who was the vice president of the United States in the
1950s, who made his name in politics at the height of the Red Scare, and

who was just a year and a half younger than Humphrey, said that the first reason was that Humphrey was a man *of* the past, who was trapped *in* the past. As such, Humphrey would not be able to restore respect in government. It was an artful reversal of the same things that were said about Nixon in 1960. Even though he and JFK were essentially the same age, it was Nixon who was seen as an artifact because he had spent the last eight years in the Eisenhower administration. Humphrey, similarly, was in the spotlight for four years as LBJ's vice president, while Nixon spent the time travelling the country, speaking to adoring crowds, and making entertainment TV appearances.

Royster trod additional familiar ground for Nixon when he asked Nixon how he would deal with the fact that, even if he won the election, he would be faced by "a large and vocal minority who will be very critical of you, who are very critical of you now." Nixon responded that he was aware of the country's racial and generation gaps. But, Nixon insisted, he was a good listener, and he would be able to build positive relations with "dissident" groups.

Royster then asked a question that was tailor-made to allow Nixon a chance to reiterate his entire campaign strategy: he was in control of his message, his audience was the adults of America, and he was going to be tough (but fair) with youthful protesters. Royster asked Nixon about the troubles of governing a place like New York City, even though it was led by a charismatic Republican mayor "who *does* communicate with the people," John Lindsay. Royster wondered if it was tough to run a city, why wouldn't it be all but impossible for Nixon to run the country. Implied in the question was that unlike Lindsay, Nixon was neither charismatic nor a good communicator. Nixon said he knew it was going to be a tough job and then he spoke, as he did on *60 Minutes*, to the issue of charisma. Nixon acknowledged he was not terribly charismatic. However, while Nixon respected people who emphasized charisma's importance, he felt action was more important than charisma and rhetoric. He said that in talking to "Black Nationalist" leaders and "student dissidents," he found that they did not want rhetoric and "over-promising." They did not want people "*taking them on a mountaintop*" and making promises that could never be kept. Instead, Nixon would tell it like it is. The time for flash was gone, Nixon was saying. It was time for real leadership.

Next, syndicated columnist Robert Novak gave Nixon another opportunity to comment on the bombing halt in Vietnam. The South Vietnamese refused to attend peace talks in Paris and Novak asked if Nixon had known ahead of time that the South Vietnamese would refuse to participate whether it would have made him less supportive of the bombing halt since the halt was supposed to spur the peace talks. Nixon said, emphatically, "I would go further: *President Johnson* would never have agreed to it."

Novak followed up, asking Nixon if he thought that Johnson was misled by the South Vietnamese government. Nixon did not directly criticize Johnson, but the message was clear: LBJ was naïve. Nixon responded that he believed LBJ fully expected South Vietnam would participate in the talks when he made the bombing halt but added that, nevertheless, Johnson had given away something significant for no gain. He said, "If you played your trump card for the right of South Vietnam to attend and then did not know that South Vietnam was going to attend, you would be giving away the card for nothing."

With both the benefit of hindsight and the work of historians, we know now what an astoundingly devious bit of politics this was by Nixon. Nixon was personally responsible for the fact that the South Vietnamese didn't participate in peace talks, working behind the scenes through his aide Anna Chennault to derail the talks by promising the South "bigger concessions if they waited to negotiate peace until after" he was elected.[31] But here, on national television just days before the election, he unashamedly suggested that LBJ had been duped, that he made a colossally bad deal, or both.

Next, *Washington Times* reporter Haynes Johnson asked Nixon a series of questions about his implication during the campaign that the United States faced "a serious security gap" and that the country's national defenses were inadequate. Johnson asked Nixon if he thought his statement would cause an escalation of the arms race with the Chinese and the Soviets. Nixon responded that he was not interested in increasing the country's *offensive* capabilities but, rather, merely making sure that it could defend itself. The country needed more weapons, he argued, to keep the peace.

Johnson followed up with a question about the cost of Nixon's defense priorities, including shifting to an all-volunteer army and winning the space race, and how these would affect the ability of the country to take care of domestic problems. Nixon spoke first of the possibility of an all-volunteer army, saying before it could be considered, the war in Vietnam needed to end. An all-volunteer army would be what he called a "peace dividend." As for domestic spending, Nixon said that the key was not necessarily more spending of the pie-in-the-sky variety Humphrey was talking about but, rather, encouraging private enterprise to provide opportunities through the use of tax credits. This was a line he used frequently on the campaign trail and in *The Nixon Answer* programs. This would not be free, Nixon said, but it would cost far less than the sort of programs his opponent was proposing and the programs that LBJ championed as president.

The next reporter to question Nixon was the show's host, Lawrence Spivak, who co-created *Meet the Press*. He referenced Nixon's lengthy 1964 essay published in *Reader's Digest*, "Cuba, Castro and Kennedy: Some Reflections on United States Foreign Policy." Regarding Vietnam, Spivak asked if Nixon was now contradicting himself in comparison to what he wrote in 1964. He reminded Nixon he wrote that victory in Vietnam was "essential to the survival of freedom" and asked Nixon to address the fact that he was now advocating a very different plan for Vietnam than he did in the essay he wrote on the eve of the 1964 election.

It was supposed to be a tough question, since Nixon was talking about "Vietnam-izing" the war, which meant extricating the United States from the war and turning the fight over to South Vietnam. But this was the end of a long campaign, and Nixon had a ready answer. He argued that his judgment had not changed at all. Nixon said that his 1964 article and all his public statements since were not arguing for the defeat of North Vietnam but, rather, the defeat of aggression. His plan would ensure South Vietnam the chance to make its own future, he said. This sort of limited victory over aggression was necessary, Nixon said, to prevent new aggression from larger enemies such as the "Communist Chinese" in a few years.

Spivak then asked Nixon if his public approval of how Johnson was handling things with the Vietnamese meant that he thought Johnson was moving toward a victory over aggression. Nixon agreed wholeheartedly, saying that he felt Johnson was being unfairly criticized, especially by members of the Democratic Party. He did not agree with Johnson on how the war had been fought but he shared the same goal: peace in Vietnam that would discourage future wars in the region. Nixon said, "I am for that; he is for that; and once this election is over, if I win it, that united front, I think, is going perhaps to have an immense effect in escalating the possibility of a peaceful settlement." The irony of these words, once again with the hindsight of history, is overwhelming. He was, even as he spoke these words, acting secretly to ensure there was no peace before the election.

Spivak told the group there were only four minutes remaining and the show ended with a series of quick questions and answers that did not allow time for follow-up. Herb Kaplow asked Nixon if he could remember any times that he disagreed publicly with Eisenhower, as Humphrey was now doing with Johnson. Nixon said yes, gave a couple of examples, and said he still wished his advice were followed.

Vermont Royster then raised the question of George Wallace's third-party campaign, asking how Nixon would govern without a majority in Congress and how he would handle the presence of George Wallace and his strong third-party effort. Nixon said that there was no need to make

a deal with Wallace but, rather, to work on building "a coalition of leaders of the New South, as well as the North and the West; Democrats and
Republicans." This answer was carefully crafted to try to appeal to everyone. Nixon told the Southerners he supported them and wanted to work
with them, while he was telling Blacks and those concerned about Wallace's racism that those ideas had no place in a Nixon administration.

Novak then asked Nixon what he would do if no one got enough electoral votes, 270, to win the election. Would he make a deal with Wallace
for electoral votes to prevent it from going to the House of Representatives? Nixon was adamant, saying, "Under no circumstances. I believe that
the best proposal to avoid this constitutional crisis is for Mr. Humphrey
to join me in my offer—which, incidentally, is unilateral; I make it in any
event—I think whoever gets the most votes, popular votes, ought to be the
next President. That, I think, will solve it once and for all." This was a fascinating answer, with no time left in the show for follow-up.

Novak, a conservative, certainly knew how Nixon would answer.
Nixon was allowed to frame the issue in completely inaccurate terms
which, thanks to the clock, went unchallenged. There would not be a Constitutional crisis if no one had a majority in the Electoral College. The
Constitution is very clear on the process. People may not like it, but it is
very simple and was used in 1800 and 1824 to elect Thomas Jefferson and
John Quincy Adams.

What Nixon was trying to do was get Humphrey to say he would give
up the obvious advantage his party held in the House of Representatives.
When the House decides the presidency, states each get one vote, meaning that the state's delegation must decide who it will vote for. In 1968, the
Democrats had a clear advantage over the Republicans in state delegations,
had it been called upon to decide the election. If Wallace won enough votes
to keep the two major party candidates from having enough votes to win,
Humphrey would have the clear, *Constitutional* advantage over Nixon.
Nixon clearly felt he had little choice but to try to influence public opinion
and begin defending against that possible scenario.

The last topic was also George Wallace–related. It was about the support South Carolina senator Strom Thurmond was giving Nixon in the
South. Haynes Johnson asked Nixon how he reconciled Thurmond's
support for him with Thurmond's opposition to school desegregation.
Did Nixon agree with Thurmond's position on desegregation? This was
another issue that dogged Nixon throughout the campaign. He needed
the support of someone like Thurmond to keep Wallace from stealing too
many votes, but he could not agree with Thurmond *too much*, lest he hurt
his support in other parts of the country.

Nixon answered in a way that walked a fine line, trying to alienate as few voters as possible, as he did throughout the campaign. He said that he did not support segregation. However, he felt that the "Office of Education," which meant "the Johnson administration," exceeded its legal authority in imposing specific penalties, such as forced busing, on districts that did not desegregate. He said, "I do not believe that you should deny funds to a particular district because they won't bus children across town and thereby, in my opinion, very detrimentally affect their education."[32]

And with that, the show was out of time and Nixon had just one last big television appearance to go—his final *Nixon Answer*. Nixon would not have the last word of the campaign be an appearance in which he was at the mercy of reporters, even friendly ones such as Novak. The last *Nixon Answer* was going to be a different kind of television event, one that was much more to Nixon's liking because he and his team controlled everything. It was to be a two-hour telethon where very little was going to be left to chance.

The Final *Nixon Answer* in Which Viewers *Ask Richard Nixon*

Nixon's last television appearance took place on the night before the election, in two live, two-hour, nationally-broadcast versions of *The Nixon Answer*, which was called *Ask Richard Nixon*. It was always going to be the way Nixon ended his campaign—on his terms, not the news media's. Treleaven planned this final broadcast in a memo written in December of 1967, before Nixon even officially announced his candidacy.[33]

There were two telethons to allow being live in the evening in as many time zones as possible. The first aired in the Eastern, Central, and Mountain time zones; the second aired an hour after the first broadcast ended in the Pacific time zone and in Hawaii. One unique feature of Nixon's broadcast was that it was the first of use of satellite transmission for a political broadcast to beam the show to Hawaii.[34]

The first *Ask Richard Nixon* aired on NBC in the heart of primetime at 9 Eastern in a time slot normally dedicated to the NBC Monday Night Movie. The show was initially planned by producer Roger Ailes. Frank Shakespeare and Paul Keyes fine-tuned some things and dramatically changed others. Every detail was considered, from camera angles, to the type of chair Nixon would sit on, to understanding that Nixon, who sweated a lot, would need the chance to mop his brow. McGinniss noted, "Paul Keyes had added a few twists to break the monotony of the answers. At one point, Bud Wilkinson walked across the room to where Julie and Tricia were answering phones and asked them what seemed to be on most callers' minds. Then David Eisenhower read a letter from his grandfather. Earnestly."[35]

The Nixon show was counter-programmed by his Democratic opponent, Vice President Hubert Humphrey, who also purchased two, two-hour blocks of time on ABC, spending about $300,000 on the final night of the campaign.[36] Humphrey's show preempted three shows: *Peyton Place, The Outcasts,* and the first half hour of *Big Valley.* To get a jump on Nixon's show, Humphrey's telethon started a half-hour before Nixon's, at 8:30 Eastern.[37] Unlike Nixon, Humphrey did not do two live shows. He taped the first and it was broadcast on the West Coast. Both Nixon and Humphrey broadcast their telethons from Los Angeles, where they spent the day making final campaign appearances. The candidates were both joined by supporters and celebrity endorsers.

There was also a 30-minute show featuring independent candidate George Wallace broadcast in the second half hour of the *Big Valley* time slot on ABC. Both Wallace and Humphrey bought 30-minute slots on CBS to air paid campaign programming. The Humphrey show aired at 7:30 Eastern and the Wallace show aired at 9 Eastern. To make room for the shows, CBS preempted the popular *Gunsmoke.*[38]

In addition to providing Nixon with advice for the broadcast, the Paul Keyes connection to the Nixon campaign also played a programming role. The show that preceded Nixon's telethon was the number one rated show in the nation, *Rowan and Martin's Laugh-In.* Humphrey, on the other hand, chose to broadcast his half-hour infomercials on CBS 30 minutes prior to primetime because his team did not want to offend viewers who liked CBS's popular Monday night line-up. His longer telethon was broadcast on ABC at least in part because ABC was a distant third in the ratings and it cost him considerably less to broadcast there than it would have on either NBC or CBS.[39]

The Nixon show began with a taped opening statement from actor Jackie Gleason, written for him by Paul Keyes. Gleason said that he loved America and, recently, he was worried a lot about the future of the country. That, he said, was why he decided to endorse Nixon even though he never publicly endorsed a candidate before. The country needed someone who saw and spoke the truth. That someone was Nixon. He then said words that researchers Druckman and Jacobs highlight in their research: Nixon would protect America.

Gleason said, "I think our country needs Dick Nixon, and we need him now. I think we'll all feel a lot safer with him in the White House." Gleason told people to watch Nixon, hear him speak, and make up their own minds. He was speaking to the Silent Majority. He said, "Never mind what everybody else tells you he said. Listen to *him* say it yourself and see if you do not agree with me. Dick Nixon's time has come. We need him. You and I need him. America needs him. The world needs him."[40] It was the message Nixon had been saying over and over: "Dick Nixon's time has come."

Celebrities, both Hollywood and political, appeared on Humphrey's telethon too. He was joined by Frank Sinatra, Buddy Hackett, Danny Thomas, Joanne Woodward, and Burt Lancaster on the set, while there was also a taped appearance by Ted Kennedy and the chairman of the Democratic National Committee, Larry O'Brien. Kennedy and O'Brien talked about how much JFK "liked and admired Hubert Humphrey."[41]

The Humphrey broadcast also included an early phone call from one of the 1968 Democratic candidates, South Dakota senator Eugene McCarthy. McCarthy, an outspoken critic of the war in Vietnam, spoke supportively of Humphrey's statements about the need to negotiate peace and urged his supporters to support Humphrey on Election Day. He said, "I hope I've cleared the way so my friends are free to vote for you, not only free but a little moved by what I've said."[42] It was not the most inspiring of speeches and one cannot help but be reminded of Bernie Sanders's lackluster efforts on Hillary Clinton's behalf in 2016. It is hard not to wonder if the close election outcome of 1968 might have been different had McCarthy been able to convince more of his young supporters to turn out to vote for Humphrey.

The two candidates' shows were both referred to as "telethons" in the press. The candidates answered call-in questions, though only a tiny fraction of the reported 130,000 calls per hour that viewers made were answered.[43] The Humphrey telethon had a more spontaneous feel. In the Humphrey show, calls were taken by both Humphrey and his running mate, Edmund Muskie. The callers were often put on the air directly with the Democratic candidates.

For Nixon, the process was much less spontaneous than it was for Humphrey. In the Nixon show, calls were screened by operators and questions were asked of Nixon by Bud Wilkinson, who continued in his role as moderator. There were also questions Nixon wanted to be sure he had the chance to answer, so they were written ahead of time by Paul Keyes. Then, when someone would call with a question that touched reasonably close to the subject matter, they would read the question written by Keyes and attribute it to the caller.[44] As with the telethon on the eve of the Oregon primary, it is impossible to know how much editing of the questions took place before they were asked of Nixon.

Another notable difference between the two shows was the fact that Nixon was not joined by his running mate as Humphrey was.[45] When Nixon appeared on *Face the Nation*, he was asked about the fact that he never mentioned Agnew in his campaign speeches. Nixon replied, somewhat facetiously, that he did not talk much about himself on the campaign trail, much less his running mate. But, he added, Agnew was a fine man the more "fair-minded" members of the news media would judge positively when they saw how well he was standing up under the pressure of the campaign.[46] On the telethon, while Agnew was not present, Nixon "praised him vigorously."[47]

The two competing panel shows or "telethons" did make a little news, providing the closest thing the campaign got to a debate when the two candidates exchanged opinions about the Vietnam War, with Humphrey responding to something he was told Nixon said on his show. As a story in the *New York Times* described, it was a debate on a single issue from television studios that were separated by 12 miles.[48]

In response to a question on his telethon, Nixon was pessimistic about the chances of successful negotiations and critical of the Johnson administration's decision to call a halt to bombing in the last days of the campaign. During his show, Nixon quoted an anonymous report from an Air Force general that the bombing halt was allowing the North Vietnamese to move supplies around Vietnam without interference on the Ho Chi Minh trail. He said, "I have read news dispatches that an Air Force general said that the North Vietnamese are moving thousands of tons of supplies down the Ho Chi Minh Trail (through Laos) and that our bombers are unable to stop them."[49] He told viewers that his previously high hopes had been ruined by the most recent negotiations, by the South Vietnamese refusal to participate in the negotiations, by the North Vietnamese bombing of the south, and by the fact that "'our men are still being killed by the hundreds.'"[50]

On his own telecast, Humphrey responded, saying Nixon's allegation was "a totally irresponsible unsubstantiated charge."[51] Humphrey added that Nixon knew LBJ's orders did not include any halt to bombing the Ho Chi Minh trail and said that "to frighten the American people at a time when delicate negotiations are under way is an irresponsible act. What you and I should be doing is giving encouragement now, not in any way spreading misinformation."[52] This was the closest the campaign got to a direct exchange between Humphrey and Nixon.

Debates were a point of contention throughout the general election season after the two parties had their nominating conventions. The situation was like what happened in 1964, though the parties reversed roles. In both election years, the candidate who most wanted to avoid debates—incumbent Johnson in 1964 and front-runner Richard Nixon in 1968—had a convenient legal wall to hide behind: the equal time rule. In 1960, Congress passed a temporary suspension of the equal time rule that allowed just the Republican and Democratic nominees to debate, leaving third parties out of the mix. In 1964, Democrats worked at LBJ's behest to prevent such legislation from passing, which allowed Johnson to say that he favored debates but did not want to open the field to every third-party candidate who might come along.

In 1968, Humphrey called for debates, but Richard Nixon resisted, saying he did not want to be forced to invite George Wallace to participate in the debates. Nevertheless, the Democrat-controlled Congress worked to pass legislation in October, which LBJ would have signed, to clear the way for debates. Republicans in both the House, led by Donald Rumsfeld, then a representative from Illinois, and in the Senate, led by Minority Leader Everett Dirksen, worked to block such legislation from passing. In the House, Rumsfeld led a time-consuming strategy of continuously asking for quorum calls and roll calls throughout the night the Speaker, John McCormack, was trying to hold a vote on the equal time bill. McCormack finally had the House chamber doors locked to keep members from wandering away and the bill was passed in the House.[53]

However, the next day in the Senate, Minority Leader Everett Dirksen had Senate Republicans refuse to come to the Senate floor for a quorum call. This maneuver prevented the Senate from convening, and after nearly two hours, Senate majority leader Mike Mansfield went to the Republican cloakroom to tell them he would not bring the bill up. This effectively killed the legislation, and no debates were scheduled.[54]

The truth of the matter is that Nixon never wanted to debate. Nixon predicted debates would become a regular part of the campaign process in *Six Crises*. Nixon asserted further that people would want them and candidates would have an obligation to participate to fully inform voters of their positions. Nixon also critiqued Robert Kennedy for saying JFK would not participate in them while running for reelection in 1964.[55] But when it was time for Nixon to be the front runner, safe in the polls, he decided not to debate. LBJ did the same in 1964 when he refused to debate Goldwater, who trailed far behind. Rather than criticize Bobby Kennedy further, Nixon took his advice. Humphrey repeatedly said he wanted debates, but the Nixon campaign saw nothing to be gained from them.[56] Debates were simply not part of Nixon's winning strategy for 1968, no matter what he said about them, right up until it was too late to hold them.

For Nixon, the *Ask Nixon* shows on the eve of the election were brilliant performances by a man who worked hard not to be seen as a performer. As McGinniss described, Nixon was happy, comfortable and at ease with the camera, and the style he had portrayed throughout the campaign was at its best.[57] Paul Keyes was especially thrilled when the show was over, saying, "Perfect! Perfect! He did it just like he said he was going

Richard Nixon in a motorcade during campaign '68.

to. He said it was nice guy time tonight. He said he wasn't going to go for punch lines. He wasn't going to go for applause. Just come in low and thoughtful. And he did it!"[58] Even Roger Ailes, who was never shy to criticize Nixon as being bad on television, was full of praise, saying, "Tonight, this was the Nixon I met on the Douglas show. This was the Nixon I wanted to work for."[59]

Nixon won the election handily in the way the Constitution says a candidate must. While he only beat Humphrey by less than a percentage point in the popular vote, he need not have been concerned about George Wallace and the effect he would have on the Electoral College vote. Nixon ended with 301 electoral votes, while Humphrey received just 191 and Wallace got 46. That victory was the culmination of two decades of political experience, strategizing, and image crafting. It was the consequence of more than six "crises." It gave birth to new ways of campaigning that have endured for 50 years.

Conclusion

In the closing pages of *Six Crises* Richard Nixon made several conclusions that added up to a blueprint for the rest of his career and set a standard for generations of politicians to follow. First, he felt the campaign of 1960 was too grueling. He wrote that he never should have done so much traveling and campaigning when broadcasting by radio and television made it possible to avoid the "physical, mental, and emotional wear-and-tear."[1]

Nixon's second conclusion was related to the first. He wrote that the need to appear well on television made it imperative that candidates save themselves for the big events and not wear themselves out on the trail.[2] There was no point in making many small campaign stops and being too worn out to perform effectively when the media moments determined the campaign. His example for this was Wendell Wilkie, the Republican nominee in 1940. Wilkie was, Nixon argued, so worn out and his voice so scratchy from long days of campaigning that he was not able to effectively speak on the radio.

Nixon's third conclusion was the most significant and one, he wrote, that he reached with regret. He concluded that in 1960 he spent too much time on substance and not enough on image, writing, "I paid too much attention to what I was going to say and too little to how I would look."[3] Television was the reason. Many people might still rely on the print media, he wrote, but a single bad camera angle could have a much larger negative impact than an even a major error in a speech that is criticized by print journalists.[4] Nixon did not like journalists, and he blamed them in large measure for losing, but what he is arguing here is that they do not really matter anymore if the visuals are right. His error had been blowing the visuals in the debates. He wrote that he did not mean that the words of a candidate *should not* be important but the reality was that "where votes are concerned, a paraphrase of what Mr. Khrushchev claims is an 'ancient Russian proverb' could not be more controlling: 'one TV picture is worth ten thousand words.'"[5]

Nixon made the visual image the focus in 1968. The strategy, learned from his six crises and the bonus crisis of running for governor of California, was do not work so hard or talk so much and worry more about the image you are beaming out to the nation. As Druckman and Jacobs so ably write about the presidency of Nixon, it was a matter of framing, but it started well before Nixon was president. Nixon learned from the crises, California, and the presidency of LBJ that he had to be the master of his own destiny when it came to sending the right image to the American people in an era when, he wrote, "one TV picture is worth ten thousand words." And now, nearly 50 years after Nixon left office, many politicians at the very highest levels seem not to worry at all about content or context.

Nixon also learned from the crises, California, and the presidency of LBJ that the news media were, by and large, against him. That was his perception, at least, and it determined much of his behavior for the rest of his career and again set a standard for many politicians in the generations that followed him. In the concluding pages of *Six Crises* Nixon related a conversation he had with a *Chicago Tribune* reporter named Willard Edwards that touched on press coverage of the campaign and newspaper endorsements of the candidates. Nixon wrote that even though many publishers were Republicans, most reporters were Democrats. He supported this with the results of informal surveys in both 1952 and 1960 which showed that large majorities of reporters preferred Stevenson and Kennedy.[6] This, Nixon argued, made the job of his press secretary, Herb Klein, much more difficult than that of JFK's press secretary, Pierre Salinger.

Nixon continued, noting that no candidate ever feels that they were treated fairly by the press and that candidates are far from objective judges of the coverage they receive. But Nixon also objected to the idea that he would have been treated better by the press if he made more effort to court them. He argued to Willard Edwards that he had been much more straightforward, honest, and fair with reporters than JFK and Pierre Salinger were. JFK's side regularly went over the heads of reporters and complained to media executives when they felt like they were being unfairly treated, Nixon said, while claiming that he never did so.[7] The problem, as Nixon saw it, was that the press was against him and for Kennedy. They were against Republicans and their ideas and for Democrats and their ideas. As he assessed the 1960 campaign, Nixon concluded that the situation would never improve until reporters "take a more favorable or at least a more tolerant view of Republican policies and principles—and not before."[8] At the end of his next campaign, in 1962, Nixon was less focused on the party and more focused on himself. Whether they were against the Republican Party or not, he *knew* they were against him.

As he saw the California campaign, the reporters actively did not like

him and campaigned against *him*. And in 1962, it was the print reporters that he felt were the most unfair to him. In his remarks he said print
reporters were less objective than broadcast reporters and thanked them
for keeping print media "a little more honest."[9] This was yet another reason for Nixon that campaigning in the future should focus on broadcasting. It reaches more people, it allows the candidate to control the image
that is projected and, if done right, it can completely close out the reporters who mean to do the candidate—Nixon—the most harm.

Another major lesson learned by Nixon from the crises, California,
and the presidency of LBJ was that taking the press on directly was not a
winning strategy. LBJ did that and it exhausted him and burned out his
administration. Nixon learned to work around the press and to say as little
as he could to let them nail him down. Later, during his presidency, Nixon
would largely forget this lesson, but he employed it with great effectiveness
in the campaign of 1968.

In 1968, as the campaign wore on, Humphrey complained about Nixon's unwillingness to get specific on the issues and his unwillingness to
meet him on a debate stage. Sometimes reporters expressed the same concern. On October 7, when Nixon was pressed by reporters about his lack
of detailed policy proposals, he dismissed the complaint, saying that presidents have a responsibility to make decisions in the interest of the country and that the judgment of the president was more important that the
"details of his proposals." This was, indeed, Nixon's 1968 philosophy: Do
not focus on the details; focus on the image. It was a strategy informed by
hard-won lessons.

When Nixon died in 1994, a political figure who became infamous in
the age of Trump, Roger Stone, wrote a tribute to Nixon for the *New York
Times* about Nixon's opinion of then-president Bill Clinton. Stone wrote
that Nixon liked Clinton and truly admired his political skills. What
Nixon focused on, according to Stone, was Clinton's ability to deliver the
right visual. As an example, Nixon talked about a common Clinton gesture, "'where he bites his lip and looks like he is pondering the question.'"
Nixon told Stone he thought it was practiced but was nevertheless "'great
television.'"

By then, being president had taught Nixon more lessons, and he told
Stone that what television could bring, it could also take away. Discussing
one of the many scandals of Clinton's presidency, Whitewater, Nixon told
Stone that although it did not seem to be hurting his popularity, he would
be in trouble as soon as televised hearings began in the Senate. This was
because, Nixon said, "'the American people don't believe anything's real
until they see it on television,'" adding, "'When Whitewater hearings are
televised, it will be Clinton's turn in the bucket.'"[10] One must take Roger

Stone, whose reputation for truth is dubious, at his word. But Stone was devoted to Nixon, and whether Nixon said exactly those words, it was certainly true that Nixon believed in the importance of the televised image and the impact it had on Americans. It saved his career at the beginning; it ruined his chance for the presidency in 1960; it made his election happen in 1968; and it was a major part of his downfall in 1974. That strongly held attitude influenced people like Stone, who went on working for politicians into the second decade of the 21st century.

In another column, the *New York Times*' Frank Rich wrote of Clinton's appearance at the 1994 White House Correspondents' Association dinner, just a day after Nixon died. Rich wrote that Clinton became Nixon-like during his remarks and "ushered ghosts of the 1962 'last press conference'" into the dinner by talking about the many ways the news media wronged him. Clinton's similarities to Nixon, on the day after Nixon's death, were striking to Rich. Clinton was angry, resentful, and self-pitying.

In closing, Rich made a serious error. He wrote that if Nixon were there, he would tell Clinton that "the prematurely bitter young politician who knocks the press for kicking him around is only asking to be kicked again."[11] But that is not true. Nixon remained angry about the press and what he saw as unfair coverage until his last breath. The solution, for Nixon, was never to smile and endure the wrath.

Scholars quite rightly study the media behavior of Nixon the president. But the very architecture of that strategy was influenced by the previous two-plus decades of his political career before he took the oath of office on January 20, 1969, finally achieving the office he worked so long and hard to achieve. And in so doing, Nixon established a model, not just as president, but as a politician and a candidate, for the generations of politicians that followed him.

Chapter Notes

Introduction

1. Nixon, Richard. *Six Crises.* New York: Doubleday, 1962, 422.

2. *Ibid.*

3. McGinniss, Joe. *The Selling of the President 1968.* New York: Trident Press, 1969, 33, 82.

4. For Theodore Roosevelt, see, for example, Kearns Goodwin, Doris. *The Bully Pulpit: Theodore Roosevelt and the Golden Age of Journalism.* New York: Simon & Schuster, 2013; for FDR, see, for example, Brands, H.W. *Traitor to His Class: The Privileged Life and Radical Presidency of Franklin Delano Roosevelt.* New York: Anchor, 2009.

5. Horner, William T. 2010. *Ohio's Kingmaker: Mark Hanna, Man and Myth.* Athens, OH: Ohio University Press.

Chapter One

1. Tulis, Jeffrey. *The Rhetorical Presidency.* Princeton: Princeton University Press, 1987.

2. Ryfe, David Michael. "Betwixt and Between: Woodrow Wilson's Press Conferences and the Transition Toward the Modern Rhetorical Presidency." *Political Communication* 16 (1999): 77–93.

3. Ryfe, David Michael. *Presidents in Culture: The Meaning of Presidential Communication.* New York: Peter Lang, 2005, 45.

4. Allen, Craig. *Eisenhower and the Mass Media: Peace, Prosperity, and Prime-Time TV.* Chapel Hill: University of North Carolina Press, 1993, 8.

5. Mitchell, Franklin D. *Harry S.*

Truman and the News Media: Contentious Relations, Belated Respect. Columbia: University of Missouri Press, 1998, 173.

6. *Ibid.*

7. Roosevelt, Franklin Delano. "Opening of the New York World's Fair." 1939. The American Presidency Project. http://www.presidency.ucsb.edu/ws/index.php?pid=15755&st=&st1=.

8. Dunlap, Jr., Orrin E. "Today's Eye-Opener: Telecast of the President at World's Fair to Start the Wheels of New Industry." *New York Times,* April 30, 1939, 186.

9. *Ibid.*

10. *Ibid.*

11. Dunlap, Jr., Orrin E. "Ceremony Is Carried by Television as Industry Makes Its Formal Bow: President Screened for First Time, Scenes at Grounds Shown—Mayor Is 'Most Telegenic' of Notables Viewed." *New York Times,* May 1, 1939, 8.

12. *Ibid.*

13. Roosevelt, Franklin D. "Roosevelt Thanks Tammany for Aid." *New York Times,* January 18, 1929, 9.

14. Brands, H.W. *Traitor to His Class: The Privileged Life and Radical Presidency of Franklin Delano Roosevelt.* New York: Anchor, 2009, 224.

15. *Ibid.,* 225.

16. Kennedy, John F. "A Force That Has Changed the Political Scene." *TV Guide,* November 14, 1959.

17. Druckman, James N., and Lawrence R. Jacobs. *Who Governs? Presidents, Public Opinion, and Manipulation.* Chicago: University of Chicago Press, 2015; Lang, Kurt, and Gladys Engel Lang. *Politics and Television.* Chicago: Quadrangle Books, 1968.

18. Iyengar, Shanto. *Is Anyone Responsible? How Television Frames Political*

Issues. Chicago: University of Chicago Press, 1991.

19. Druckman has published many articles on framing. See, for example, Druckman, James. "The Implications of Framing Effects for Citizen Competence." *Political Behavior* 23 (2001): 225–56.

20. Druckman and Jacobs, 13.

21. *Ibid.*, 14.

22. *Ibid.*, 76.

23. *Ibid.*

24. *Ibid.*, 81.

25. *Ibid.*, 76–77.

26. *Ibid.*, 77.

27. *Ibid.*

28. *Ibid.*, 81.

29. *Ibid.*, 78–81.

30. *Ibid.*, 93.

Chapter Two

1. "Nixon Writing Book About 'Six Crises.'" *New York Times*, June 29, 1961, 37.

2. Sorensen, Theodore C. *Counselor: A Life at the Edge of History.* New York: Harper, 2008, 148–51.

3. *Ibid.*, 151.

4. Lardner, Jr., George. "Behind the Statesman, a Reel Nixon Endures." *Washington Post*, June 17, 1997, A1.

5. Ambrose, *Nixon: The Education of a Politician*, 637–38.

6. Nixon, *Six Crises*, xi–xii.

7. Ambrose, Stephen. *Nixon: The Education of a Politician, 1913–1962.* New York: Simon & Schuster, 1987, 636–37.

8. *Ibid.*

9. Nixon, *Six Crises*, xii.

10. Ambrose, *Nixon: The Education of a Politician*, 637.

11. Nixon, *Six Crises*, xiii.

12. *Ibid.*, xvi.

13. *Ibid.*, 183.

14. *Ibid.*, 300.

15. Brogan, Denis William. "Six Crises, by Richard Nixon: The Problems of Richard Nixon." *Commentary*, September 1, 1962.

16. Herblock was political cartoonist Herbert Lawrence Block, a multiple Pulitzer Prize winner who spent the majority of his career writing for the *Washington Post*.

17. Brogan, "Six Crises."

18. *Ibid.*

19. *Ibid.*

20. *Ibid.*

21. Ryan, Edward F. "Hiss Confronts Chambers; Each Calls Other a Liar." *Washington Post,* August 26, 1948, 1.

22. Nixon, Richard. *Six Crises.* New York: Doubleday, 1962, 41.

23. *Ibid.*, 67.

24. *Ibid.*, 69.

25. *Ibid.*

26. *Ibid.*, 70.

27. *Ibid.*

Chapter Three

1. Nixon, *Six Crises*, 73–74.

2. *Ibid.*, 80–81.

3. Hill, Gladwin. "Nixon Affirms Getting Fund of $16,000 from Backers." *New York Times*, September 19, 1952, 1.

4. *Ibid.*

5. "Nixon Should Withdraw." *Washington Post*, September 20, 1952, 8.

6. "The Nixon Fund." *Chicago Daily Tribune*, September 20, 1952, 11.

7. "The Nixon Fund." *New York Times*, September 20, 1952, 14.

8. "Nation's Press Divided on Nixon; Disapproval Expressed by 2 to 1: Press of Nation Divided on Nixon." *New York Times*, September 21, 1952, 1.

9. "Press Stand on Nixon Issue Is Wait and See." *Washington Post*, September 21, 1952, M6.

10. "Mr. Nixon's Explanation." *New York Times*, September 21, 1952, E10.

11. *Ibid.*

12. "Sparkman Defends Hiring Wife in Office." *New York Times*, September 21, 1952, 68.

13. "Senate Probe of Nixon Asked by Sparkman." *Chicago Daily Tribune*, September 22, 1952, 2.

14. "Asks Nixon Be Told to Quit." *New York Times*, September 19, 1952, 11.

15. "Truman as Historian Errs on Pierce's Vice President." *Washington Post*, September 21, 1952, M2.

16. *Ibid.*

17. "New Fund Bared; It's Adlai's." *Chicago Daily Tribune*, September 23, 1952, 1.

18. *Ibid.*

19. "List of Donors to Nixon Fund: No One Asked for Favors, Senator Says." *Chicago Daily Tribune*, September 21, 1952, 1.

20. Nixon, *Six Crises*, 92–93.

21. Eisenhower, Dwight. "Text of General Eisenhower's Speech at Kansas City Auditorium." *New York Times*, September 20, 1952, 8.

22. Nixon, *Six Crises*, 94.

23. *Ibid.*, 95.

24. *Ibid.*, 96.

25. *Ibid.*, 97.

26. *Ibid.*

27. *Ibid.*

28. *Ibid.*, 86.

29. *Ibid.*, 86–87.

30. *Ibid.*, 87.

31. *Ibid.*, 98–99.

32. *Ibid.*, 100.

33. *Ibid.*

34. Korman, Seymour. "Nixon to Bare 'Life's Finances' on Air Tonight: Radio-TV talk to Go Out to Nation at 8:30 P.M." *Chicago Daily Tribune*, September 23, 1952, 3.

35. *Ibid.*

36. Nixon, *Six Crises*, 95.

37. Nixon, Richard. "Address of Senator Nixon to the American People: The 'Checkers Speech.'" September 23, 1952. http://www.presidency.ucsb.edu/ws/index.php?pid=24485.

38. "Western Union's Wires Jammed by Nixon Appeal; Nothing Like It, Says One Official." *Wall Street Journal*, September 25, 1952, 8.

39. "Donor of Puppy to Nixons Says It Had 'No Price Tag.'" *New York Times*, September 25, 1952, 27.

40. "What Is He Hiding?" *Washington Post*, September 25, 1952, 14.

41. *Ibid.*

42. *Ibid.*

43. "Press Reaction Split on Nixon." *Washington Post*, September 25, 1952, 4.

44. "Senator Nixon's Error." *Washington Post*, September 25, 1952, 14.

45. *Ibid.*

46. *Ibid.*

47. Nixon, *Six Crises*, 85.

48. *Ibid.*

49. "Two Funds." *New York Times*, September 25, 1952, 30.

50. "Excerpts from Editorial Comment on Nixon's Explanation of Fund." *New York Times*, September 25, 1952, 28.

51. Clark, William A. "The Nixon Who Left Missoula Had a New Attitude Toward Ike." *Wall Street Journal*, September 25, 1952, 1.

52. *Ibid.*

53. *Ibid.*

54. Nixon, *Six Crises*, 122.

55. "Texts of Addresses by General Eisenhower and Nixon." *New York Times*, September 25, 1952, 21.

56. *Ibid.*

57. *Ibid.*

58. *Ibid.*

59. *Ibid.*

60. *Ibid.*

61. "Nixon Emerges." *Chicago Daily Tribune*, September 25, 1952, 16.

62. *Ibid.*

63. *Ibid.*

64. Nixon, *Six Crises*, 124.

65. *Ibid.*, 125.

66. "How Nation's Editors React to Nixon Speech." *Chicago Daily Tribune*, September 25, 1952, 4.

67. *Ibid.*

68. Mattson, Kevin. *Just Plain Dick*. New York: Bloomsbury USA, 2012, 212.

69. Nixon, *Six Crises*, 127.

70. *Ibid.*, 128.

71. *Ibid.*, 128–29.

72. *Ibid.*, 129.

73. *Ibid.*

74. *Ibid.*, 134. Emphasis added.

75. *Ibid.*, 143.

76. *Ibid.*

77. *Ibid.*, 143–44.

78. *Ibid.*, 148.

79. *Ibid.*

80. *Ibid.*, 152.

81. *Ibid.*, 153.

82. *Ibid.*, 158.

83. *Ibid.*, 159.

84. *Ibid.*, 165.

85. *Ibid.*, 166.

86. *Ibid.*

Chapter Four

1. Nixon, *Six Crises*, 186.

2. *Ibid.*, 187.

3. *Ibid.*

4. Bradshaw, Stanford. "'Neexon' Turns Jeers into Cheers, Wins Debate with Uruguayan Critic." *Washington Post*, April 30, 1958, A1.

5. "Uruguayans Jeer and Cheer Nixons: Crowds, Officials Demand Revision of U.S. Policies to Bolster Economy." *New York Times*, April 29, 1958, 3.

6. Nixon, *Six Crises*, 187.

7. *Ibid.*, 188.

8. Bradshaw, "'Neexon' Turns Jeers into Cheers."

9. Nixon, *Six Crises,* 188.

10. *Ibid.*, 189.

11. "Frondizi Takes Reins; Hoots Greet Nixon." *Chicago Daily Tribune*, May 2, 1958, 11.

12. Nixon, *Six Crises*, 190.

13. *Ibid.*

14. *Ibid.*, 192.

15. *Ibid.*

16. Hinshaw, Joseph U. "Nixon on Goodwill Tour Surprised by Lack of It." *Chicago Daily Defender*, May 8, 1958, 4.

17. Nixon, *Six Crises*, 193.

18. *Ibid.*, 195.

19. *Ibid.*, 197–98.

20. *Ibid.*, 199.

21. *Ibid.*, 202.

22. *Ibid.*

23. Bradshaw, Stanford. "Nixon Is Jeered, Stoned; Cancels Speech in Peru." *Washington Post*, May 9, 1958, A1.

24. Nixon, *Six Crises,* 205.

25. *Ibid.*

26. "The Nixon Incidents." *New York Times*, May 11, 1958, E8.

27. Nixon, *Six Crises*, 212.

28. *Ibid.*, 213.

29. *Ibid.*, 218.

30. *Ibid.*, 219.

31. Kipling, Rudyard. "If—" in *Rewards and Faeries*, 1910.

32. Nixon, *Six Crises*, 223.

33. *Ibid.*, 228.

34. Feeley, Connie. "Thousands to Acclaim Nixons' Return Today: Capital Hails Nixons Today." *Washington Post*, May 15, 1958, A1.

35. Nixon*, Six Crises*, 230–31.

36. *Ibid.*, 234.

Chapter Five

1. Nixon, *Six Crises*, 236.

2. *Ibid.*

3. *Ibid.*, 252.

4. Herbert G. Klein recorded interview by Timothy J. Naftali and David Greenberg, February 20, 2007, the Richard Nixon Oral History Project of the Richard Nixon Presidential Library and Museum, 20.

5. Nixon, *Six Crises*, 253.

6. Herbert G. Klein interview, 20.

7. Nixon, *Six Crises,* 254.

8. Safire, William. *Before the Fall: An Inside View of the Pre-Watergate White House.* New York: Doubleday, 1975, 3.

9. Nixon, *Six Crises*, 255.

10. Herbert G. Klein interview, 20.

11. Nixon, *Six Crises,* 258.

12. Nixon, *RN*, 209.

13. Herbert G. Klein interview, 20.

14. Shepard, "Debate Goes on TV Over Soviet Protest."

15. Gould, "TV: Debate in Moscow."

16. *Ibid.*

17. Safire, 6.

18. *Ibid.*

Chapter Six

1. For information about Susskind's career, see, for example, Battaglio, Stephen. "A Talk Show Pioneer, Before TV Talk Was Toxic." *New York Times*, April 15, 2001, AR31; Ferretti, Fred. "A Chat with a Master of Televised Talk." *New York Times*, October 17, 1982, H29; Unger, Arthur. "David Susskind, TV's Senior Talk-Show Host, Looks Over Today's Medium." *Christian Science Monitor*, October 15, 1980; Battaglio, Stephen. *David Susskind: A Televised Life.* New York: St. Martin's Press, 2010.

2. Ferretti, Fred. "A Chat with a Master of Televised Talk." *New York Times*, October 17, 1982, H29.

3. Battaglio, Stephen. *David Susskind: A Televised Life.* New York: St. Martin's Press, 2010, 57.

4. Shanley, John P. "Mr. Nixon on Camera: Vice President to Answer Susskind's Questions on 'Open End' Tonight." *New York Times*, May 15, 1960, X15.

5. Battaglio, *David Susskind*, 57.

6. Gardner, Frederick H. "David Susskind." *Harvard Crimson*, April 29, 1963.

7. Shanley, John P. "Mr. Nixon on Camera: Vice President to Answer Susskind Questions on 'Open End' Tonight." *New York Times*, May 15, 1960, X15.

8. *Ibid.*

9. "Excerpts from Nixon's TV Interview." *New York Times*, May 16, 1960, 20.

10. *Ibid.*

11. *Ibid.*

12. *Ibid.*

13. *Ibid.*

14. *Ibid.*

15. *Ibid.*

16. Battaglio, *Susskind*, 57.

17. *Ibid.*

18. *Ibid.*

19. Reston, James. "Washington: Kennedy Starts to Work on the Vice President." *New York Times*, June 15, 1960, 40.

20. "JFK on Jack Paar show, 1960." June 16, 1960. https://www.youtube.com/watch?v=eIkZK-Z21Pw.

21. "John F. Kennedy's Pre-Presidential Voting Record & Stands on Issues." John F. Kennedy Presidential Library and Museum. https://www.jfklibrary.org/Research/Research-Aids/Ready-Reference/JFK-Fast-Facts/Voting-Record-and-Stands-on-Issues.aspx.

22. "Scott Sends Kennedy 'Official' Hill Report." *Washington Post*, June 19, 1960, A13.

23. "Kennedy Gets Needle in 'Dear Jack' Letter.'" *Chicago Daily Tribune*, June 19, 1960, 5.

24. *Ibid.*

25. *Ibid.*

26. Adams, Val. "'The Red Balloon' Is Bought for TV—French Film Fantasy Listed for 'G.E. Theatre'—Nixon Declines C.B.S. Invitation." *New York Times*, October 25, 1960, 71.

27. Shanley, John P. "TV: Limiting the Debate." *New York Times*, August 23, 1960, 59.

28. Duscha, Julius. "Ike Signs Bill, Paar to Show Nixon Today." *Washington Post*, August 25, 1960, A2.

29. Loftus, Joseph A. "Nixon Mixes Jokes and Politics on TV; Denies Policy Role." *New York Times*, August 26, 1960, 1.

30. Edwards, Willard. "Vice President Swaps Views and Humor." *Chicago Daily Tribune*, August 26, 1960, 1.

31. *Ibid.*

32. Eisenhower, Dwight D. "The President's News Conference." August 24, 1960. www.presidency.ucsb.edu/ws/index.php?pid=11915.

33. *Ibid.*

34. "Excerpts from Nixon's Appearance on 'The Jack Paar Show.'" *New York Times*, August 26, 1960, 6.

35. *Ibid.*

36. *Ibid.*

37. Shepard, Richard F. "Nixon Hails Paar." *New York Times*, August 31, 1960.

38. Eisen, Jack. "Prestige Issue False, Lodge States in N.Y." *Washington Post*, November 2, 1960, A8.

39. Dales, Douglas. "Brooklyn Rally Acclaims Lodge." *New York Times*, November 2, 1960, 25.

40. Eisen, "Prestige Issue False."

41. Gould, Jack. "TV: Paar as Symptom." *New York Times*, September 11, 1961, 49.

42. Reston, James. "Who Can Sit Down with Jack Paar." *New York Times*, August 28, 1960, E10.

43. *Ibid.*

44. *Ibid.*

45. There were eventually four hours with of debates in the fall 1960 campaign, one hour each in Chicago (Sept. 26), Washington, D.C. (Oct. 7), a split-screen with Nixon in LA and Kennedy in New York (Oct. 13), and in New York (Oct. 21). Each debate attracted more than 60 million viewers at a time that the U.S. population was 179.3 million, according to the 1960 U.S. Census.

46. *Ibid.*

Chapter Seven

1. Ambrose, Vol. 2, 314.

2. Nixon, *Six Crises*, 294.

3. *Ibid.*, 298.

4. *Ibid.*, 306.

5. *Ibid.*, 307.

6. Kennedy, John F. "A Force That Has Changed the Political Scene." *TV Guide*, 1959.

7. *Ibid.*

8. https://www.fcc.gov/media/policy/statutes-and-rules-candidate-appearances-advertising.

9. Lang, Kurt, and Gladys Engel Lang. *Politics and Television*. Chicago: Quadrangle Books, 1968, 216.

10. Nixon, *Six Crises*, 323.

11. *Ibid.*

12. Seltz, Herbert A., and Richard D. Yoakam. "Production Diary of the Debates" in *The Great Debates: Background, Perspective, Effects*, Sidney Kraus, ed., 1962, 95.

13. *Ibid.*

14. *Ibid.*
15. *Ibid.*
16. Nixon, *Six Crises,* 340.
17. *Ibid.*
18. *Ibid.*
19. *Ibid.,* 334.
20. *Ibid.,* 324.
21. Lang, Kurt, and Gladys Engel Lang. *Politics and Television.* Chicago: Quadrangle Books, 1968, 233.
22. The presidential debate commission number of viewers for the debates are as follows: 66.4 million, 61.9. 63.7, and 60.4. Each of these audiences represented about ⅓ of the total U.S. population for 1960, truly massive audiences.
23. Ben-Zeev, Saul, and Irving S. White. "Effects and Implications" in *The Great Debates: Background, Perspective, Effects,* Sidney Kraus, ed., 1962, 332–333.
24. *Ibid.*
25. Nixon, *Six Crises,* 357.
26. *Ibid.*
27. *Ibid.,* 323.
28. *Ibid.*

Chapter Eight

1. "What's News." *Wall Street Journal,* March 14, 1961, 1.
2. Nixon, *RN,* 238.
3. *Ibid.,* 241.
4. *Ibid.,* 239.
5. Reston, 34.
6. Davies, Lawrence E. "Nixon Accuses Brown of Untruths on Loan." *New York Times,* October 2, 1962, 34.
7. Pearson, Drew. "The Press and Don Nixon's Loan: 'Nothing Found' Truth Barely Leaks." *Washington Post,* October 8, 1962, B19.
8. Pearson, Drew. "Some New Facts on Don Nixon Loan." *Washington Post,* October 9, 1962, B27.
9. Pearson, Drew. "Faked Photos in Golden State." *Washington Post,* November 2, 1962, D11.
10. Nixon, Richard. "Richard Nixon, Press Conference, November 7, 1962." http://languagelog.ldc.upenn.edu/myl/RichardNixonConcession.html (see also "Transcript of Nixon's News Conference on His Defeat by Brown in Race for Governor of California." *New York Times,* November 8, 1962, p. 18).

11. *Ibid.*
12. Being called out this way made Greenberg extremely uncomfortable, and he offered his resignation to the *Los Angeles Times.* In an article titled "The Undesired Kiss," *Time Magazine* noted: "Thus, in his bitter political swan song, California's defeated Republican candidate for Governor lifted to national attention a hitherto obscure political reporter for the *Los Angeles Times.* No man desired the distinction less" ("The Press: The Undesired Kiss," *Time,* November 23, 1962).
13. Nixon, "Press Conference."
14. *Ibid.*
15. *Ibid.*
16. *Ibid.*
17. *Ibid.*
18. *Ibid.*
19. *Ibid.*
20. *Ibid.*
21. Lewis, Joe. "California Loser Angry at Press." *Washington Post,* November 8, 1962, A1.
22. Hill, Gladwin. "Nixon Denounces Press as Biased." *New York Times,* November 8, 1962, 1.
23. Nixon, *RN: Memoir of Richard Nixon,* 246.
24. One author, Anthony Summers, did interview Dr. Arnold Hutschnecker, the only psychologist who ever treated Nixon. He interviewed him shortly before Hutschnecker's death at the age of 102 in 2001. Summers, Anthony. *The Arrogance of Power: The Secret World of Richard Nixon.* New York: Penguin, 2001. In it, Hutschnecker told Summers that Nixon was not mentally ill but neurotic.

Chapter Nine

1. Transcript, Helen Thomas Oral History Interview I, 4–19–77, by Joe B. Frantz, Internet Copy, LBJ Library, 14.
2. Dallek, 288.
3. Transcript, Helen Thomas Oral History Interview, 14.
4. Woods, 647.
5. Johnson, Lyndon. "Remarks in Chicago Before the National Association of Broadcasters." April 1, 1968. http://www.presidency.ucsb.edu/ws/index.php?pid=28774&st=&st1=.

6. Gowran, Clay. "Broadcasters Told of Dangers to News." *Chicago Tribune*, April 2, 1968, 8.

7. McFadden, "Johnson Dismay at TV Disclosed."

8. *Ibid.*

9. *Ibid.*

10. Transcript, John Chancellor Oral History Interview I, 4–25–69, by Dorothy Pierce McSweeney, Internet Copy, LBJ Library, 4.

11. Leuchtenburg, William E. "A Visit with LBJ." *American Heritage Magazine* 41, no. 4 (May/June 1990). www.american heritage.com/content/visit-lbj.

12. *Ibid.*

13. McFadden, "Johnson Dismay at TV Disclosed."

14. Transcript, Helen Thomas Oral History Interview I, 4–19–77, by Joe B. Frantz, Internet Copy, LBJ Library, 4.

15. Transcript, John Chancellor Oral History Interview, 6.

16. Transcript, Helen Thomas Oral History Interview, 17.

17. Transcript, John Chancellor Oral History Interview, 20–21.

18. *Ibid.*, 21.

19. *Ibid.*, 21–22.

20. *Ibid.*, 22.

21. *Ibid.*, 23–24.

22. Transcript, Helen Thomas Oral History Interview, 4.

Chapter Ten

1. "Nixon Criticizes Kennedy on Cuba." *New York Times*, March 9, 1963, 2.

2. *Ibid.*

3. *Ibid.*

4. *Ibid.*

5. *Ibid.*

6. *Ibid.*

7. Nixon on *The Jack Paar Show*, March 8, 1963. http://www.youtube.com/watch?v=x-ihI5_Vg6a.

8. McLuhan, Marshall. *Understanding Media: The Extensions of Man.* New York: McGraw Hill, 1964, 309.

9. Kolbert, Elizabeth. "Whistle-Stops a la 1992: Arsenio, Larry, and Phil: Media." *New York Times*, June 5, 1992, A1.

10. *Ibid.*

11. Ifill, Gwen. "The 1992 Campaign: Youth Vote; Clinton Goes Eye to Eye with MTV Generation." *New York Times*, June 17, 1992, A1.

12. Maraniss, David. "Tooting His Own Horn: Clinton's Team Sees 'Arsenio' Gig as Triumph." *Washington Post*, June 5, 1992, C1.

13. Kurtz, Howard. "The Woman Who Put Clinton on 'Arsenio': Consultant Mandy Grunwald and Her Populist Approach." *Washington Post*, August 10, 1992, B1.

14. *Ibid.*

15. *Ibid.*

16. "Filling in for Piers Morgan, guest host Arsenio Hall recalls the time Bill Clinton played the sax on his show." March 16, 2012. https://www.youtube.com/watch?v=7LhgGs4TrYA.

17. *Ibid.*

18. Gould, Jack. "Nixon Returning as a Guest on TV." *New York Times*, January 30, 1963, 6.

19. *Ibid.*

20. Nixon, Richard. "Text of Address to Newspaper Editors by Richard M. Nixon: In Different Role." *Washington Post*, April 21, 1963, A12.

21. *Ibid.*

22. *Ibid.*

23. *Ibid.*

24. *Ibid.*

25. *Ibid.*

26. *Ibid.*

27. *Ibid.*

28. Nixon, Richard M. "Introduction of Barry Goldwater." Republican National Convention, July 16, 1964.

Chapter Eleven

1. Liebovich, Louis W. "American Dreamers: The Wallaces and Reader's Digest: An Insider's Story." *The Journal of American History* 84, no. 2 (1997): 705–706. See also Canning, Peter. *American Dreamers: The Wallaces and Reader's Digest: An Insider's Story.* New York: Simon & Schuster, 1996; Sharp, Joanne P. *Condensing the Cold War: Reader's Digest and American Identity.* Minneapolis: University of Minnesota Press, 2000.

2. Ambrose, 52.

3. Nixon, Richard M. "Cuba, Castro and John F. Kennedy: Some Reflections on United States Foreign Policy." *Reader's Digest* 85, no. 511 (November 1964): 282.

4. *Ibid.*, 284.

5. *Ibid.*, 288.

6. *Ibid.*, 291.

7. *Ibid.*, 295.

8. *Ibid.*

9. *Ibid.*

10. *Ibid.*

11. *Ibid.*, 297–98.

12. *Ibid.*, 298.

13. *Ibid.*

14. *Ibid.*, 299.

15. *Ibid.*

16. *Ibid.*

17. *Ibid.*, 300.

18. *Ibid.*

19. Nixon, Richard. "Why Not Negotiate in Vietnam?" *Reader's Digest* 86, no. 524 (1965): 49.

20. *Ibid.*

21. *Ibid.*, 49–50.

22. *Ibid.*, 53.

23. *Ibid.*

24. *Ibid.*, 54.

25. *Ibid.*

26. Nixon, Richard. "What Has Happened to America?" *Reader's Digest,* October 1967, 49–54.

27. *Ibid.*

28. *Ibid.*

29. *Ibid.*

30. *Ibid.*

Chapter Twelve

1. Johnson, Lyndon B. "The President's News Conference." November 4, 1966.

2. Gelman, Irwin F. *The President and the Apprentice.* New Haven: Yale University Press, 2015, 568–569.

3. Carlos Pena Romulo was a former Filipino general and served in the Philippines as an official for the U.S. government when it was still a U.S. territory and helped lead the nation's transition to independence. He then served several decades in the Philippines government, mostly under Ferdinand Marcos.

4. ABC News. *Issues and Answers,* November 6, 1966.

5. Nixon on *Firing Line with William F Buckley, Jr.,* "The Future of the GOP," September 14, 1967.

6. "Nixon Calls Makeup on TV a Big Factor in His 1960 Defeat." *New York Times,* November 23, 1967, 28.

7. Nixon on *The Tonight Show,* November 22, 1967. http://www.youtube.com/watch?v=mQ_jRIJJOiw.

8. *The Merv Griffin Show,* January 18, 1966.

9. "Dodd Assails Percy Over Fund-Raising." *Chicago Tribune,* November 30, 1967.

10. Pearson, Rick. "Former U.S. Sen. Charles Percy Dies." *Chicago Tribune,* September 17, 2011.

11. Treleaven in McGinniss, 236.

12. "Nixon Unperturbed." *New York Times,* July 26, 1968, 36.

13. Humphrey, Hal. "Candidates Short on Wit for Talk Shows." *Chicago Tribune,* August 11, 1968, SA1.

Chapter Thirteen

1. McGinniss, 58.

2. *Ibid.*, 181.

3. For example, see Chapter Two, "Media Hot and Cold." McLuhan, Marshall. *Understanding Media.* New York: McGraw-Hill, 1964.

4. *Ibid.*, 313–14.

5. *Ibid.*, 319.

6. McGinniss, 35–36.

7. Gavin, William. "Analysis" in McGinniss, 1967, pp. 187–89.

8. Haldeman, Bob. "Bob Haldeman Memo to Richard Nixon Outlining a Campaign Strategy for 1968," 1967, Richard Nixon Presidential Library, Nixon Presidential Returned Materials Collection: White House Special Files, Box 33, Folder 12, 1.

9. *Ibid.*

10. Haldeman, 2–3.

11. *Ibid.*, 3.

12. *Ibid.*, 4.

13. *Ibid.*

14. *Ibid.*, 5.

15. *Ibid.*, 6.

16. *Ibid.*, 7.

17. *Ibid.*

18. Haldeman, cover letter.

19. *Ibid.*

20. Ambrose, 139.

21. Reston, James. "Washington: Richard Nixon's Farewell: A Tragic Story." *New York Times,* November 9, 1962, 34.

22. Gavin, William. "Memorandum" in McGinniss, 1968, pp. 207–217.

23. Ambrose, Stephen. *Nixon: Volume Two, The Triumph of a Politician, 1962–1972.* New York: Simon & Schuster, 1989, 138.

24. Herbert G. Klein recorded interview by Timothy J. Naftali and David Greenberg, February 20, 2007, the Richard Nixon Oral History Project of the Richard Nixon Presidential Library and Museum, p. 12.

25. Kenworthy, E.W. "'The Richard Nixon Show' on TV Lets Candidate Answer Panel's Questions." *New York Times,* September 22, 1968, 69.

26. Nixon, Richard M. "Richard Nixon's Letter to the Citizens of New Hampshire Announcing His Presidential Candidacy," 1968.

27. Chester, Lewis, Godfrey Hodgson, and Bruch Page. *An American Melodrama: The Presidential Campaign of 1968.* New York: Viking, 1969, 100.

28. Chester, et al., 101.

29. Ambrose, 138–39.

30. Chester, et al., 139.

31. See the American Presidency Project. https://www.presidency.ucsb.edu/statistics/data/presidential-news-conferences, retrieved June 4, 2019.

32. *A Time to Begin: Nixon in New Hampshire, 1968.* https://www.youtube.com/watch?v=9aiGt2_4xy4.

33. Apple, Jr., R.W. "Rockefeller Not to Run, but Would Accept Draft." *New York Times,* March 22, 1968, 1.

34. Apple, Jr., R.W. "'Choice Offered by Rockefeller as He Joins Race." *New York Times,* May 1, 1968, 1.

35. Chester, et al., 207.

36. *Ibid.,* 208.

37. Korman, Seymour. "Nixon Begins Aiming at Big G.O.P. States." *Chicago Tribune,* May 27, 1968, 9.

38. *Ibid.*

39. Broder, David. "Nixon Was Patient." *Washington Post,* August 9, 1968, A1.

40. Chester, et al., 453.

41. *Ibid.,* 455.

42. *Ibid.*

43. Just, Ward. "Nixon Serene, Genial: Meets Delegates, Weighs Soviet Trip." *Washington Post,* August 7, 1968, A1.

44. *Ibid.*

45. *Ibid.*

46. Chapman, William. "How Nixon Held Southern Delegations." *Washington Post,* August 9, 1968, A10.

47. Chester, et al., 464.

48. Chapman, "How Nixon Held…"

49. Nixon, *RN,* 312.

50. Chester, et al., 485–87.

51. "…And His First Decision." *Washington Post,* August 9, 1968, A20.

52. Nixon used the phrase "silent majority" in a speech delivered on November 3, 1969, about the war in Vietnam. Nixon was not the first to use the phrase "silent majority." Other examples include supporters of the campaign of Calvin Coolidge in 1920, but Nixon gave the phrase staying power in American politics.

53. Nixon, Richard M. "Remarks on the CBS Radio Network: 'A New Alignment for American Unity.'" CBS Radio, May 16, 1968.

54. *Ibid.*

55. Janson, Donald. "Nixon Discerns a New Coalition." *New York Times,* May 17, 1968, 25.

56. Nixon, "Remarks on the CBS Radio Network."

57. *Ibid.*

58. *Ibid.*

59. *Ibid.*

60. *Ibid.*

61. Nixon was, indeed, worried that Reagan could appeal to conservatives and steal the nomination away from him. To prevent that from happening, Nixon made a trip to the Atlanta on the last day of May to meet with Southern Republican leaders such as Strom Thurmond. As Ambrose documents, "Nixon assured them that he would slow the pace of integration … and that he would not make the South into a whipping boy for national problems.… He promised Thurmond he would use tariffs against textile imports to protect South Carolina's mills, and he promised a strong national defense policy.… Nixon was telling him what he wanted to hear." Ambrose, 155.

62. Nixon, "A New Alignment."

63. Janson, Donald. "Nixon Discerns a New Coalition." *New York Times,* May 17, 1968, 25.

64. Childs, Marquis W. "Nixon Tailors His Generalities to U.S. Frustration on Problems of Ghettos, Negro Joblessness." *St. Louis Post-Dispatch,* May 28, 1968, 1C.

65. Wicker, Tom. "People Indifferent

to Urban Crisis." *St. Louis Post-Dispatch*, May 28, 1968, 3C.
66. *Ibid.*
67. Nixon, "A New Alignment."
68. *Ibid.*
69. *Ibid.*
70. Childs, "Nixon Tailors."
71. Wicker, Tom. "People Indifferent."
72. Edwards, Williard. "Nixon Performance Recalls 1960: Same Eloquence, Acclaim." *Chicago Tribune*, August 9, 1968, 1.
73. Chester, et al., 498.
74. "Pledges End of War, Toughness on Crime." *New York Times*, August 9, 1968, 1.
75. Freeburg, Russell. "Nixon Vows G.O.P. Victory." *Chicago Tribune*, August 9, 1968, 1.
76. Edwards, Willard. "Nixon Performance Recalls 1960: Same Eloquence, Acclaim." *Chicago Tribune*, August 9, 1968, 1.
77. Chester, et al., 495.
78. *Ibid.*
79. *Ibid.*, 495–96.
80. Just, Ward. "Covering Oregon Can Be a Killer." *Washington Post*, May 28, 1968, 20.

Chapter Fourteen

1. Kenworthy, E.W., "The Richard Nixon Show."
2. Ambrose, Vol. 2, 139.
3. Kenworthy, "The Richard Nixon Show."
4. Ambrose, Vol. 2, 139.
5. Kenworthy, "The Richard Nixon Show."
6. Treleaven, Harry. "Notes on Television Advertising in New Hampshire." December 18, 1967, in McGinniss, 226–27.
7. Treleaven, Harry. "Notes re. Nixon Advertising after September," in McGinniss, 237–38.
8. *Ibid.*
9. *Ibid.*
10. Fuller, Smith, and Ross, in McGinniss, 230–31.
11. Windeler, Robert. "Nixon's Television Aide Says Candidate 'Is Not a Child of TV.'" *New York Times*, October 9, 1968.
12. Fuller, Smith, and Ross in McGinniss, 231.

13. McGinniss, 103.
14. In 1972, Jones switched teams and joined the McGovern campaign as the ad buyer for that effort. See "Buyer of Air Time for Nixon Drives Switches to Muskie." *New York Times*, February 12, 1972.
15. McGinniss 54.
16. *Ibid.*, 58.
17. *Ibid.*, 66.
18. Richard Nixon Foundation. "The Nixon Answer: Southern Town Hall." October 1, 1968. https://www.youtube.com/watch?v=MzCrkvvDyhQ, transcribed by the author.
19. "Here Is a Partial Text of Nixon's Answers to TV Panel on What He Would Do If Elected." *Chicago Tribune*, September 5, 1968, 2.
20. McGinniss, 106.
21. *Ibid.*, 109.
22. Kenworthy, "'The Richard Nixon Show.'"
23. *Ibid.*
24. Littlewood, Tom. "Nixon is Strongly Advised to Avoid Television Debates." *Washington Post*, September 17, 1968, A2.
25. *Ibid.*
26. *Ibid.*
27. *Ibid.*
28. Windeler.
29. Reston, James. "Cats and Dogs: Mr. Nixon and the Press." *New York Times*, October 30, 1968, 46.

Chapter Fifteen

1. "Rowan and Martin." *Time* 92, no. 15 (October 11, 1968), 58.
2. McGinniss, 24.
3. Oliver, Myrna. "Paul W. Keyes, 79; Comedy Writer and Producer for Classic TV Shows." *Los Angeles Times*, January 8, 2004. http://articles.latimes.com/2004/jan/08/local/me-keyes8.
4. Kihss, Peter. "Nixon, Happy as New Yorker, Says Job is Law, Not Politics." *New York Times*, December 29, 1963, 1.
5. Donovan had an illustrious career. He is most famous for his book, *PT-109*, about JFK's naval heroics, and is credited with reviving Truman's reputation with a two-volume biography published in the early 1980s. He was the president of the White House correspondents' association

and was the White House correspondent for the *Los Angeles Times*. See Ramirez, Anthony "Robert J. Donovan, 90, the Author of 'PT-109.'" *New York Times*, August 10, 2003.

6. Donovan, Robert J. "Over-Nominated, Under-Elected, Still a Promising Candidate." *New York Times*, April 25, 1965, SM14.

7. *Ibid.*

8. McGinnis, 24–25.

9. "Nixon on Weekend Cruise, Sees Coast Guard Rescue." *New York Times*, August 29, 1971, 56.

10. "Nixon Flies to the Bahamas from Key Biscayne, Fla." *New York Times*, May 6, 1973, 47.

11. Ambrose, Stephen. *Nixon: Volume Three, Ruin and Recovery, 1973–1990*. New York: Simon & Schuster, 1991, 66.

12. Nixon, Richard. *RN: The Memoirs of Richard Nixon*. New York: Grosset & Dunlap, 1978, 865.

13. *Ibid.*, 868.

14. *Ibid.*

15. Ross, Steven J. *Hollywood Left and Right: How Movie Stars Shaped American Politics*. New York: Oxford University Press, 2011, 154.

16. Allen, Craig. *Eisenhower and the Mass Media*. Chapel Hill: University of North Carolina Press, 1993, 26–27.

17. McGinniss, 37.

18. Ambrose, 314.

19. McGinniss, 77.

20. For an excellent history of the political fights of the Smothers Brothers and their variety show, see Bianculli, David. *Dangerously Funny: The Uncensored Story of "The Smothers Brothers Comedy Hour."* New York: Touchstone, 2010.

21. MacDonald, 128.

22. *Ibid.*, 171.

23. *Ibid.*, 174.

24. John Wayne appeared on the show 14 times.

25. Kent, Leticia. "They'll Leave you Laughing—and Thinking." *New York Times*, March 11, 1973, 135.

26. Burke, 29.

27. Interview with Lorne Michaels, October 2010.

28. Wiedrich, Robert. "Tower Ticker." *Chicago Tribune*, December 16, 1968, 18.

29. Barthell, Joan. "Hilarious, Brash, Flat, Peppery, Repetitious, Topical and in Borderline Taste." *New York Times*, October 6, 1968, SM32.

30. *Ibid.*

31. *Ibid.*

32. See http://www.youtube.com/watch?v=EoafIREAMD4.

33. Kolbert, Elizabeth. "Stooping to Conquer." *The New Yorker*, April 19, 2004, 2. www.newyorker.com/archive.2004/04/19/040419fa_fact1?currentpage=1.

34. Archerd, Army. "1969: Nixon Bows in 'Laugh-In.'" *Variety*, January 8, 2009. www.variety.com/article/VR1117998206?refCatId=1924.

35. See, for example, http://www.youtube.com/watch?v=NLjgqVQpFHg.

36. McGinniss, 128.

37. MacDonald, 69.

38. Archerd, www.variety.com/article/VR1117998206?refCatId=1924.

39. Kolbert, 2.

40. Perlstein, Rick. *Nixonland: The Rise of a President and the Fracturing of America*. New York: Scribner's, 2009. 333.

41. For an in-depth examination of Ford, Nessen and *SNL*, as well as the election of 1976, see Horner, William T., and M. Heather Carter. *Saturday Night Live and the 1976 Presidential Election: A New Voice Enters Campaign Politics*. Jefferson, NC: McFarland, 2018.

42. Oberdorfer, Don. "Nixon Twits Humphrey on McCarthy Support: Campaign '68." *Washington Post*, October 10, 1968, A2.

43. "Viewers Rap Nixon's TV AD About Hubert." *Chicago Tribune*, October 29, 1968, A10.

44. For an excellent examination of the "Daisy" ad, see Mann, Robert. *Daisy Petals and Mushroom Clouds: LBJ, Barry Goldwater, and the Ad That Changed American Politics*. Baton Rouge: Louisiana State University Press, 2011.

45. "GOP TV Commercial Evokes Protests on Image of Humphrey." *New York Times*, October 29, 1968, 35.

46. "Ad on HHH Withdrawn by GOP." *Washington Post*, October 30, 1968, A5.

47. Clarity, James F. "G.O.P. Cancels Commercial Showing Humphrey Grinning Amid Distress." *New York Times*, October 30, 1968, 28.

48. "Nixon Forces Drop Hubert Commercial: TV Spot Called Smear by Democrats." *Chicago Tribune*, October 30, 1968, 5.

49. "A Very Sick Joke." *Washington Post*, October 30, 1968, A24.

50. *Ibid.*

51. Clarity, "G.O.P. Cancels Commercial."

52. *Ibid.*

Chapter Sixteen

1. "Mr. Muskie vs. Mr. Agnew." *New York Times*, October 20, 1968, E14.

2. *Ibid.*

3. *Ibid.*

4. *Ibid.*

5. "Mr. Agnew's Fitness." *New York Times*, October 26, 1968, 36.

6. *Face the Nation*, October 26, 1968. https://www.youtube.com/watch?v=5CHELZAZW18&t=176s.

7. *Ibid.*

8. Franklin, Ben A. "Old Issues Revived as Investigators Study Agnew's Past: Land Purchase and Bank Directorship Weighed Anew. Political Rivals and Newsmen Search Maryland Data." *New York Times*, October 22, 1968, 29.

9. "Gutter Politics." *New York Times*, October 29, 1968, 46.

10. Reston, "Cats and Dogs."

11. *Ibid.*

12. "G.O.P. Officials Continue Their Attacks on *The Times* for Criticism of Agnew and Nixon." *New York Times*, October 31, 1968, 31.

13. *Ibid.*

14. "Governor Agnew's Integrity." *Washington Post*, October 30, 1968, A24.

15. Kraft, Joseph. "Nixon Appears on Defensive in Closing Days of Campaign." *Washington Post*, October 29, 1968, A17.

16. "Agnew Presses *Times* to Retract Critical Editorials." *New York Times*, October 30, 1968, 27.

17. *Ibid.*

18. "Mr. Agnew's Unfitness." *New York Times*, October 30, 1968, 30.

19. "The Election (II)—Agnew & Muskie." *Washington Post,* November 1, 1968, A22.

20. *Ibid.*

21. *Ibid.*

22. "Points in the Agnew-*Times* Dispute Are Clarified." *New York Times*, November 2, 1968, 22.

23. "Agnew Buys *Times* Full Page to Deny Its Conflict Charges." *Chicago Tribune*, November 5, 1968, 4.

24. "The Truth Hurts at *Times.*" *New York Times*, November 4, 1968, 41.

25. *Ibid.*

26. "*The Times* Replies to Mr. Agnew's Advertisement." *New York Times*, November 4, 1968, 46.

27. *Ibid.*

28. McGinniss, 143.

29. *Ibid.*, 136–37.

30. *Ibid.*, 137.

31. This was long rumored but documents proving Nixon's actions came to light in early 2017 and were covered extensively in the press. For example: Daley, Jason. "Notes Indicate Nixon Interfered With 1968 Peace Talks." *Smithsonian Magazine*, January 2, 1968, www.smithsonianmag.com/smart-news/notes-indicate-nixon-interfered-1968-peace-talks-189061627/.

32. *NBC's Meet the Press: America's Press Conference of the Air*, September 3, 1968.

33. Treleaven, in McGinnis, 227.

34. DuBrow, Rick. "Politicians Gobbling Up Bulk of Prime Time." *St. Louis Post-Dispatch*, October 25, 1968, 10F.

35. McGinniss, 157.

36. Beckman, Aldo. "Hubert Ends Campaign in Los Angeles; Flies to Minnesota After Big Rally." *Chicago Tribune*, November 5, 1968, 1.

37. Laurent, Lawrence. "Politics Eat Up Monday Prime Time." *Washington Post*, October 26, 1968, B11; Semple, Robert B. "Nixon Urges 'Fresh Ideas.'" *New York Times*, November 5, 1968, 1.

38. DuBrow, "Politicians Gobbling."

39. *Ibid.*

40. "Jackie Gleason for Richard Nixon." November 4, 1968. https://www.youtube.com/watch?v=1_C9vGEJXTU

41. Beckman, "Hubert Ends Campaign."

42. Apple, Jr., R.W. "100,000 Cheer Humphrey: Democrats are Elated; 100,000 on the Coast Cheer Humphrey." *New York Times*, November 6, 1968, 1.

43. Ambrose, Vol. 2, 218.

44. McGinniss, 149–50.

45. Semple, Jr., Robert B. "Nixon Urges 'Fresh Ideas': Republican Stresses Paris." *New York Times*, November 5, 1968, 1.

46. *Face the Nation*, October 26, 1968.

https://www.youtube.com/watch?v=5CHELZAZW18&t=176s.

47. Semple, "Nixon Urges 'Fresh Ideas.'"

48. "Humphrey Assails Nixon War Report in Remote 'Debate.'" *New York Times*, November 5, 1968, 28.

49. *Ibid.*

50. Dudman, Richard. "Nixon Flies East to Wait for Returns." *St. Louis Post-Dispatch*, November 5, 1968, 1.

51. "Humphrey Assails Nixon War Report."

52. Dudman, "Nixon Flies East."

53. Lyons, Richard L. "House GOP Accused of Foiling TV Debate." *Washington Post*, October 9, 1968, A1; Yunger, James. "Rumsfeld Loses One, but Keeps Fighting." *Chicago Tribune*, October 10, 1968, 3.

54. Albright, Robert C. "GOP Ploy Kills TV Debates: GOP Move Kills Debate Bill in Senate." *Washington Post*, October 11, 1968, A1.

55. Nixon, *Six Crises*, 323.

56. Littlewood, "Nixon Is Strongly Advised."

57. McGinniss, 157.

58. *Ibid.*, 159.

59. *Ibid.*

Conclusion

1. Nixon, *Six Crises*, 422.

2. *Ibid.*

3. *Ibid.*

4. *Ibid.*

5. *Ibid.*, 423.

6. *Ibid.*, 396.

7. *Ibid.*

8. *Ibid.*, 397.

9. Nixon, Richard M. "Transcript of Nixon's News Conference on His Defeat in Race for Governor of California." *New York Times*, November 8, 1962, 18.

10. Stone, Roger. "Nixon on Clinton." *New York Times*, April 28, 1994, A23.

11. Rich, Frank. "'I Am Not a Comedian.'" *New York Times*, April 28, 1994, A23.

Bibliography

Adams, Val. "Many Issues, Some Answers." *New York Times,* September 5, 1965, X11.

Adams, Val. "'The Red Balloon' Is Bought for TV—French Film Fantasy Listed for 'G.E. Theatre'—Nixon Declines C.B.S. Invitation." *New York Times,* October 25, 1960, 71.

Adams, Val. "Sweet Deal May Sour." *New York Times,* December 4, 1966, X23.

Albright, Robert C. "GOP Ploy Kills TV Debates: GOP Move Kills Debate Bill in Senate." *Washington Post,* October 11, 1968, A1.

Albright, Robert C. "U.S. Policy Shift Urged by Kennedy." *Washington Post,* June 15, 1960, A1.

Allen, Craig. *Eisenhower and the Mass Media: Peace, Prosperity and Prime-Time TV.* Chapel Hill: University of North Carolina Press, 1993.

Ambrose, Stephen. *Nixon: Volume One, The Education of a Politician, 1913–1962.* New York: Simon & Schuster, 1987.

Ambrose, Stephen. *Nixon: Volume Three, Ruin and Recovery, 1973–1990.* New York: Simon & Schuster, 1991.

Ambrose, Stephen. *Nixon: Volume Two, The Triumph of a Politician, 1962–1972.* New York: Simon & Schuster, 1989.

American Presidency Project. "Presidential Press Conferences." https://www.presidency.ucsb.edu/statistics/data/presidential-news-conferences.

Ansolabehere, Stephen, Roy Behr, and Shanto Iyengar. *The Media Game: American Politics in the Television Age.* New York: Macmillan, 1993.

Apple, R.W. "Choice Offered by Rockefeller as He Joins Race." *New York Times,* May 1, 1968, 1.

Apple, R.W. "100,000 Cheer Humphrey: Democrats Are Elated." *New York Times,* November 6, 1968, 1.

Apple, R.W. "Rockefeller Not to Run, But Would Accept Draft." *New York Times,* March 22, 1968, 1.

Archerd, Army. "1968: Nixon Bows in 'Laugh-in.'" *Variety,* January 8, 2009.

Barthell, Joan. "Hilarious, Brash, Flat, Peppery, Repetitious, Topical and in Borderline Taste." *New York Times,* October 6, 1968, SM 32.

Battaglio, Stephen. "A Talk Show Pioneer, Before TV Talk Was Toxic." *New York Times,* April 25, 2001, AR 31.

Beckman, Aldo. "Hubert Ends Campaign in Los Angeles; Flies to Minnesota After Big Rally." *Chicago Tribune,* November 5, 1968, 1.

Belair, Felix, Jr. "Eisenhower Asks Equal-Time Curb." *New York Times,* March 19, 1959, 1.

Ben-Zeev, Saul, and Irving S. White. "Effects and Implications," in Sidney Kraus, ed., *The Great Debates: Background, Perspective, Effects.* Bloomington: Indiana University Press, 1962.

Berquist, Goodwin F., Jr. "The Kennedy-Humphrey Debate: To Talk Sense or to Talk Politics?" *Today's Speech* 8, no. 3, 1960.

Bradshaw, Stanford. "'Neexon' Turns Jeers into Cheers, Wins Debate with Uruguayan Critic." *Washington Post,* April 30, 1958, A1.

Bradshaw, Stanford. "Nixon Is Jeered, Stoned; Cancels Speech in Peru." *Washington Post,* May 9, 1958, A1.

Brands, H.W. *Traitor to His Class: The Privileged Life and Radical Presidency of Franklin Delano Roosevelt.* New York: Anchor Press, 2009.

Broder, David. "Nixon Was Patient." *Washington Post,* August 9, 1968, A1.

Brogan, Denis William. "Six Crises, by Richard Nixon: The Problems of Richard Nixon." *Commentary,* September 1, 1962.

Burd, Laurence. "FCC Refuses to Alter Rule on Equal Time: Ike Presses Fight in Radio-TV Case." *Chicago Daily Tribune,* March 19, 1959, 1.

Canning, Peter. *American Dreamers: The Wallaces and Reader's Digest: An Insider's Story.* New York: Simon & Schuster, 1996.

Caro, Robert A. *The Years of Lyndon Johnson: The Passage of Power.* New York: Alfred A. Knopf, 2012.

Cathcart, Henry. "Inside Washington: Kintner's Departure Is Blow to LBJ." *New York Times,* July 6, 1967, 17.

Cathcart, Henry. "Inside Washington: White House Team's Turn Over." *New York Times,* May 16, 1966, 13.

Chapman, William. "How Nixon Held Southern Delegations." *Washington Post,* August 9, 1968, A10.

Chester, Lewis, Godfrey Hodgson, and Bruce Page. *An American Melodrama: The Presidential Campaign of 1968.* New York: Viking, 1969.

Chicago Daily Defender. "Delay Suit Against Paar, Kennedy." *Chicago Daily Defender,* August 17, 1960, 4.

Chicago Daily Tribune. "Boo Lar Daly on Paar Show: Gets Unwelcome Time to Answer Kennedy." July 8, 1960, 1.

Chicago Daily Tribune. "Frondizi Takes Reins; Hoots Greet Nixon." May 2, 1958, 11.

Chicago Daily Tribune. "Groucho Demands Equal Time." September 11, 1960, NW15.

Chicago Daily Tribune. "How Nation's Editors React to Nixon Speech." September 25, 1952, 4.

Chicago Daily Tribune. "Kennedy Gets Needle in 'Dear Jack' Letter." June 19, 1960, 5.

Chicago Daily Tribune. "Lar Daly Asks FCC For 22 Minutes 'More' Equal Time." July 9, 1960, W2.

Chicago Daily Tribune. "Lar Daly Gets 47 Minutes on Paar TV Show." July 7, 1960, L11.

Chicago Daily Tribune. "List of Donors to Nixon Fund: No One Asked for Favors, Senator Says." September 21, 1952, 1.

Chicago Daily Tribune. "New Fund Bared; It's Adlai's." September 23, 1952, 1.

Chicago Daily Tribune. "Nixon Emerges." September 25, 952, 16.

Chicago Daily Tribune. "The Nixon Fund." September 20, 1952, 11.

Chicago Daily Tribune. "Sen. Humphrey Insists He Has Chance to Win." May 5, 1960, 4.

Chicago Daily Tribune. "Sen. Kennedy, Humphrey to Debate on TV." May 4, 1960, 8.

Chicago Daily Tribune. "Senate Probe of Nixon Asked by Sparkman." September 22, 1952, 2.

Chicago Daily Tribune. "Set Debate in West Virginia: Kennedy, Humphrey to Meet on TV." May 4, 1960, 8.

Chicago Tribune. "Agnew Buys *Times* Full Page to Deny Its Conflict Charges." November 1, 1968, 16.

Chicago Tribune. "Banker Asks Agnew Retraction by *Times.*" November 1, 1968, 1.

Chicago Tribune. "Dodd Assails Percy Over Fund-Raising." November 30, 1967.

Chicago Tribune. "Here Is a Partial Text of Nixon's Answers to TV Panel on What He Would Do If Elected." September 5, 1968, 2.

Chicago Tribune. "Nixon Forces Drop Hubert Commercial: TV Spot Called Smear by Democrats." October 30, 1968, 5.

Chicago Tribune. "Viewers Rap Nixon's TV AD About Hubert." October 29, 1968, A10.

Childs, Marquis. "Nixon in Crisis: A Joyless Fighter." *Washington Post,* April 4, 1962, A16.

Childs, Marquis. "Nixon Tailors His Generalities to U.S. Frustration on Problems of Ghettos, Negro Joblessness." *St. Louis Post-Dispatch,* May 28, 1968, 1C.

Clarity, James F. "G.O.P. Cancels Commercial Showing Humphrey Grinning Amid Distress." *New York Times,* October 30, 1968, 28.

Clark, William A. "The Nixon Who Left Missoula Had a New Attitude Toward Ike." *Wall St. Journal,* September 25, 1952, 1.

Cronkite, Walter. "Commentary." CBS News Special Report. February 27, 1968.

Dales, Douglas. "Brooklyn Rally Acclaims

Lodge." *New York Times,* November 2, 1960, 25.

Daley, Jason. "Notes Indicate Nixon Interfered with 1968 Peace Talks." *Smithsonian Magazine,* January 2, 2017.

Dallek, Robert. *An Unfinished Life: John F. Kennedy, 1917–1963.* Boston: Back Bay Books, 2004.

Davies, Lawrence E. "Nixon Accuses Brown of Untruths on Loan." *New York Times,* October 2, 1962, 34.

Donovan, Robert J. "Over-Nominated, Under-Elected, Still a Promising Candidate." *New York Times,* April 25, 1965, SM14.

Druckman, James. "The Implication of Framing Effects for Citizen Competence." *Political Behavior* 23, 225–256, 2001.

Druckman, James N., and Lawrence R. Jacobs. *Who Governs? Presidents, Public Opinion, and Manipulation.* Chicago: University of Chicago Press, 2015.

Drummond, Roscoe. "A Chance for Television to Shine." *Washington Post,* April 24, 1960, 24.

DuBrow, Rick. "Politicians Gobbling Up Bulk of Prime Time." *St. Louis Post-Dispatch,* October 25, 1968, 10F.

Dudman, Richard. "Nixon Flies East to Wait for Returns." *St. Louis Post-Dispatch,* November 5, 1968, 1.

Dunlap, Orrin E., Jr. "Ceremony Is Carried by Television as Industry Makes Its Formal Bow. President Screened for First Time, Scenes at Grounds Shown—Mayor Is Most Telegenic of Notables Viewed." *New York Times,* May 1, 1939, 8.

Dunlap, Orrin E., Jr. "Today's Eye Opener: Telecast of the President at the World's Fair to Start the Wheels of New Industry." *New York Times,* April 30, 1939, 186.

Duscha, Julius. "Ike Signs Bill, Paar to Show Nixon Today." *Washington Post,* August 25, 1960, A2.

Edwards, Willard. "Nixon Performance Recalls 1960: Same Eloquence, Acclaim." *Chicago Tribune,* August 9, 1968, 1.

Edwards, Willard. "Vice President Swaps Views and Humor." *Chicago Daily Tribune,* August 26, 1960, 1.

Eisen, Jack. "Prestige Issue False, Lodge States in N.Y." *Washington Post,* November 2, 1960, A8.

Eisenhower, Dwight D. "The President's News Conference." August 2, 1960.

Eisenhower, Dwight D. "Text of General Eisenhower's Speech at Kansas City Auditorium." *New York Times,* September 20, 1952, 8.

Evans, Rowland, and Robert D. Novak. *Lyndon B. Johnson: The Exercise of Power; a Political Biography.* New York: New American Library, 1966.

Farmers Educ. & Co-op Union v. WDAY, Inc., 360 U.S. 525, 1959.

Farrell, John A. *Richard Nixon: The Life.* New York: Doubleday, 2017.

Feeley, Connie. "Thousands to Acclaim Nixons' Return Today: Capital Hails Nixons Today." *Washington Post,* May 15, 1958, A1.

Ferretti, Fred. "A Chat with a Master of Televised Talk." *New York Times,* October 17, 1982, H29.

Folliard, Edward T. "Nixon Fund Story Splits Ike Advisers: Eisenhower Leaves Way Open to Own Decision But Terms Running Mate Honest. Eisenhower Advisers Divided on Nixon Fund Disclosure." *Washington Post,* September 20, 1951, 1.

Franklin, Ben A. "Old Issues Revived as Investigators Study Agnew's Past: Land Purchase and Bank Directorship Weighed Anew. Political Rivals and Newsmen Search Maryland Data." *New York Times,* October 22, 1968, 29.

Frantz, Joe B. "Transcript, Helen Thomas Oral History Interview 1." LBJ Library, April 19, 1977.

Freeburg, Russell. "Nixon Vows G.O.P. Victory." *New York Times,* August 9, 1968, 1.

Gardner, Frederick H. "David Susskind." *The Harvard Crimson,* April 29, 1963.

Garfield, James A. "The Press: Address Delivered Before the Ohio Editorial Association, July 11, 1878," in Burke A. Hinsdale, *The Works of James Abram Garfield, Vol. II.* Boston: James R. Osgood.

Gelman, Irwin F. *The President and the Apprentice.* New Haven: Yale University Press, 2015.

Gent, George. "C.B.S. President Backs War News: Protests 'News by Handout.' Asks Honesty on Vietnam." *New York Times,* January 29, 1966, 55.

Goodwin, Doris Kearns. *Lyndon Johnson*

& The American Dream. New York: Signet, 1976

Gould, Jack. "Kintner Urges TV Networks to Expand Newscasts." *New York Times,* December 6, 1966, 95.

Gould, Jack. "Nixon Returning as a Guest on TV." *New York Times,* January 30, 1963, 6.

Gould, Jack. "Radio-TV: Debaters; WNTA and Channel 5 Scoop Networks on Kennedy and Humphrey Meeting." *New York Times,* May 5, 1960, 71.

Gould, Jack. "TV: Debate in Moscow: Taped Exchange Between Nixon and Khrushchev Personalizes History." *New York Times,* July 27, 1959, 47.

Gould, Jack. "TV: Disturbing Khrushchev TV Interview: Visit to 'Open End Is Assayed by Critic; Susskind Seen Debating Rather Than Inquiring." *New York Times,* October 11, 1960, 91.

Gould, Jack. "TV: Equal Time Issue." *New York Times,* June 17, 1959, 71.

Gould, Jack. "TV: Foreign Policy—N.B.C. Deserves Credit for a Good Try, But Topic Needs Deeper Treatment." *New York Times,* June 14, 1967, 44.

Gould, Jack. "TV: Jack Paar as Symptom." *New York Times,* September 11, 1961, 49.

Gould, Jack. "TV: Jack Parr Shows Amateur Movies of His Trips to Far-Away Places." *New York Times,* February 1, 1961, 71.

Gould, Jack. "TV: Khrushchev Stays—Premier's Impromptu Exchange with Susskind Is Better Than Main Show." *New York Times,* October 10, 1960, 62.

Gould, Jack. "TV: 225-Minute Telethon with Vice President Nixon." *New York Times,* May 17, 1960, 75.

Gowran, Clay. "Broadcasters Told of Dangers to News." *Chicago Tribune,* April 2, 1968, 8.

Haldeman, Robert. "Bob Haldeman Memo to Richard Nixon Outlining a Campaign Strategy for 1968." Richard Nixon Presidential Library. Nixon Presidential Returned Materials Collection. White House Special Files, Box 33, Folder 12, 1, 1967.

Hill, Gladwin. "Nixon Affirms Getting Fund of $16,000 From Backers." *New York Times,* September 19, 1952, 1.

Hill, Gladwin. "Nixon Denounces Press as Biased." *New York Times,* November 8, 1962, 1.

Hinshaw, Joseph U. 1958. "Nixon on Good will Tour Surprised by Lack of It." *Chicago Daily Defender,* May 8, 1958, 4.

Horner, William T., and M. Heather Carver. *Saturday Night Live and the 1976 Presidential Election: A New Voice Enters Campaign Politics.* Jefferson, NC: McFarland, 2018.

Humphrey, Hal. "Candidates Short on Wit for Talk Shows." *Chicago Tribune,* August 11, 1968, SA 1.

Ifil, Gwen. "The 1992 Campaign: Youth Vote; Clinton Goes Eye to Eye with MTV Generation." *New York Times,* June 17, 1992, A1.

Iyengar, Shanto. *Is Anyone Responsible? How Television Frames Political Issues.* Chicago: University of Chicago Press, 1991.

Iyengar, Shanto, and Donald R. Kinder. *News That Matters: Television and American Opinion.* Chicago: University of Chicago Press, 1987.

The Jack Paar Show. "JFK on the Jack Paar Show." June 16, 1960. Accessed on YouTube at https://www.youtube.com/watch?v=elkZK-Z21Pw.

Janson, Donald. "Nixon Discerns a New Coalition." *New York Times,* May 17, 1968, 25.

Johnson, Lyndon B. "The President's News Conference." November 4, 1966. American Presidency Project.

Johnson, Lyndon B. "Remarks in Chicago Before the National Association of Broadcasters." April 1, 1968. American Presidency Project.

Johnson, Lyndon B. "Text of President Johnson's Address to the U.N." *New York Times,* June 26, 1965, 2.

Johnson, Lyndon B. "Transcript of the President's News Conference on Foreign and Domestic Matters." *New York Times,* April 1, 1966, 18.

Johnson, Lyndon B. *Vantage Point: Perspectives of the Presidency, 1963–1968.* New York: Popular Library, 1971.

Johnson, Lyndon B. Daily Diary Back-up Files. LBJ Library. April 25, 1968.

Johnston, Richard J.H. "Humphrey Calls Debate a Success." *New York Times,* May 6 1960, 12.

Just, Ward. "Covering Oregon Can Be a Killer." *Washington Post,* May 28, 1968, 20.

Just, Ward. "Nixon Serene, Genial: Meets

Delegates, Weighs Soviet Trip." *Washington Post,* August 7, 1968, A1.

Kennedy, John F. "Address: 'The President and the Press' Before the American Newspaper Publishers Association, New York City." April 27, 1961. American Presidency Project.

Kennedy, John F. "A Force That Has Changed the Political Scene." *TV Guide,* November 14, 1959.

Kennedy, John F. "John F. Kennedy's Pre-Presidential Voting Record & Stands on Issues." John F. Kennedy Presidential Library and Museum. https://www.jfklibrary.org/Reserch/Reserch-Aids/Ready-Reference/JFK-Fast-Facts/Voting-Record-and-Stands-on-Issues.aspx

Kennedy, John F. *Profiles in Courage.* New York: Harper and Brothers, 1955.

Kennedy, John F. "Text of Kennedy's Speech to Senate Advocating New Approach on Foreign Policy." *New York Times,* June 15, 1960, 32.

Kent, Leticia. "They'll Leave You Laughing—and Thinking." *New York Times,* March 11, 1973, 135.

Kenworthy, E.W. "Kennedy Proposes Treaty To Check Nuclear Spread." *New York Times,* June 24, 1965, 1.

Kenworthy, E.W. "'The Richard Nixon Show' on TV Lets Candidate Answer Pane's Questions." *New York Times,* September 22, 1968, 69.

Kihss, Peter. "Nixon, Happy as New Yorker, Says Job Is Law, Not Politics." *New York Times,* December 29, 1963, 1.

Kilpatrick, Carroll. "Humphrey, Kennedy Find TV Debate Accord." *Washington Post,* April 23, 1960, A10.

Kilpatrick, Carroll. "2 See Eye to Eye Except on Taxes." *Washington Post,* May 5, 1960, A1.

Kipling, Rudyard. "If-." *Rewards and Faeries.* London: Macmillan, 1910.

Kolbert, Elizabeth. "Stooping to Conquer." *The New Yorker,* April 19, 2004, 2.

Kolbert, Elizabeth. "Whistle-Stops a la 1992: Arsenio, Larry, and Phil: Media." *New York Times,* June 5, 1992, A1.

Korman, Seymour. "Nixon Begins Aiming at Big G.O.P. States." *Chicago Tribune,* May 27, 1968, 1.

Korman, Seymour. "Nixon to Bare 'Life's Finances' on Air Tonight: Radio-TV Talk to Go Out to Nation at 8:30 P.M."

Chicago Daily Tribune, September 23, 1952, 3.

Kraft, Joseph. "Nixon Appears on Defensive in Closing Days of Campaign." *Washington Post,* October 29, 1968, A17.

Kurtz, Howard. "The Woman Who Put Clinton on 'Arsenio': Consultant Mandy Grunwald and Her Populist Approach." *Washington Post,* August 10, 1992, B1.

Lang, Kurt, and Gladys Engel Lang. *Politics and Television.* Chicago: Quadrangle Books, 1968.

Lardner, George, Jr. "Behind the Statesmen, A Reel Nixon Endures." *Washington Post,* June 17, 1997, A1.

Laurent, Lawrence. "Politics Eat Up Monday Prime Time." *Washington Post,* October 26, 1968, B11.

Lawrence, W.H. "C.B.S. Show Bars Humphrey to Avoid Equal-Time Demands." *New York Times,* July 17, 1959, 1.

Leuchtenburg, William F. "A Visit with LBJ." *American Heritage Magazine* 41, no. 4, May/June 1990.

Lewis, Anthony. 1959. "Test on TV Libel Up in High Court." *New York Times,* March 23, 1959, 19.

Lewis, Joe. "California Loser Angry at Press." *Washington Post,* November 8, 1962, 1.

Liebovich, Louis W. "American Dreamers: The Wallaces and Reader's Digest: An Insider's Story." *The Journal of American History* 84.

Littlewood, Tom. "Nixon Is Strongly Advised to Avoid Television Debates." *Washington Post,* September 17, 1968, A2.

Loftus, Joseph A. "Nixon Mixes Jokes and Politics on TV; Denies Policy Role." *New York Times,* August 26, 1960, 1.

Lyons, Richard L. "House GOP Accused of Foiling TV Debate." *Washington Post,* October 9, 1968, A1.

Mann, Robert. *Daisy Petals and Mushroom Clouds: LBJ, Barry Goldwater, and the Ad That Changed American Politics.* Baton Rouge: Louisiana State University Press.

Maraniss, David. "Tooting His Own Horn: Clinton's Team Sees 'Arsenio Gig as Triumph." *New York Times,* June 5, 1992, A1.

Mattson, Kevin. *Just Plain Dick.* New York: Bloomsbury USA, 2012.

McGinniss, Joe. *The Selling of the President 1968.* New York: Trident Press, 1969.

McLuhan, Marshall. *Understanding Media: The Extensions of Man*. New York: McGraw-Hill, 1964.

Mitchell, Franklin D. *Harry S. Truman and the New Media: Contentious Relations, Delated Respect*. Columbia: University of Missouri Press, 1998.

Morris, John D. "Bill on Equal Time Passed by Senate." *New York Times*, July 20, 1959, 1.

Naftali, Timothy J., and David Greenberg. "Herbert G. Klein Interview." The Richard Nixon Oral History Project of the Richard Nixon Presidential Library and Museum, February 7, 2007.

Naftali, Timothy J., and David Greenberg. "William L. Safire Interview." The Richard Nixon Oral History Project of the Richard Nixon Presidential Library and Museum, March 27, 2008.

National Public Radio. "Tortuous Wording." www.npr.org, June 26, 2009.

New York Times. "Adviser to the President: Robert Edmonds Kintner." April 1, 1966, 19.

New York Times. "Agnew Presses *Times* to Retract Critical Editorials." October 30, 1968, 27.

New York Times. "Asks Nixon Be Told to Quit." September 19, 1952, 11.

New York Times. "Broadcasters Ask Congress to Relax Equal-Time Rule." April 2, 1968, 31.

New York Times. "Buyer of Air Time for Nixon Drives Switches to Muskie." February 12, 1972.

New York Times. "C.B.S. Won't Carry Democratic Debate." April 29, 1960, 62.

New York Times. "Donor of Puppy to Nixons Say It Had 'No Price Tag.'" September 25, 1952, 27.

New York Times. "Excerpts from Editorial Comment on Nixon's Explanation of Fund." September 25, 1952, 28.

New York Times. "Excerpts from Nixon's Appearance on 'The Jack Paar Show.'" August 26, 1960, 6.

New York Times. "Excerpts from Nixon's TV Interview." May 16, 1960, 20.

New York Times. "G.O.P. Officials Continue Their Attacks on *The Times* for Criticism of Agnew and Nixon." *New York Times*, October 22, 1968, 29.

New York Times. "GOP TV Commercial Evokes Protests on Image of Humphrey." October 29, 1968, 35.

New York Times. "Gutter Politics." October 29, 1968, 46.

New York Times. "Humphrey Assails Nixon War Report In Remote 'Debate.'" November 5, 1968, 28.

New York Times. "The *Times* Replies to Mr. Agnew's Advertisement." November 4, 1968, 46.

New York Times. "JFK Restored Nation's Confidence, Attorney General Says in TV Appeal." March 13, 1964, A13.

New York Times. "Kintner Ready to Quit Johnson Staff." June 14, 1967, 44.

New York Times. "Lar Daly Loses Plea." November 5, 1960, 15.

New York Times. "Lar Daly Wins Fight to be on Paar Show." July 7, 1960, 18.

New York Times. "Maryland Bank Defends Agnew: Asks *Times* for a Retraction of Editorial on Governor." November 1, 1968, 50.

New York Times. "Mr. Agnew's Fitness." October 26, 1968, 36.

New York Times. "Mr. Agnew's Unfitness." October 30, 1968, 30.

New York Times. "Mr. Muskie vs. Mr. Agnew." October 20, 1968, E14.

New York Times. "Mr. Nixon's Explanation." September 21, 1952, M6.

New York Times. "Nation's Press Divided on Nixon: Disapproval Expressed by 2 to 1: Press of Nation Divided on Nixon." September 21, 1952, 1.

New York Times. "Nixon Calls Makeup on TV a Big Factor in His 1960 Defeat." November 23, 1967, 28.

New York Times. "Nixon Criticizes Kennedy on Cuba." March 9, 1963, 2.

New York Times. "Nixon Flies to the Bahamas From Key Biscayne, Fla." May 6, 1973, 47.

New York Times. "The Nixon Fund." September 20, 1952, 14.

New York Times. "The Nixon Incidents." May 11, 1958, E8.

New York Times. "Nixon on Weekend Cruise, Sees Coast Guard Rescue." August 29, 1971, 56.

New York Times. "Nixon Unperturbed." July 26, 1968, 36.

New York Times. "Nixon Writing Book About Six Crises." June 29, 1961, 37.

New York Times. "Pledges End of War, Toughness on Crime." August 9, 1968, 1.

New York Times. "Points in the Agnew-

Times Dispute Are Clarified." November 5, 1968, 4.

New York Times. "President Describes Decision Not to Run as Effort to Save Integrity of His Office." April 2, 1968, 30.

New York Times. "President to Speak Before U.N. Friday at San Francisco." June 26, 1965, 1.

New York Times. "Sparkman Defends Hiring Wife in Office." September 21, 1952, 68.

New York Times. "Texts of Addresses by General Eisenhower and Nixon." September 25, 1952, 21.

New York Times. "The Truth Hurts at *Times*." November 4, 1968, 41.

New York Times. "Two Funds." September 25, 1952, 30.

New York Times. "Uruguayans Jeer and Cheer Nixons: Crowds, Officials Demand Revision of U.S. Policies to Bolster Economy." April 29, 1958, 3.

Nixon, Richard. "Address of Senator Nixon to the American People: The Checkers Speech." , September 23, 1952. The American Presidency Project.

Nixon, Richard. "Richard Nixon's Letter to the Citizens of New Hampshire Announcing His Presidential Candidacy." January 31, 1968.

Nixon, Richard. *RN: The Memoirs of Richard Nixon.* New York: Grosset & Dunlap, 1978.

Nixon, Richard. *Six Crises.* New York: Doubleday and Company, 1962.

Nixon, Richard. "Text of Address to Newspaper Editors by Richard M. Nixon: In Different Role." *Washington Post,* April 21, 1963, A12.

Nixon, Richard. "Transcript of Nixon's News Conference on His Defeat by Brown in Race for Governor of California." *New York Times,* November 8, 1962, 18.

Nixon, Richard. "What Has Happened to America?" *Reader's Digest,* October 1967, 49–54.

Nixon, Richard. "Why Not Negotiate in Vietnam?" *Reader's Digest* 86, no. 524, December 1965, 49.

Nixon, Richard M. "Cuba, Castro, and John F. Kennedy: Some Reflections on United States Foreign Policy." *Reader's Digest* 85, no. 11, November 1964.

Nixon, Richard M. "Remarks on the CBS Radio Network: A New Alignment for American Unity." May 16, 1968. American Presidency Project.

Nixon, Richard N. "Introduction of Barry Goldwater." Republican National Convention, July 16, 1964.

Oliver, Myrna. "Paul W. Keyes, 79; Comedy Writer and Producer for Classic TV Shows." *Los Angeles Times,* January 8, 2004.

Orberdorfer, Don. "Nixon Twits Humphrey on McCarthy Support: Campaign '68." *Washington Post,* October 10, 1968, A2.

Pearson, Drew. "Bickering Besets Adlai's Camp." *Washington Post,* November 3, 1952, 27.

Pearson, Drew. "Faked Photos in Golden State." *Washington Post,* November 2, 1962, D11.

Pearson, Drew. "Ike Grapples with Nixon 'Bombshell.'" *Washington Post,* September 23, 1952, 31.

Pearson, Drew. "Nixon Fund, Vote Record Compared." *Washington Post,* September 24.

Pearson, Drew. "Nixon vs. Corrupt Practices Act." *Washington Post,* September 24, 1952, 43.

Pearson, Drew. "The Press and Don Nixon's Loan." *Washington Post,* October 9, 1962, B27.

Pearson, Drew. "Questions Nixon Hasn't Answered." *Washington Post,* October 30, 1952, 41.

Pearson, Drew. "Some New Facts on Don Nixon Loan." *Washington Post,* October 9, 1962, B27.

Pearson, Rick. "Former U.S. Sen. Charles Percy Dies." *Chicago Tribune,* September 17, 2011.

Perlstein, Rick. *Nixonland: The Rise of a President and the Fracturing of America.* New York: Scribner's, 2009.

Pierce, Dorothy McSweeney. "Transcript, John Chancellor Oral History Interview." LBJ Library, April 19 1977.

Pilat, Oliver. *Drew Pearson: An Unauthorized Biography.* New York: Harper & Row, 1973.

Pomfret, John D. "Kintner and Rostow Get Posts as Johnson Aides." *New York Times,* April 1, 1966, 1.

Ramirez, Anthony. "Robert J. Donovan, 90, the Author of 'Pt-109.'" *New York Times,* August 10, 2003.

Reed, Roy. "Johnson Regrets Kintner's Leaving." *New York Times,* June 15, 1967, 60.

Reston, James. "Cats and Dogs: Mr. Nixon and The Press." *New York Times,* October 30, 1968, 46.

Reston, James. "Washington: Kennedy Starts to Work on the Vice President." *New York Times,* June 15, 1960, 40.

Reston, James. "Washington: Richard Nixon's Farewell: A Tragic Story." *New York Times,* November 9 1962, 34.

Reston, James. "Washington: The Causes of World Tension." *New York Times,* June 23, 1965, 40.

Reston, James. "Who Can Sit Down with Jack Paar." *New York Times,* August 28, 1960, E10.

Rich, Frank. "I Am Not a Comedian." *New York Times,* April 28, 1994, A23.

Richard Nixon Foundation. "The Nixon Answer: Southern Town Hall." October 1, 1968.

Roosevelt, Franklin D. "Opening of the New York World's Fair." 1939. The American Presidency Project.

Roosevelt, Franklin D. "Roosevelt Thanks Tammany for Aid." *New York Times,* January 18, 1929, 9.

Ross, Steven J. *Hollywood Left and Right: How Movie Stars Shaped American Politics.* New York: Oxford University Press, 2011.

Rowan, Ford. *Broadcast Fairness: Doctrine, Practice, Prospects.* New York: Longman, 1984.

Ryan, Edward F. "Hiss Confronts Chambers; Each Calls the Other a Liar." *Washington Post,* August 26, 1948, 1.

Ryfe, David Michael. "Betwixt and Between: Woodrow Wilson's Press Conferences and the Transition Toward the Modern Rhetorical Presidency." *Political Communication* 16, 77–93.

Ryfe, David Michael. *Presidents in Culture: The Meaning of Presidential Communication.* New York: Peter Lang, 2005.

Safire, William. *Before the Fall: An Inside View of the Pre-Watergate White House.* New York: Doubleday, 1975.

Schlesinger, Robert. *White House Ghosts: Presidents and their Speechwriters.* New York: Simon & Schuster, 2008.

Schoen, Douglas. *The Nixon Effect: How Richard Nixon Changed American Politics.* New York: Encounter Books, 2016.

Seitz, Herbert A., and Richard D. Yoakam. "Production Diary of the Debates," in Sidney Kraus, ed., *The Great Debates: Background, Perspective, Effects.* Bloomington: Indiana University Press, 1962.

Semple, Robert B., Jr. "Nixon Urges 'Fresh Ideas': Republican Stresses Paris." *New York Times,* November 5, 1968, 1.

Shanley, John P. "Mr. Nixon on Camera: Vice President to Answer Susskind's Questions on 'Open End' Tonight." *New York Times,* May 15, 1960, X15.

Shanley, John P. "TV: Limiting the Debate." *New York Times,* August 23, 1960, 59.

Sharp, Joanne P. *Condensing the Cold War: Reader's Digest and American Identity.* Minneapolis: University of Minnesota Press, 2000.

Shepard, Richard F. "Debate Goes on TV Over Soviet Protest: Khruschev-Nixon Debate Aired on TV Here Over Soviet Protest." *New York Times,* July 26, 1959, 1.

Shepard, Richard F. "Khrushchev Set as Guest Sunday on TV 'Open End.'" *New York Times,* October 6, 1960, 82.

Shepard, Richard F. "Nixon Hails Paar." *New York Times,* August 31, 1960, 59.

Shepard, Richard F. "Senator Kennedy to Be Paar Guest." *New York Times,* June 9, 1960, 67.

Sherrill, Robert. "The Happy Ending (Maybe) of 'The Selling of the Pentagon.'" *New York Times,* May 16, 1971, SM25.

Smith, Margaret Chase. *Declaration of Conscience.* New York: Doubleday, 1972.

Sorenson, Theodore C. *Counselor: A Life at the Edge of History.* New York: Harper, 2008.

Stone, Roger. "Nixon on Clinton." *New York Times,* November 8, 1962, 18.

Summers, Anthony. *The Arrogance of Power: The Secret World of Richard Nixon.* New York: Penguin, 2001.

Tankersly, Bazy McCormick. "Sidelights from Nation's Capital." *Chicago Daily Tribune,* May 6, 1962, 12.

Thomas, Evan. *Being Richard Nixon: The Fears and Hopes of an American President.* New York: Random House. 2016.

Thompson, Howard. "'A Face of War' Offers Intimate Record of 97 Days with G.I.s." *New York Times,* May 11, 1968, 28.

Time. "Rowan and Martin." *Time* 92, no. 15, October 11, 1968, 58.

Tulis, Jeffrey. *The Rhetorical Presidency.* Princeton: Princeton University Press, 1987.

Unger, Arthur. "David Susskind, TV's Senior Talk-Show Host, Looks Over Today's Medium." *Christian Science Monitor,* October 15, 1980.

Wall Street Journal. "Western Union's Wires Jammed by Nixon Appeal *Washington Post.* "$16,0000 Aid Given Nixon as Senator." September 19, 1952, 1.

Wall Street Journal. "What's News." March 14, 1961, 1.

Warren, James. "Nixon, Graham anti–Semitism on tape." *Chicago Tribune,* March 1, 2002, 8.

Washington Post. "Ad on HHH Withdrawn By GOP." October 30, 1968, A5.

Washington Post. "...And His First Decision." August 9, 1968, A20.

Washington Post. "The Election (II)—Agnew and Muskie." November 1, 1968, A22.

Washington Post. "GOP Attacks 'Debate,' Demands Equal Time." May 6, 1960, A2.

Washington Post. "Governor Agnew's Integrity." October 30, 1968, A24.

Washington Post. "Nixon Should Withdraw." September 20, 1952, 8.

Washington Post. "Press Reaction Split on Nixon." September 25, 1952, 4.

Washington Post. "Reds Fail to Halt U.S. Broadcasts." July 26, 1959, A2.

Washington Post. "Scott Sends Kennedy 'Official' Hill Report." June 19, 1960, A13.

Washington Post. "Senator Nixon's Error." September 25, 1952, 14.

Washington Post. "Truman as Historian Errs on Pierce's Vice President." September 21, 1952, M2.

Washington Post. "U.S. Attacks Equal-Time Rule of FCC: Attorney General Files Brief After Seeing President." May 8, 1959, 1.

Washington Post. "What Is He Hiding?" September 25, 1952, 14.

Weaver, Warren, Jr. "Nixon Favors TV Debates by Nominees in 1968." *New York Times,* November 28, 1967, 32.

Wicker, Tom. "People Indifferent to Urban Crisis." *St. Louis Post-Dispatch,* May 28, 1968, 3C.

Wicker, Tom. "Turning Points for a Man in the Running." *New York Times,* April 1, 1962, 234.

Wiedrich, Robert. "Tower Ticker." *Chicago Tribune,* December 16, 1968 18.

Wolters, Larry. "Paar Returns as a Hero and Gets Censored Again." *Chicago Daily Tribune,* March 8, 1960, 1.

Yerxa, Fendall W. "Johnson to Talk to Truman Today." *New York Times,* October 21, 1964, 30.

Yunger, James. "Rumsfeld Loses One, but Keeps Fighting." *Chicago Tribune,* October 1, 1968, 3.

Zullo, Joseph. "Two Kennedy Brother Get on Paar Show." *Chicago Daily Tribune,* March 8, 1960, 1.

Index

Numbers in **_bold italics_** indicate pages with illustrations